MW00800227

THE HISTORY OF AL-ṬABARĪ

AN ANNOTATED TRANSLATION

VOLUME VI

Muḥammad at Mecca

The History of al-Ṭabarī

Editorial Board

Ihsan Abbas, University of Jordan, Amman

C. E. Bosworth, The University of Manchester

Jacob Lassner, Wayne State University, Detroit

Franz Rosenthal, Yale University

Ehsan Yar-Shater, Columbia University *(General Editor)*

SUNY

SERIES IN NEAR EASTERN STUDIES

Said Amir Arjomand, Editor

The general editor acknowledges with gratitude the support received for the execution of this project from the Division of Research Programs, Translations Division of the National Endowment for the Humanities, an independent federal agency.

Bibliotheca Persica
Edited by Ehsan Yar-Shater

The History of al-Ṭabarī
(Ta'rīkh al-rusul wa'l-mulūk)

VOLUME VI

Muḥammad at Mecca

translated and annotated
by

W. Montgomery Watt

University of Edinburgh, Emeritus

and

M. V. McDonald

University of Edinburgh

State University of New York Press

The preparation of this volume was made possible by a grant from the Division of Research Programs of the National Endowment for the Humanities, an independent federal agency.

Published by
State University of New York Press, Albany

For information, address State University of New York Press, State University Plaza, Albany, N. Y. 12246
Library of Congress Cataloging in Publication Data

Ṭabarī, 838?– 923.
Muḥammad at Mecca

(The history of al-Tabarī=Ṭa'rīkh al-rusul wa'l-mulūk; v. 6) (SUNY series in Near Eastern studies) (Bibliotheca Persica)
Translation of extracts from: Ta'rīkh al-rusul wa-al-mulūk.
Bibliography: p.
Includes index.
1. Muhammad, Prophet, d. 632. 2. Muslims—Saudi Arabia—Biography. I. Watt, W. Montgomery (William Montgomery) II. McDonald, M. V. (Michael V.) III. Title. IV. Series: Ṭabarī, 838?– 923. Ta'rīkh al-rusul wa-al-mulūk. English ; v. 6. V. Series: SUNY series in Near Eastern studies. VI. Series: Bibliotheca Persica (Albany, N.Y.)
DS 38. 2.T 313 1985 vol. 6 [BP 77. 4] 909'. 1 s 87- 17949
ISBN 0- 88706- 706- 9
ISBN 0- 88706- 707- 7 (pbk.)
10 9 8 7 6 5 4 3 2

Preface

THE HISTORY OF PROPHETS AND KINGS (*Ta'rīkh al-rusul wa'l-mulūk*) by Abū Ja'far Muhammad b. Jarīr al-Tabarī (839–923), here rendered as the *History of al-Tabarī*, is by common consent the most important universal history produced in the world of Islam. It has been translated here in its entirety for the first time for the benefit of the non-Arabists, with historical and philogical notes for those interested in the particulars of the text.

Ṭabari's monumental work explores the history of the ancient nations, with special emphasis on biblical peoples and prophets, the legendary and factual history of ancient Iran, and, in great detail, the rise of Islam, the life of the Prophet Muhammad, and the history of the Islamic world down to the year 915. The first volume of translation will contain a biography of al-Ṭabarī and a discussion of the method, scope, and value of his work. It will also provide information on some of the technical considerations that have guided the work of the translators.

The *History* has been divided into 38 volumes, each of which covers about two hundred pages of the original Arabic text in the Leiden edition. An attempt has been made to draw the dividing lines between the individual volumes in such a way that each is to some degree independent and can be read as such. The page numbers of the original in the Leiden edition appear on the margins of the translated volumes.

Al-Ṭabarī very often quotes his sources verbatim and traces the chain of transmission *(isnād)* to an original source. The chains of transmitters are, for the sake of brevity, rendered by only a dash (—) between the individual links in the chain. Thus, according to Ibn Ḥumayd–Salamah–Ibn Isḥāq means that al-Ṭabarī received the report from Ibn Ḥumayd who said that he was told by Ibn Isḥāq, and so on. The numerous subtle and important differences in the original Arabic wording have been disregarded.

The table of contents at the beginning of each volume gives a brief survey of the topics dealt with in that particular volume. It also includes the headings and subheadings as they appear in al-Ṭabarī's text, as well as those occasionally introduced by the translator.

Well-known place-names, such as, for instance, Mecca, Baghdad, Jerusalem, Damascus, and the Yemen, are given in their English spellings. Less-common place-names, which are the vast majority, are transliterated. Biblical figures appear in the accepted English spelling. Iranian names are usually translated according to their Arabic forms, and the presumed Iranian forms are often discussed in the footnotes.

Technical terms have been translated wherever possible, but some, such as dirham and imām, have been retained in Arabic forms. Others which cannot be translated with sufficient precision have been retained and italicized as well as footnoted.

The annotation aims chiefly at clarifying difficult passages, identifying individuals and place-names, and discussing textual difficulties. Much leeway has been left to the translators to include in the footnotes whatever they consider necessary and helpful.

The bibliographies list all the sources mentioned in the annotation.

The index in each volume contains all the names of persons and places referred to in the text, as well as those mentioned in the notes as far as they refer to the medieval period. It does not include the names of modern scholars. A general index, it is hoped, will appear after all the volumes have been published.

For further details concerning the series and acknowledgments, see Preface to Volume 1.

Ehsan Yar-Shater

Contents

Translator's Foreword

The Sources and Their Reliability

The sources

In the latest and most complete history of Arabic literature by Fuat Sezgin, nearly fifty pages are devoted to works on the history of pre-Islamic Arabia and the life of the Prophet, solely for the period up to about the year 1000 A.D.[1]

There are notices of over seventy writers, even if many of these are now known only through quotations from them by later authors. This gives some idea, however, of the large amount of written material available to Ṭabarī. For the present volume, he had three main sources.

The earliest and most important of those sources is Ibn Isḥāq, whose book on the Prophet is usually known as the *Sīrah*. This has been preserved primarily in the recension of a later scholar, Ibn Hishām (d.218/833).[2] It is known, however, that there were at least fifteen recensions of Ibn Isḥāq's work by various pupils of his, and there is a little information about how these differed from that of Ibn Hishām.[3] Ibn Hishām derived his version mainly from Ziyād b. 'Abdallāh al-Bakkā'ī (d.183/299). Ṭabarī, on the other hand, knew Ibn Isḥāq through the recension of Salamah b. al-Fadl al-Abrash

1. *Geschichte des arabischen Schrifttums (GAS)*, vol. I, Leiden 1967, pp. 257–302.
2. Ed. Ferdinand Wüstenfeld, Göttingen 1858, 1859. For other editions and further details about Ibn Hishām, see Sezgin, I:297-99.
3. J. Fück, *Muhammed b. Ishāq*, Frankfort 1925.

(d.191/206), which was transmitted to him by Ibn Ḥumayd, but he also sometimes consulted the recension of Yūnus b. Bukayr (d.199/214). The *Sīrah* of Ibn Isḥāq is accessible to English readers in the translation of Alfred Guillaume.[4] Guillaume aimed at reconsituting the text of Ibn Isḥāq as far as it still exists. He took out of the main text the notes and editorial comments of Ibn Hishām (of whom he had a poor opinion) and placed these in an Appendix. Then he incorporated into his main text the passages omitted by Ibn Hishām which he was able to recover mainly from Ṭabarī, though there are also one or two from other sources.[5]

Muḥammad b. Isḥāq b. Yasār was born in al-Madīnah about 85/704. His grandfather Yasār, who had been held as a prisoner by the Persian emperor, was captured by the Muslims at ʿAyn al-Tamr in Iraq in 12/633 and sent to al-Madīnah as a slave. On professing Islam, he was manumitted. His sons Isḥāq and Mūsā became scholars with special knowledge of the anecdotes about the Prophet and the early history of Islam. Occasionally, Ibn Isḥāq gives his father as the source for a piece of information. In 119/737, when he was over thirty, he went to Alexandria to study under Yazīd b. Abī Ḥabīb. He seems to have returned to al-Madīnah after a year or two, but had to go away again, probably because of the hostility of the jurist Mālik b. Anas (though there are some discrepancies in the accounts). He then taught for several years in a number of places, including al-Kūfah, al-Baṣrah, and al-Rayy, before settling in Baghdad. His move to Baghdad can hardly have been before 146/763, since it was only about that year that the Caliph, al-Manṣur, and his administration took up residence in their new city. Ibn Isḥāq died there, probably in 151/768.

Ibn Isḥāq's great work was the *Sīrah* of the Prophet, though there are reports and fragments of other works. The *Sīrah* as a whole may have been called *Kitāb al-Maghāzī* (The Book of the Expeditions), but the name is also used for the third part dealing with Muḥammad's career from the hijrah to his death. The first part was *al-Mubtada'* (The Beginning), and went from the creation of the world through stories of early prophets to accounts of South Arabian affairs up to the time of the Prophet. The second part,

---

4. *The Life of Muhammad: a Translation of (Ibn) Isḥāq's "Sīrat Rasūl Allāh,"* translated by A. Guillaume, London 1955.

5. Op.cit., xxxi-xxxiii.

al-Mab'ath (The Sending, sc. of the Prophet), covered the period from Muḥammad's birth until his arrival in al-Madīnah.

The earlier section of *al-Mubtada'* was omitted by Ibn Hishām, though fragments of it are found in other authors. He retained a genealogy of Muḥammad back to Adam, but then passed immediately to the Arab descendants of Ishmael (Ismā'īl) through 'Adnān, with a reference to the parallel line through Qaḥṭān. A number of stories then follow about the kings of South Arabia, but not much of this material is relevant to Mecca and Yathrib (as al-Madīnah was then called). The story of the expedition of the Elephant, however, is told in some detail. This was an expedition against Mecca led by Abrahah, the Abyssinian viceroy, or ruler, of the Yemen, which included a fighting elephant to terrify the Arab tribesmen. In Sūrah 105 of the Qur'ān, the failure of the expedition is attributed to God. Muḥammad is reported to have been born in "the year of the elephant," which is usually taken to be the year A.D. 570.

In the second part of the *Sīrah,* events are given a rough dating according to Muḥammad's age. Ibn Hishām has omitted some anecdotes (1161f.; 1171–73) which present 'Alī as playing an important role in the earliest days of Islam (and so were felt to be pro-Shī'ite), and also the story of the "satanic verses" (1192–95), which was perhaps thought to be slightly discreditable to the Prophet. Ibn Hishām may well have omitted more passages of which we are unaware, since Ṭabarī does not report many of the minor topics found in Ibn Isḥāq.

The great reputation of Ibn Isḥāq as a biographer of the Prophet is due to his wide knowledge of the relevant material, to his wise judgement in selecting the more reliable accounts of events, and to his ability to form the whole into a single connected narrative. Criticisms of him by later Muslim scholars are not of his work as a historian but of his collection of Ḥadīth (anecdotes about Muḥammad's sayings and doings to be used for legal purposes). Ibn Isḥāq usually gives a source for his historical material, though not always with a complete *isnād* or chain of transmitters. In the case of some major events he names several sources which he has used, but does not specify the source or sources of each detail of the account.

Ṭabarī clearly regarded Ibn Isḥāq very highly, and in many parts of his narrative uses him as his main source, while inserting variant accounts from other sources. Where Ibn Hishām omitted passages from Ibn Isḥāq which he thought unduly favorable to Shī'ism (as noted above), Ṭabarī retained such passages but balanced them by other material. Thus, where Ibn Isḥāq only had material showing that 'Alī was the first male Muslim, Ṭabarī added other sources which claimed that honor for Abū Bakr or Zayd b. Ḥārithah.

In the section dealing with Muḥammad's ancestry Ibn Isḥaq follows a chronological order, but, as already noted, introduces many incidents from South Arabian history which have little relevance to the Prophet's ancestors. It has been suggested that attention was paid to South Arabia because this was a matter of pride for the Muslims of al-Madīnah, who regarded themselves as descended from the South Arabian or Yemenite tribes, whereas the Muslims of Mecca, who by Ibn Isḥāq's time held most of the power in the Islamic state, belonged to the northern Arabs. Ṭabarī includes some of the South Arabian material from Ibn Isḥāq at an earlier point in his narrative.[6] When he comes to Muḥammad's ancestors, he reverses the chronological order; he begins with Muḥammad's father, then goes to his grandfather, then to his great-grandfather, and so on. The difference between the two historians may be seen from the following table:

Ancestors	Ibn Isḥāq	Ṭabarī
Adam to 'Adnān	3	1113–23
'Adnān, Ma'add	3–7	1111–13
Nizār	49	1111
Muḍar, Ilyās	50	1108–10
Mudrikah to Lu'ayy	60–62	1101–8
Ka'b to Quṣayy	67–68	1092–1101
'Abd Manāf	68, 84	1091–92
Hāshim	87	1088–91
'Abd al-Muṭṭalib	88	1082–88
'Abdallāh, Muḥammad's conception	98–101	1074–82

A second important source is Muḥammad b. 'Umar (as Ṭabarī

6. This will be found in the previous volume of the present translation.

usually calls him), generally known as al-Wāqidī.[7] Al-Wāqidī was born in al-Madīnah in 150/747, and studied under the scholars there, notably Mūsā b. ʿUqbah, Maʿmar b. Rāshid and Abū Maʿshar.[8] In 180/796 he went to Baghdad, obtained the support of the wazīr Yaḥyā b. Khālid al-Barmakī, and was appointed by the caliph Hārūn al-Rashīd as judge for the east side of Baghdad; later he had other similar posts. He died in Baghdad in 207/823. His most important work is the *Kitāb al-Maghāzī*, which deals with the "expeditions" of Muḥammad, and thus covers most of the events of the period between the hijrah and Muḥammad's death. There are many references to this in the next two volumes of the present translation of Ṭabarī's history. Al-Wāqidī paid special attention to chronology, and his dating of the expeditions in general is superior to that of Ibn Isḥāq and to be accepted. He must have known the work of Ibn Isḥāq , but does not make use of it in his *Maghāzī*, though he uses it for earlier and later matters. He was also regarded as an authority on the early Islamic conquests, but was not so highly thought of in respect of pre-Islamic history. Some of the historical material he collected has been preserved not in his own works but in those of his pupil Ibn Saʿd. There is now an excellent text of the *Maghāzī* edited by Marsden Jones. Previously scholars had to rely on the accurate summary of the work in German by Julius Wellhausen entitled *Muhammed in Medina*.

Muḥammad b. Saʿd was born in al-Baṣrah in 168/784, but moved to al-Madīnah and other centers of learning. It was presumably in Baghdad that he studied under al-Wāqidī. Though he had studied under other scholars, including Hishām b. al-Kalbī, he became specially attached to al-Wāqidī and was known as his *kātib* or secretary. He died in Baghdad in 230/845. Virtually his only extant work is the *Kitāb al-Ṭabaqāt al-Kabīr* (The Great Book of Classes).[9] The "classes" are the various generations of those who transmitted anecdotes, historical or legal, about Muḥammad. The first "class" consists of the Companions *(Ṣaḥābah)*, those who had known and conversed with Muḥammad. Thus there are bio-

---

7. Sezgin, I:294-97; the notices of his three teachers are on pp. 286, 290, and 291.
8. *Kitāb al-Maghāzī*, ed. Marsden Jones, 3 vols., London 1966; *Muhammed in Medina*, abbreviated German translation by J. Wellhausen, Berlin 1882.
9. Sezgin, *GAS*, I:300f.

graphical notices of all the 300-odd men who had taken part in the battle of Badr. Altogether Ibn Sa'd has notices of some 4,250 persons, including about 600 women, though some of the notices in the later "classes" are sketchy, occasionally only a name. The *Ṭabaqāt* proper are preceded by a collection of information about the earlier part of Muḥammad's life, but the *Maghāzī* are not dealt with in detail, presumably because of the existence of al-Wāqidī's book, though there are accounts of tribal deputations and texts of treaties not found in al-Wāqidī. The material relevant to the period up to the hijrah is found in the first half of the first volume of the European edition. Ṭabarī quotes the *Ṭabaqāt* from al-Ḥārith b. Abī Usāmah (d. 282/895).

A third important source is Ibn al-Kalbī, or more fully, Hishām b. Muḥammad b. al-Sā'ib al-Kalbī.[10] His father Muḥammad (d.146/763) was already an authority on pre-Islamic Arabia, and the son added to his store of knowledge. He was born in al-Kūfah about 120/737, and died there in 204/819. Ṭabarī's normal description of this source is: Hishām b. Muḥammad from his father. They were regarded as the chief authorities on Arab genealogy and many other aspects of the pre-Islamic history of Arabia. Two books relevant to the life of Muḥammad by the philologist Muḥammad b. Ḥabīb (d.245/860), *al-Muḥabbar* and *al-Munammaq*, rely heavily on Ibn al-Kalbī.[11]

It may also be noted that from one of his minor sources Ṭabarī reproduces an early document, a letter from the scholar 'Urwah b. al-Zubayr to 'Abd al-Malik (Caliph from 685 to 705).[12] 'Urwah was a son of al-Zubayr, who along with Ṭalḥah was defeated by 'Alī at the Battle of the Camel in 35/656. His brother 'Abdallāh b. al-Zubayr, some thirty years his senior, set himself up as counter-Caliph in Mecca from 61/80 to 73/692. Though 'Urwah had supported his brother in Mecca against the Umayyads, he managed to have good relations with the Umayyad 'Abd al-Malik. He was reckoned to have a wide knowledge of early Islamic history, and some of this has been transmitted by later scholars such as Muḥammad b. Shihāb al-Zuhrī (d.124/742) and Abū al-

10. Ibid., 268–71.

11. C. Brockelmann, *Geschichte der arabischen Literatur, (GAL)*[2] Leiden 1943, I:105 (106).

12. See 1180f., 1284-88 below.

Aswad al-Asadī (d.131/748).[13] Al-Zuhrī was one of the teachers of Ibn Isḥāq.

The reliability of the materials used

For a century or so, some Western scholars have been sceptical about the historical value of much of the material about the career of Muḥammad. This scepticism may be said to have reached its culmination in two works published in 1977. One was a book on the Qur'ān by John Wansbrough, in which he maintained that the text of the Qur'ān did not attain its present form until a century and a half after Muḥammad.[14] The other book was by two pupils of Wansbrough's who attempted to show that all the early Muslim sources for the life of Muḥammad were to be rejected, and that the earliest phase of his religion was not Islam as it is now known but something different which they called "Hagarism".[15] Neither book has been favorably received by scholars in general, since both are based on many unjustified assumptions, and there seems little point in offering a detailed criticism of them. Nevertheless, since they allege that the entire contents of this and the two or three following volumes of Ṭabarī's history are without historical value, it seems worth while to give some arguments to justify the belief that most of the materials used by Ṭabarī are reliable. A form of these arguments has already been published under the title "The Reliability of Ibn Isḥāq's Sources",[16] and since Ibn Isḥāq was Ṭabarī's main source, they will also apply to Ṭabarī. It will be useful, however, to show more particularly how this is so.

One of the earliest exponents of sceptical views was Ignaz Goldziher, who in 1890, in the second volume of his *Muhammedanische Studien*, suggested that much of what was contained in the vast collections of Ḥadīth was not historically

---

13. Sezgin, I:280-83, 284f.

14. *Quranic Studies, Sources and Methods of Scriptural Interpretation*, London 1977.

15. Patricia Crone and Michael Cook, *Hagarism, the Making of the Islamic World*, Cambridge 1977.

16. In *La vie du prophète Mahomet* (Colloque de Strasbourg, 1980), Paris 1983, pp.31-43; see also Watt. "The Materials used by Ibn Isḥāq," in *Historians of the Middle East*, ed. B. Lewis and P.M. Holt, London 1962, pp.23-34.

true.[17] This line of thought was further elaborated by Joseph Schacht in *The Origins of Muhammadan Jurisprudence.*[18] The corpus of Ḥadīth is primarily concerned with legal and liturgical matters, and to a lesser extent with theological concerns, but other scholars expressed similar criticisms of the more purely historical material. The leaders among them were Henri Lammens and Carl Heinrich Becker, and their views were widely accepted up to a point. Becker expressed his conclusions by saying that the *Sīrah* of Ibn Isḥāq consisted primarily of "the already existing dogmatic and juristic Ḥadīth ... collected and chronologically arranged," and he held that to these had been added expanded versions of historical allusions in the Qur'ān[19] Following Lammens and Becker, Régis Blachère argued that the only reliable source for the life of Muḥammad was the Qur'ān itself.[20]

One serious defect of the Lammens-Becker view is that it does not explain where the chronology comes from. Ḥadīth do not normally give an indication of chronology, and there are no "chronological" Ḥadīth. Thus Ḥadīth cannot be used to arrange Ḥadīth chronologically. The other serious defect is that "the already existing dogmatic and juristic Ḥadīth," even if they are true, have no importance for the historian of Muḥammad's career. They do not convey the sort of information which the historian requires. It is plausible to suppose that "anecdotes about what Muḥammad said and did" must be at the heart of his biography, but this is not so with those in the corpus of Ḥadīth. A saying which is of dogmatic or juristic interest is usually irrelevant to the historian. Thus there is a well-known story about how Muḥammad passed a man beating a slave and told him not to do so because "God made Adam in his (the slave's) image." This is dogmatically important, since it replaces the usual Jewish and Christian interpretation of the phrase "God made Adam in His image" as being God's image—a phrase which, in other Ḥadīth, Muḥammad is said to have uttered. For the historian, however, this story is of no importance.

It is essential to realize that, though originally there may have

17. Halle 1890; English translation edited by S.M. Stern, *Muslim Studies* London 1971.

18. Oxford 1950.

19. C.H. Becker, *Islamstudien,* Leipzig 1924, I:520f. (reprinted from *Der Islam,* IV [1913]: 263ff.)

20. *Le problème de Mahomet,* Paris 1952.

been some overlap between the study of Ḥadīth and the study of the *Sīrah,* the two studies soon became distinct disciplines with different methodologies. This is made obvious by a glance at Arent Jan Wensinck's *Handbook of Early Muhammadan Tradition.*[21] At the beginning of the work he lists the titles—about four hundred in all—of the separate "books" or sections in eight standard collections of Ḥadīth. Most of these books deal with legal or liturgical matters such as "marriage" or "ablutions." A few deal with dogmatic questions under such headings as "faith" (*īmān)* and "predestination" (*qadar).* Only three "books" could be regarded as historical, two in the collection of al-Bukhārī (d. 256/870) entitled "expeditions" (*maghāzī)* and "the merits of the Companions" (*faḍā'il al-ṣaḥābah),* and one in the collection of Muslim (d.261/875) with the latter title. Bukhārī's "book" on the "expeditions" is lengthy, but the difference between his methodology and that of the historians can be illustrated from his first paragraph. He quotes both a Companion and a later scholar as saying that the first expedition in which Muḥammad took part personally was that of al-ʿUshayrah, but then he gives the statement of Ibn Isḥāq that Muḥammad had taken part in two expeditions before that of al-ʿUshayrah.[22] Bukhārī thought it worthwhile retaining the assertion of the Companion and the later scholar, although it seems to be valueless after that of Ibn Isḥāq. Historians like Ibn Isḥāq, on the other hand, did not repeat assertions they held to be clearly mistaken. When Ṭabarī gives alternative views, as he sometimes does, it is probably because he is not sure which is correct. The conclusion to which these considerations lead is that the critique of Ḥadīth by Goldziher, Schacht, and others does not necessarily apply to the materials used in the *Sīrah.* Most of these materials may be brought under four headings: a chronological framework and outline of events, anecdotes other than Ḥadīth, Qur'ānic elaborations, and poetry.

The first type of material consists of a basic chronological framework and an outline of the main events. This applies particularly to the period after the hijrah where the framework is the chronological order of the expeditions and is accompanied by brief account of what happened in each. (A word will be said later

21. Leiden 1927.
22. Cf. Ibn Hishām, *Sīrah,* 415f., 421f.; Ṭabarī, I:1269-71.

about the chronology of the period before the hijrah.) Ibn Isḥāq usually introduces each expedition with a description of it in his own words, without naming any source. Thus for the first expedition in which Muḥammad participated he says

> Then he went out raiding in Ṣafar (August) at the beginning of the twelfth month from his arrival in al-Madīnah, and proceeded as far as Waddān. This is the expedition of al-Abwā' against Quraysh and Banū Ḍamrah,...during which Banū Ḍamrah made an agreement with him through their chief Makhshī b. 'Amr. Then the Messenger of God returned to al-Madīnah without meeting hostile action, and remained there for the rest of Ṣafar and the first part of Rabī' I (September).[23]

This account raises the question: What was the source of Ibn Isḥāq's information, and why does he not name a source? The answer is almost certainly that these were matters of widespread and generally accepted common knowledge, and a little reflection will show how this came to be so. At the time Muḥammad died, all Muslims of long standing and many more recent Muslims presumably knew the order of the main events since the hijrah, namely: the battle of Badr, the battle of Uḥud, the siege of al-Madīnah, the expedition of al-Ḥudaybiyah, the conquest of Khaybar, the conquest of Mecca, the battle of Ḥunayn, and the expedition to Tābūk. Those who had taken part in some of the other expeditions presumably knew more or less how these fitted into the basic framework, because Arab society was primarily an oral and not a literate society. This common knowledge would be carefully treasured. As the Islamic state expanded into a more literate world, literacy must have grown. There are grounds for thinking that a few men had begun to write down something of the early history within about thirty years of Muḥammad's death; perhaps even before then. Fuat Sezgin's list of early historians has already been mentioned; and it is noteworthy that of those dealing with the *Sīrah*, the first two were born a year or two after the hijrah, and the next four within ten years of Muḥammad's death;

23. Ibn Hishām, *Sīrah*, 415f. As Guillaume assumes, the statement that Sa'd b. 'Ubādah was left in charge of al-Madīnah is probably from Ibn Hishām, though it is not indicated as such in the text.

and these men appear to have left written reports. They may, even before they were twenty years old, have heard informal lectures or talks in the mosques about the early days of Islam; there certainly were such lectures on the history of pre-Islamic times. If by the time they were twenty they were interested in studying the subject, there would be great numbers of older men whom they could ask about points they found obscure.

Of the scholars described above, 'Urwah b. al-Zubayr would reach the age of twenty about 46/665 and al-Zuhrī about 71/690. These dates are important for comparative purposes. A person aged eighty today (1987) probably remembers something of the beginning of the First World War in 1914, perhaps also of the sinking of the "Titanic" in 1911, and of the order of the two events; and these happened over seventy years ago. Such a person would have heard parents and elders talking about events twenty or thirty years earlier still. If we apply this consideration to early Islam, then 'Urwah could certainly have spoken to a number of men who had lived through the events of the first ten years after the hijrah, and even al-Zuhrī might have met one or two. Moreover, 'Urwah and al-Zuhrī by the time they were twenty would already have learnt something of the *Sīrah* from older scholars, so that their work was not the construction of a chronological framework but the refining of one that already existed. Thus when Ibn Isḥaq gives a statement about an expedition such as the one quoted, he will have learnt most of it from al-Zuhrī and his other teachers, and it will represent the distillate of the work of several generations of scholars. It cannot be attributed to a single source, since it is the result of many scholars sifting masses of evidence from dozens or even hundreds of informants. The final result of this process is what is meant by "the basic chronological framework and outline of events", and the bulk of it must have been accepted by all scholars, though some might have had fuller knowledge than others of certain parts, and there might have been divergencies on minor matters. For the period after the hijrah, Ṭabarī has the chronology of both Ibn Isḥāq and al-Wāqidī to follow, and he also notes where they differ, as in respect of some of the earlier expeditions.

For the period between Muḥammad's birth and the hijrah, there is only a meager chronological framework. Doubtless this was because there were fewer outstanding events and fewer people capable of giving information by the time the scholars were beginning to ask questions. Some dating is provided by Muḥammad's age: the war of the Fijār took place when he was twenty, his marriage to Khadījah when he was twenty-five, the rebuilding of the Kaʿbah when he was thirty-five, and the beginning of his prophethood when he was forty or forty-three. The fact that these are multiples of five suggests that they are only approximations. For the period after the call to be a prophet, there is virtually no attempt to give dates, though the order is probably correct in the case of such events as the emigration to Abyssinia and the boycott of the clan of Hāshim. Ṭabarī sometimes introduces an event by a brief statement in his own words—presumably saying what is generally accepted—before going on to quote sources. An example of this is in his introduction to the rebuilding of the Kaʿbah (1130) where he notes that it happened ten years after Muḥammad's marriage to Khadījah; he then quotes Ibn Isḥāq as saying that it was when Muḥammad was thirty-five, and he follows with a longer account also from Ibn Isḥāq.

The importance of genealogy for the Arabs will be further discussed below, but it may be noted here that it provided a rough chronological structure for pre-Islamic events, as can be seen in the *Sīrah* of Ibn Isḥāq. Ṭabarī disregards genealogy in this respect, since he treats Muḥammad's ancestors in reverse order; and in the previous volume, he mixed in a few events in Arabian history with the accounts of the Persian kings.

A second type of historical material is provided by anecdotes other than Ḥadīth. It would be only natural that families would remember with pride the exploits of their older members in the battles of Badr and Uḥud and similar events. A notable example is the story of a man called Qatādah b. al-Nuʿmān, who was beside Muḥammad in the battle of Uḥud when he was wounded. When Muḥammad's bow broke, Qatādah picked it up and kept it. At the same time, his own eye was partly pulled out, but Muḥammad replaced it and in later life Qatādah declared that this eye was better than the other.[24] This is the sort of anecdote which would be treasured within a family, especially if the bow had become a family heirloom. It is in fact recorded by Qatādah's grandson, ʿĀṣim b.

24. Ṭabarī, pp. i, 1414, from Ibn Hishām, *Sīrah*, 573f.

'Umar b. Qatādah (d.120/737), who was a student of the *Sīrah* and produced some written works.[25] The story may well have been touched up in the course of transmission; for example, the wound to the eye may have been less serious than the description suggests, but Qatādah may well have claimed that he saw better with it. The story tells us nothing about the course of the battle, except that at one point Muḥammad used a bow, but Ibn Isḥāq may have included it because it seemed to show that Muḥammad had unusual healing powers.

Joseph Schacht regarded what he called a "family *isnād*" as an invention to give an appearance of authenticity to Ḥadīth where there was no proper *isnād*.[26] This may well be so in legal Ḥadīth where there is no question of family pride, but there seems to be no reason why it should apply to historical anecdotes, especially when these were of incidents which a family took pride in remembering. An example from the present volume is found in the long accounts from Abū Bakr's daughters of how Muḥammad told Abū Bakr that the time for his hijrah had come and how they arranged things.[27] These accounts are fitted into the narrative of the hijrah and the events leading up to it, which belong to the basic framework. This is in part a family *isnād*, since 'Ā'ishah, from whom 'Urwah heard the story, was his maternal aunt, while her sister Asmā' was his mother. When 'Ā'ishah died in 58/678 'Urwah was over thirty, so that he may have heard the story from her many times. Whether such anecdotes about minor incidents come with a family *isnād* or some other form, they cannot be rejected out of hand. Each, however, should be considered on its merits and examined for inherent improbabilities and the presence of distorting motives. Many of these anecdotes, however, appear to be genuine, and they may serve a useful purpose in adding flesh to the basic framework.

The third type of material is the text itself of the Qur'ān, together with expansions of it. When C. H. Becker spoke of "exegetical elaborations of Qur'ānic allusions," he presumably meant chiefly what Muslim scholars know as "occasions of revelation" (*asbāb al-nuzūl*), that is, accounts of the particular occasion on

---

25. Sezgin, I:279f.
26. *Origins*, 170.
27. Ṭabarī, pp. 1237-41.

which a certain passage was revealed. Thus Sūrah 80 begins with the words "He frowned and turned away, because the blind man came to him," and the occasion of this is said to have been that Muḥammad was talking to one or two important Meccan merchants (who are named), trying to convince them of the truth of Islam, when a blind man, already a believer, came and asked some questions. The blind man was Ibn Umm Maktūm, who came from a good family and was later adjudged a suitable person to be left in charge of al-Madīnah once or twice when Muḥammad was absent on an expedition. This incident must have happened in the earlier part of Muḥammad's prophethood at Mecca, but no date is assigned, and Ṭabarī neglects the story in his history. As historical material, the "occasions of revelation" are in a similar position to the anecdotes just considered; they are possibly true, but each must be examined separately. An example may be given from Ṭabarī where the alleged "occasion" has to be rejected.[28] In a passage where he speaks in his own person, he states that Muḥammad received permission for himself and the Muslims to fight the pagans by the revelation of the verse: "Fight them until there is no more *fitnah* (persecution), and the religion is God's alone" (Qur'ān 8:39). This appears to have been just before the Muslims from al-Madīnah took the Pledge of War at the pilgrimage of 622 A.D. The dating of passages of the Qur'ān is notoriously difficult, but this verse occurs in a group of verses which were almost certainly revealed after the battle of Badr.[29] This means that the Pledge of War and the impending hijrah cannot have been the "occasion" for its revelation.

Ibn Isḥāq quotes many verses from the Qur'ān in respect of important events like the battles of Badr and Uḥud, also paraphrasing and otherwise expanding them; but Ṭabarī is sparing in such quotations, and indeed there are hardly any which are relevant to the period before the hijrah, apart from some which speak of the character of Muḥammad's prophethood, which is not really a matter for a history such as the present. Any use of the Qur'ān for historical purposes necessarily presupposes the chronological framework of events, so that verses with a clear historical refer-

---

28. I:1227; See also 1225, where the emphasis is on *fitnah.*

29. The almost identical verse 2:193 seems to have been revealed shortly before the conquest of Mecca.

ence can be fitted into that. Most of the information to be derived from the Qur'ān concerns not the outward shape of events but the attitudes of the participants. Apart from this, however, much can be learnt from the Qur'ān about various aspects of the background of the events described by the historians.[30]

Not much need be said about a fourth type of material, the poetry. There has been much discussion, from the days of Ibn Hishām down to modern times, of the authenticity of the poetry quoted by Ibn Isḥāq and Ṭabarī.[31] A proportion of the poetry would seem to be by the persons to whom it is attributed, but by no means all. The poetry, like the Qur'ān, does not tell us much about the outward events, but it gives some insight into people's feelings and attitudes, including the attitudes of a tribe or clan toward its rivals. Even when poems are not by the authors to whom they are ascribed, the information they give about attitudes may still be accurate.

This review of the types of material used by historians like Ibn Isḥāq and Ṭabarī points to the conclusion that their presentation of the career of Muḥammad and the early history of the Islamic state is largely sound. The historians are, of course, subject to various limitations imposed by the general intellectual outlook of their time, as well as by personal idiosyncrasies, and for these, allowance must be made. To suggest, however, that the whole corpus of material found in the historians was invented several generations after the events is ludicrous when one becomes aware of the vastness of this corpus. Thus besides the biographical notices of the more important Companions of Muḥammad found in Ibn Saʿd, there are later biographical dictionaries of Companions by Ibn al-Athīr (d. 630/1233) and al-Dhahabī (d. 748/1348) which contain something like 10,000 names with longer or shorter biographical notices. Naturally in all this plethora of material there are differences and discrepancies, but it is amazing how much of it fits together in an interlocking whole. The problem facing scholars today is how to use all this material critically and creatively so

30. Some of this background information has been collected in Watt, *The Meccan Prophet in the Qur'ān*, Edinburgh 1987.

31. See Guillaume, *Life of Muhammad*, Introduction, xxv-xxx; W. Arafat, "Early Critics of the Authenticity of the Poetry of the Sīra," in *Bulletin of the School of Oriental and African Studies*, xxi (1958):453-63.

as to gain an understanding of the beginnings of Islam which will be relevant to the needs of Muslims in the twenty-first century

Comment on the Events

The present volume of the translation of al-Ṭabarī's history is the first of four dealing with the life of Muḥammad. In this volume al-Ṭabarī first describes the ancestors of Muḥammad, and then the main events in his life until his Hijrah or emigration to Medina in 622. The following comments deal with the chief points and issues involved.

Genealogy

The first section of this volume (pp.1073–1123 of the Leiden text) deals with the ancestry of Muḥammad. Where Ibn Isḥāq deals with the individual men more or less in chronological order, Ṭabarī reverses this and works backwards from Muḥammad's father to his grandfather, then to his great-grandfather and so on.[32]

Genealogy played an important part in the cultural tradition of the Arabs. It was the basic structure which was then clothed with stories and memories, or, to vary the metaphor, it was the skeleton for which particular events and incidents provided the flesh. Thus, for the Arabs of the period round about 600 A.D., genealogy was the heart of their traditional lore. Every individual wanted to be sure that the tribe of which he was a member was an honorable one, and its honor was bound up with the great names in its past. Maintaining the honor of the tribe was a deep spring of action among the Arabs of the desert.

Abū Bakr, Muḥammad's chief lieutenant, was an expert genealogist, and this probably meant that he also had a thorough knowledge of the internal politics of the various tribes. Genealogy continued to be studied by the early Muslim scholars, and they collected material from all available sources. What had been oral tradition was set down in writing. The matter was naturally complicated, since groups often made conflicting claims about their ancestry. By about the year 800, largely due to the work of Ibn al-Kalbī, the genealogical system had been established in a way

32. See the table on p. xiv above.

that satisfied most people. On points of detail, of course, there were still many disagreements and uncertainties. Western scholars of the late nineteenth century were inclined to think that some parts of this genealogical system had been manipulated in order to justify alliances between tribes which developed in parts of the Umayyad empire during the first Islamic century. There may be some truth in this at one or two points, but scholarly opinion now tends to think that the standard system is, broadly speaking, a true reflection of genealogical facts.

According to this system, the existing Arab tribes are descended from two distinct ancestors, ʿAdnān and Qaḥṭān. The descendants of ʿAdnān are spoken of as northern Arabs, and those of Qaḥṭān as southern Arabs or Yemenites.[33] The southern Arabs had at one time lived as a settled population in the Yemen, but as the result of a great disaster they had had to give up settled life and had taken to the desert; many had moved northwards.[34] In Arabian tradition the disaster is spoken of as the breaking of the dam of Ma'rib, and is mentioned in the Qur'ān (34:16). Remains of the great dam are still extant, and inscriptions have been found recording breakings in the middle of the fifth and sixth centuries A.D. It is now thought, however, that the breaking of the dam, which really means a breakdown of the irrigation system, was not the cause but rather the effect of a general decline of the civilization of South Arabia owing to economic and social factors.[35]

With Arab interest in genealogy being strong, it was natural that attempts should be made to link the traditional Arab system with the genealogies in the Bible, especially since the Qur'ān had associated Abraham and Ishmael with Mecca. The Biblical genealogies are found as follows: *Genesis* 5, Adam to Noah; *Genesis* 10:1-11:26, descendants of Noah; *Genesis* 25:12-16, descendants of Ishmael; 1 *Chronicles* 1:1-31, Adam to the sons of Ishmael. The Muslim scholars held ʿAdnān to be a descendant of Ishmael either through his son Nābit (Nebaioth) or through his son Qaydhar (Kedar). Qaḥṭān is sometimes held to be descended from Ishmael, but is usually identified with Joktan son of Eber and Noah's

33. The best short account is in *EI*, s.v. ʿArab (Djazīrat al-), sect. vi.
34. There is a reference to this on p. 1132 (Leiden); see also n. 68 to the text.
35. Philip K. Hitti, *History of the Arabs*, London 1960, p. 64f.

great-great-great-grandson.[36] At some points Ṭabarī admits that these genealogies have been taken from "the people of the first Book," but most Muslim scholars disliked admitting borrowings from Jews and Christians and omitted any mention of the ultimate source. The Hebrew names are mostly recognizable in Arabic despite the fact that they may not have been taken directly from Hebrew but through either Syriac or Greek.

The early history of Mecca

In the course of his description of Muḥammad's ancestors, Ṭabarī gives some stories and other material relevant to the early history of Mecca. It is not known when the Ka'bah was first regarded as sacred. The earliest statement with even a modicum of historical value is that the tribe of Jurhum exercised some sort of control over the Ka'bah, presumably benefiting in some way from the visits of pilgrims. Jurhum probably had no houses but lived in tents, and were not necessarily at Mecca throughout the year. The statement (on p. 1131) that Ishmael married a woman of Jurhum seems to be no more than an attempt to fill the gap between Ishmael and Jurhum. Ṭabarī tells (1132) how the control of the Ka'bah passed from Jurhum to Khuzā'ah after the latter had come from the Yemen; and this suggests a date in the fifth or sixth century A.D., and it seems unlikely that Jurhum would have been in control for more than a century of two. Ishmael, on the other hand, is now dated by scholars at about 1800 B.C., so that the gap between him and Jurhum is considerable. Muslim scholars thought that Jurhum had completely disappeared, but there are one or two traces of it in the early Islamic period.

In his account of Quṣayy (1092–99) Ṭabarī tells how Khuzā'ah in their turn were deprived of control of the Ka'bah by Quṣayy and his allies. This was the real founding of the town of Mecca, since Quṣayy brought his supporters and settled them in the area round the Ka'bah, presumably in permanent dwellings. In the"valley" or torrent-bed *(baṭḥā')* immediately round the Ka'bah, he gave land to the more important groups of supporters, and these became known as Quraysh al-Biṭāḥ, while less important groups, Quraysh al-Ẓawāhir, were at a greater distance. These supporting

36. *Genesis* 10:25-30; *I Chronicles* 1:19-23.

groups were probably related to Quṣayy, but possibly not so precisely as the standard genealogy suggests (of which an abbreviated version is given below).

Though the name Quraysh is sometimes given to an ancestor, either Fihr or al-Naḍr, in its origin it seems to have been a nickname which was given to the supporters of Quṣayy as a whole, perhaps meaning "the little collection," though other meanings were suggested by later scholars (as the text shows). Associated with control of the Ka'bah were various offices or privileges, doubtless intended to ensure that things went smoothly during the time of pilgrimage. Among the offices mentioned in Ṭabarī's material were: the *siqāyah* or ensuring of a water supply, especially for the pilgrims; the *rifādah* or seeing that there was food for the pilgrims; the *liwā'*, which was either carrying the standard in battle or arranging for this; and the *nasī'* or arranging when a month was to be intercalated.[37]

The existence of the sanctuary and the habit of pilgrimage gave Mecca some advantages for commerce. In the later sixth century, possibly because of the warfare between the Byzantine and Persian empires, the merchants of Mecca seem to have gained something like monopoly control over the trade between South Arabia (and the Indian Ocean?) and the Mediterranean coast, and they had become very prosperous. There were two or three rival goups, but commercial interests made them work together. Though most Meccans shared in the prosperity, some fared very much better than others, and there was growing social malaise as the wealthy came to disregard aspects of traditional morality. Islam may be said to have developed as an answer to the problems resulting from Meccan commercial prosperity.

Events up to Muhammad's call (1123–39)

The story of Muḥammad's encounter with the Christian monk Baḥīrā, like some of the other stories about Muḥammad in this volume, is to be regarded as primarily a way of reassuring people that Muḥammad was really a prophet. After the Arabs had conquered Syria, Egypt, and Iraq, they were in contact with Christians who used various arguments to show that Muḥammad was not

37. See n. 71 to the text.

The Clans of Quraysh.
(Names in capitals are those of groups commonly spoken of as clans.)

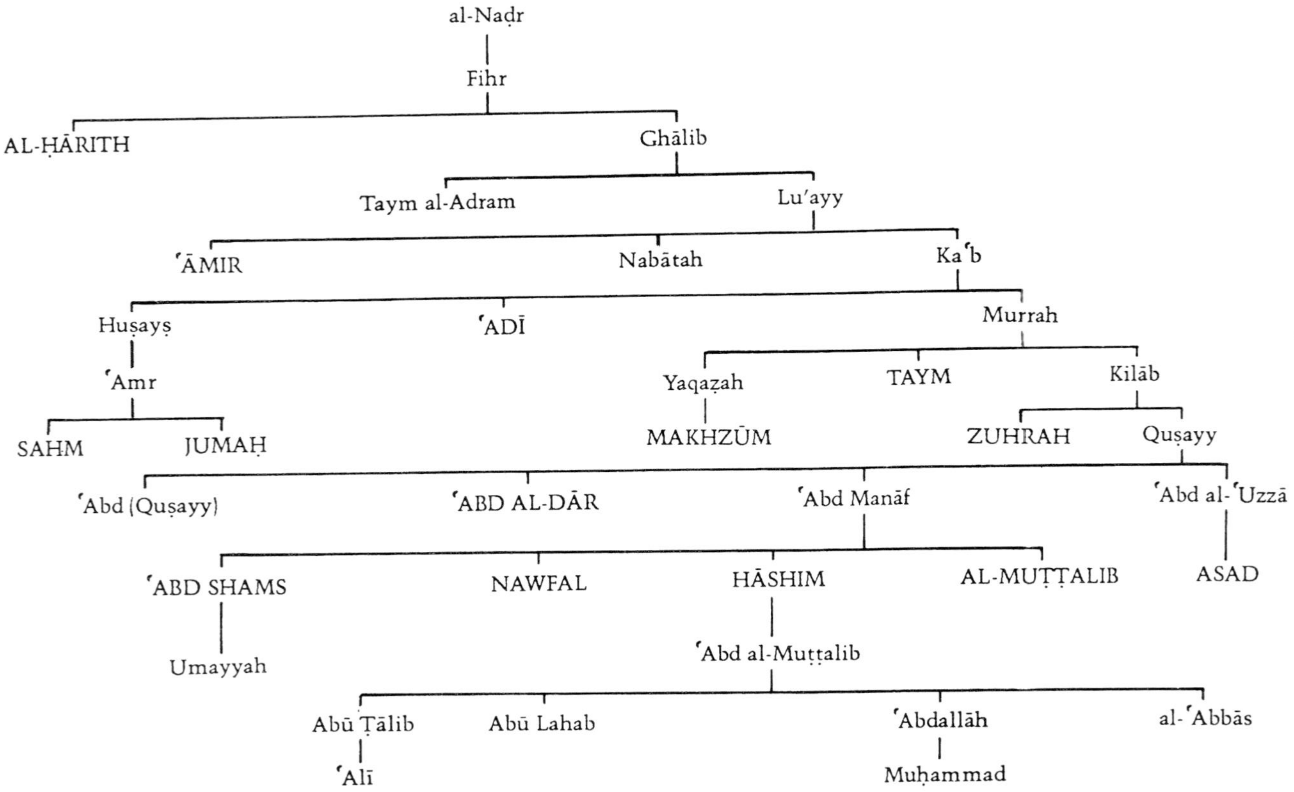

a prophet; for example, that he had performed no miracles, and that his coming had not been foretold. It is almost certain that Muḥammad travelled more than once with Abū Ṭālib and others to Gaza and Damascus, and he may well have had some contacts with Christian monks; but the details of the story must be treated as hagiography.

Muḥammad's marriage to Khadījah was a turning point in his career. The system of inheritance customary among the Arabs at this time allowed only mature persons to inherit, and thus Muḥammad received nothing from either his father or his grandfather. This meant that he was unable to engage in trading on his own account as most of his relatives did. It is not known what social arrangements made it possible for Khadījah to be a merchant in her own right, though at least one other woman merchant is mentioned in the sources. After the marriage Muḥammad continued to trade with Khadījah's capital, though presumably now as her partner rather than as her agent. We are told that he had as a business associate al-Sā'ib b. Abī al-Sā'ib of the clan of Makhzūm, a nephew of Khadījah's second husband. These arrangements made it possible for Muḥammad to make some use of his administrative skills, but Khadījah seems to have been only moderately wealthy and Muḥammad was probably still excluded from the most lucrative enterprises.

It appears that Khadījah also appreciated the qualities in Muḥammad which made it possible for him to be a prophet; and after some of his earliest prophetic experiences, when he was uncertain what to make of these and anxious about the future, her encouragement and support helped him to overcome his difficulties. She had a cousin, Waraqah b. Nawfal, who is said to have become a Christian, and she may have learnt something about Christianity from him. Waraqah, when talking to Khadījah about Muḥammad, is reported to have identified Muḥammad's experiences with those of Moses in the Bible. It is doubtful whether Waraqah ever spoke to Muḥammad about this, but his ideas may have been conveyed by Khadījah, for in the end Muḥammad was convinced that he was continuing the line of Biblical prophets.

The story of Muḥammad's part in the rebuilding of the Ka'bah is probably intended to show that he was a person of high character before his call to be a prophet. There may be some truth in the story, in that many of the merchants may have realized that Muḥammad was unusually skilled in handling difficult personal situations.

The call to be prophet

It will be convenient to treat under a single heading all the matters covered in pages 1139–57, since they are closely interconnected, besides being the most important part of the present volume. The historian can hardly avoid asking what light this material throws on the origins of a religion professed by perhaps a seventh of the world's population.

It is necessary first of all to say something about religious attitudes in Mecca at the time, and in particular to call attention to a feature which was ovelooked in my book *Muḥammad at Mecca.* This is the existence in Mecca of a belief in Allah as a "high god," that is, as one god among many, though in some respects superior to the others.[38] The fact is clearly stated in two passages of the Qur'ān and referred to in several others.

> If you ask them who created the heavens and the earth, and made the sun and moon subservient, they will certainly say, Allāh. . . . And if you ask them who sent down water from heaven and thereby revived the earth after its death, they will certainly say, Allāh. . . . And when they sail on the ship they pray to Allāh as sole object of devotion, but when he has brought them safe to land they "associate" (*yushrikūn*) others with him (29:61–65).
>
> If you ask them who created the heavens and the earth, they will certainly say, Allāh. Say: Do you then consider that what you call upon apart from Allāh, those (female beings), are able, if God wills evil to me, to remove this evil, or, if he wills mercy for me, to hold back this mercy (39:38)?

This last passage is possibly a reference to the belief that the other deities intercede with Allāh on behalf of their worshippers, a belief which is clearly stated in 10:18: "they serve apart from Allāh what neither harms nor benefits them, and they say, These

38. See Watt, "Belief in a 'high god' in pre-Islamic Mecca," *Journal of Semitic Studies*, xvi (1971): 35-40; "The Qur'ān and Belief in a 'High God'," *Der Islam*, lvi (1979): 205-11. See also n. 4 to the text.

are our intercessors (*shufa'ā'*) with Allāh."[39] Once it is admitted that there was this belief in Allāh as a "high god," it will be found that there are many other passages of the Qur'ān, descriptive of pagans, in which it may be implicit.

While it is clear that such beliefs were widespread among Muḥammad's contemporaries, it is impossible to know what proportion of the people held them. Similar beliefs are known to have been held throughout the Semitic Near East during the Graeco-Roman period.[40] Something of the kind is also to be found in the Bible, for according to recent interpreters, *Psalm* 16:2f. runs as follows:

> To Yahweh you say, "My Lord, you are my fortune, nothing else but you," yet to these pagan deities in the land, "My princes, all my pleasure is in you."[41]

Muḥammad must have been aware of this belief in Allāh as a "high god" even if he did not fully share in it. There is no way of discovering how much he knew about Judaism and Christianity before his revelations began. He presumably knew all that was commonly known in Mecca, and he may have discussed religious matters with Christians on his visits to Syria. Khadījah, too, may have known something about Christianity through her cousin Waraqah who is said to have been a Christian. The word Allāh, however, was presumably used by Jews and Christians when speaking about God in Arabic; and this must have made it difficult for serious-minded people in Mecca to understand how Allāh as worshipped by Jews and Christians differed from Allāh as worshipped by their pagan contemporaries.

Relevant to this matter is a significant point which does not seem to have been noticed by Western scholars, namely, that the word Allāh does not occur in the earliest passages of the Qur'ān, or does so only rarely. The relative dating of the Qur'ān is, of course, a notoriously difficult matter about which Western scholars are not agreed, while few Muslims accept the Western approach to chronology. The absence of the word Allāh in early sūrahs can be

39. See also 36:23 and 43:86.
40. See J. Teixidor, *The Pagan God: Popular Religion in the Greco-Roman Near East*, Princeton 1977.
41. Jerusalem Bible.

illustrated from the latest attempt to place the sūrahs in chronological order, that of Régis Blachère in his French translation.[42] In what he reckons to be the first seventeen sūrahs, the word Allāh occurs only three times, namely, in his seventh (91:13), his tenth (95:8) and his sixteenth (87:7); and of these, he considers the verses 91:13 and 87:7 to be later than the rest of the sūrah. Instead of Allāh, one finds "your Lord" (rabbuka) as in 96:1,3 or "we" as in 94:14. The word Allāh occurs, of course, in the invocation at the beginning of each sūrah, but this would be added later.

The story of the "satanic verses" (1192–96) shows the persistence of some confusion between Allāh conceived monotheistically and Allāh as "high god." The truth of the story cannot be doubted, since it is inconceivable that any Muslim would invent such a story, and it is inconceivable that a Muslim scholar would accept such a story from a non-Muslim. It also appears to be vouched for by a verse from the Qur'ān (22:52). Many Muslims reject the story as unworthy of Muḥammad, but there is nothing unworthy of him in holding that his knowledge and understanding of "his Lord" developed during the early years of his prophethood as the revelations multiplied.

The core of the story is that one day Muḥammad received a revelation (as he supposed) in which three goddesses were mentioned and permission was given to use them as intercessors. He communicated this to the leading men of Quraysh, and they all joined with him in Islamic worship. Later he realized that the verses permitting intercession were not from God but must have been put into his mind by Satan. When the change was communicated to Quraysh, their opposition became even fiercer. Some versions state that the realization of the falsity of the supposed revelation came to Muḥammad on the evening of the same day, but this is unlikely if one accepts the further story about some Emigrants returning from Abyssinia. There would thus appear to have been an interval between the "revelation" of the verses and their cancellation.

The point to be emphasized here is that Muḥammad did not immediately appreciate that there was a contradiction between this permission for intercession and a genuine monotheism. This does

42. First edition, Paris 1949.

not necessarily mean that he accepted the idea of the believers in Allāh as "high god" that there were other deities which could intercede with him Some of those who heard the verses might certainly have understood them in this way, but Muḥammad himself probably thought of the three goddesses as angels. It is to be noted that verse 26 of the same sūrah speaks of the possibility of intercession by angels: "How many angels there are in the heavens whose intercession is of no avail save after God gives leave to those whom he chooses and accepts!" The full story of the rejection of the "satanic verses" will never be known. What is certain is that a fresh revelation cancelled them and replaced them by others. It is from this time, too, that the revelations emphasize that "there is no deity but God" and that he must be the sole object of worship.[43] Even the possibility that the goddesses might be angels is rejected: "they are but names which you have named, you and your fathers" (53:23). Thus, in the end, the Qur'ān decisively rejected the belief in Allāh as "high god," but it is part of the background against which the accounts of Muḥammad's call must be considered.

There is much to be said for accepting the statement of 'Ā'ishah that first beginning of revelation for the Messenger of God was true vision (*al-ru'yā al-sādiqah*); it used to come upon him like the dawn".[44] It seems very probable that this refers to the two visions described in Sūrah 53:1–8:

> By the Star when it sets,
> your comrade neither errs nor is deceived,
> nor does he speak from (his own) fancy.
> It is naught but a revelation revealed,
> which one of mighty powers taught him,
> a vigorous one; he grew clear to view
> while being on the uppermost horizon.
> Then he drew near and came down
> till he was (distant) two bows' length or nearer
> and revealed to his slave what he revealed.
> The heart lied not (in seeing) what it saw.

43. Emphasis on the unicity of God is not found in the early passages of the Qur'ān; see Watt, *Muhammad at Mecca*, 60-85.
44. P. 1147.

Will you dispute with him concerning what he sees?

Indeed he saw him yet another time
by the lote tree of the utmost boundary,
near which is the Garden of Abode,
when the lote tree was strangely shrouded.
The eye turned not aside nor yet was overbold.
He saw one of the greatest signs of his Lord.

In Islamic tradition, the second vision is often identified with the "night journey," of which more will be said later. This is unlikely, however, since the vision of 53:13–18 appears to be very early, whereas the "night journey" is generally held to come late in the Meccan period. The words here translated "reveal" and "revelation" (*awḥā, waḥy)* are those which became the standard terms for these concepts; but in this passage they are used in a more general sense, which could perhaps be rendered by "suggested" or "indicated", and of which there are several examples in the Qur'ān.[45] This means that these visions were not the beginning of the verbal revelations which constitute the Qur'ān. It should also be noted that the word "slave" (*ʿabd)* in verse 10 implies that the object seen was a divine being and not an angel, since "slave" would be inappropriate in the latter case. When, after the hijrah, it came to be the accepted view that the angel Gabriel was the agent of revelation, he was taken to be the object of the visions; but many of the early commentators allow that it was a vision of God. It may be, however, that Muḥammad thought of him only as "his Lord" and not as Allāh.

The text of Ṭabarī (1245–50) shows that there were two strong bodies of opinion about Muḥammad's age when he was called to be a prophet, one maintaining that he was forty, the other that he was forty-three. It would seem probable that there is some truth underlying both views, and that they refer to two stages in his becoming aware of himself as a prophet. The problem then becomes how to distinguish between the full prophethood from the age of forty-three onwards and what happened in the previous three years. There are two main possibilities. One is that the revelation of the Qur'ān began soon after the visions but that he did not pro-

45. Watt, *Bell's Introduction to the Qur'ān*, 20-23.

claim the revelations publicly until after three years. The other is that during the three years he was not receiving verbal revelations (or at least not until near the end), but that he had some other kind of religious experience. This second possibility may be connected with the statement that during the three years his visitant was the angel Isrāfīl (1248f.). This would mean that during these years Muḥammad was coming to a deeper understanding of religious truth and working out a system of religious practice, such as the details of the formal prayer. The statement that these were demonstrated to him by Gabriel (1156f.) is unlikely to be a description of the original experience, since Gabriel does not seem to have played any part in Muḥammad's thinking until after the hijrah. The statement would be more plausible if Isrāfīl was substituted for Gabriel; but on the whole, it is likely that Isrāfīl was brought in by a later Muslim scholar. Nevertheless, it would be true that Muḥammad must have had religious experiences through which he learnt such matters as the details of the formal prayer, and he may have done so only gradually. Since the details of the prayer are not prescribed in the Qur'ān, they must have come to Muḥammad through some form of nonverbal inspirational experience. This tends to support the second of the two possibilities, namely, that for most of the three-year period Muḥammad was not receiving Qur'ānic revelations but was having experiences of another kind.

There is not much of clear historical value in the remaining material about the call to prophethood. The story of the revelation by Gabriel of the first part of Sūrah 96 cannot be accepted as it stands, since there are strong grounds for holding that it was only after the hijrah that Muḥammad came to think of Gabriel as the agent of revelation. The receiving of passages of the Qur'ān does not seem to have been accompanied by any visual experience, and so it is possible that Muḥammad thought that it was "his Lord" himself who was putting the Qur'ān into his heart. Interpreted in this way, the story may be essentially true, at least in those versions in which the words *mā aqra'u* are taken to mean "what shall I recite?" At some point a Muslim scholar realized that these words could also mean "I do not recite" or "do not read." By this time, in order to counter Christian claims that Muḥammad had taken stories from the Bible, it had become a point of Muslim apologetic that Muḥammad was unable to read; and so the story of the first revelation was sometimes modified to support this line of apologetic. Such modifications are certainly not original.

Even if the central point of the story is accepted, the question has still to be asked whether the beginning of Sūrah 96 was in fact the first revelation. Some nineteenth-century scholars, like Sir William Muir and Hubert Grimme, thought that several sūrahs had been revealed before this passage. It can also be argued that it would be easy for a later Muslim scholar to think that a sūrah beginning "recite" *(iqra') must* have been the beginning of a book called "recitation" (*qur'ān* - the verbal noun from the same root), and then to invent a story to substantiate this. On the other hand, when the core of the story is accepted, it does sound like a new beginning.

The contents of the passage, however, seem to show that it cannot have been the first revealed. The words "your Lord... taught by the pen, taught man what he did not know" are almost certainly a reference to previous scriptures, that is, to the Bible. This is not meant to suggest that Muḥammad had himself read any of the Bible, for it is unlikely that it had been translated into Arabic, and doubtful if anyone in Mecca had a copy of it in any language. The point is that Muḥammad had had two visions and other strange experiences, and sometimes was not sure what to make of them. He needed to be assured by someone with the requisite knowledge that what he had experienced was similar to what had been experienced by the prophets of the Bible. There are many discrepancies in the versions of the story about Waraqah, but the central point is the assurance to Muḥammad that what had come to him was the great Nāmūs which had come to Moses (1151f.). Western scholars have tended to identify the Nāmūs with the Mosaic law because of the resemblance to the Greek *nomos* (law). The identification with Gabriel is impossible for the reason given above, but suggests that Waraqah may have been saying that the "Lord" of Muḥammad's experience was God who had come to Moses. Certainly throughout his prophetic career Muḥammad never doubted that he and the Jews and the Christians were all alike worshippers of God. So, in a sense, it was because of what "his Lord" had taught by the pen to men like Waraqah that Muḥammad was able to have the assurance that he stood within a great prophetic tradition. This does not prove that there had been verbal revelations to Muḥammad before Sūrah 96, but it makes it not unlikely that there had been some. If this were so, then the *iqra'* of 96:1 could be a command to recite revealed passages as part of the formal prayer, and in this respect would mark a new beginning.

Early in the material from al-Zuhrī on page 1147 there occur the words, "the Truth (that is, God) came to him unexpectedly and said, Muḥammad, you are the Messenger of God", and "he" repeated the words shortly afterwards in Khadījah's chamber. A line or two later the same words are spoken to Muḥammad by Gabriel; and on page 1155, Gabriel comes to him after the "gap" in the revelation and says "you are the Prophet of God." The name of Gabriel cannot be original here, since he belongs to the period after the hijrah. If there is a genuine experience underlying the story, it is to be found in the version which speaks of "the Truth," for this could be identified with Muḥammad's "Lord" and the divine being of the visions.

Further, if through this experience Muḥammad came to some understanding of his vocation, it could not have been by means of the term "Messenger of God" *(rasūl Allāh)*. Apart from the fact that he seems to have been uncertain whether to think of "his Lord" as identical with Allāh, the term *rasūl* would probably not have had much meaning for him at this period. He certainly came to believe that he had a divinely given vocation, but he would have thought of it in other terms. In the earliest passages of the Qur'ān, he is told to warn or to admonish, and is then spoken of as a "warner" *(nadhīr)* or "admonisher" *(mudhakkir)*.[46]

Some Muslim scholars held that the first passage of the Qur'ān to be revealed was the beginning of Sūrah 74: "O you enveloped in a cloak, Rise and warn." Others held that this was not the first of all revelations but was the one marking the beginning of public preaching. The words "rise and warn" certainly imply communicating the message to people in general; but then they could not be the first of all revelations unless there were none for communication only to believers.

The idea that Muḥammad thought of committing suicide must

46. E.g., 74:2 and 87:9 (commands). See also *Muhammad at Mecca,* 71f.

have come originally from himself, though it may not have been so definite as it appears to be in the stories, but was perhaps rather a mood of dejection and despair. Sūrah 93 *(al-Ḍuḥā)* gives encouragement to Muḥammad to rise above such a mood. The reason for such depression could be perplexity at the strange experiences through which he was passing and uncertainty whether to accept them at their face value. After Muḥammad had received a number of revelations, there was a period known as the "gap" *(fatrah)* when none came to him; and this also he found worrying. It should be remembered, too, that there was a widespread feeling among Semitic peoples that the near approach of the divine could have disastrous consequences for the individual, and so was to be feared. To be covered with a cloak seems to have been regarded as offering some protection against the danger. This is the most likely explanation of the description of Muḥammad as "enveloped or enwrapped in a cloak" in the opening verses of Sūrahs 73 and 74. The words *muzzammil* and *muddaththir* are similar in meaning as well as in form. It is possible that the stories in which Muḥammad asks to be covered were invented to explain the two words.

Close examination, then, of the material presented by Ṭabarī about Muḥammad's call to be a prophet shows that much of it has little historical value. This should not, however, obscure the fact that most of the main points in the presentation as a whole are almost certainly true. Muḥammad had meditated deeply on the social, moral, and religious problems of Mecca. He had two visions which moved him profoundly and other religious experiences. He became convinced first that God had called him to be a "warner" to his community, then later that he had called him to be not just a prophet, but a prophet in the line of the biblical prophets. He began to receive messages or revelations from God, and these continued to come to him at short intervals. He communicated these to other people, and those who believed them came to form a religious community.

The night journey (1157–59)

Popular Islamic tradition has greatly elaborated and expanded the story of Muḥammad's "night journey" and ascent to heaven *(isrā', mi'rāj)*. There is much more to it than the brief account given by Ṭabarī. In many versions, Muḥammad is first of all carried from Mecca to Jerusalem. and then from Jerusalem taken up to the seventh heaven. It is claimed that these are fuller descriptions of what is briefly referred to in the Qur'ān (17:1):

> Glorified be he who carried his servant by night from the Inviolable Mosque to the Furthest Mosque, whose neighborhood we have blessed, that we might show him our signs.

This presumably refers to a dream or something similar, and is far from justifying the plethora of material about the "night journey" of Muḥammad.[47]

The first Muslims (1159–69)

The material on the question of who was the first male to become a Muslim is not so much history as political propaganda. For Shī'ites, the assertion that "'Alī was the first male Muslim is an additional mark of his superiority to Abū Bakr and further support for his claim to be the rightful successor of Muḥammad as caliph. 'Alī may well have been the first male to accept Islam and join in the prayer; but he was only ten at that time. The assertion that Abū Bakr was first is doubtless a Sunnite claim that he was best fitted to succeed Muḥammad; though he became Muḥammad's chief lieutenant, he was not necessarily his best friend at the time of his call, and, if not, probably not the first Muslim. The statement that fifty accepted Islam before him but that he was the best Muslim looks like a Sunnite admission that he was not first. Zayd b. Ḥārithah, as a member of Muḥammad's household, may well have been the first adult male.

The opposition to Muḥammad in Mecca (1169–99)

It was probably a year or two after the beginning of Muḥammad's public preaching that he and his followers came to experience serious opposition from the leading merchants of Mecca. Some older Western scholars thought that the reason for the opposition was that the leading merchants considered that Muḥammad's attack on idols would put an end to the sacredness of the Ka'bah and of Mecca generally. This idea is without founda-

---

47. There is much more material in Ibn Hishām, *Sīrah* 263-71; see also *EI(S)*, art. Mi'rādj (Horovitz).

tion. There is no record of Muḥammad doing other than respecting the sacredness of the Ka'bah and of Mecca. Though the Qur'ānic attack on idols would apply to the idol Hubal who was kept in the sacred area round the Ka'bah, the men of Quraysh are called upon (Sūrah 106:3) to worship "the Lord of this House"; and this last phrase implies that for Muslims the Ka'bah is a temple of the one true God, and therefore eminently sacred. Since the three goddesses of the "satanic verses" had each a shrine not far from Mecca, at al-Ṭā'if, Nakhlah, and al-Mushallal, respectively, the cancellation of the verses would mean primarily that worship at these shrines was no longer permitted, but would not affect the status of the Ka'bah. There is nothing here to suggest that the pilgrimage would be adversely affected and trade destroyed.

The reasons for the Meccan opposition are to be sought rather in the main themes found in the earlier passages of the Qur'ān. In *Muhammad at Mecca,* pages 60–85, the passages were carefully examined and the main themes shown to be: God's goodness and power, the return to God for Judgement, the requirement that men should respond by gratitude and worship, and also by being generous with their wealth and "purifying" themselves. The requirement of generosity implied a critique of the merchants' unscrupulous pursuit of profit and their disregard of traditional obligations to kinsmen. The call to men to believe in God, to be grateful to Him, and to worship Him went counter to the firm conviction of the merchants that their own economic and political powers were the ultimate determinant of events. The merchants probably also felt that Muḥammad was threatening their political control of Meccan affairs. He was collecting round him devoted followers, and if this process continued and his followers became a sizeable proportion of the people of Mecca, it would be difficult for the merchant's council to go against rulings given by Muḥammad.

Credence should also be given to the statement in the letter of 'Urwah to the caliph 'Abd al-Malik (p.1180) that Quraysh were not wholly averse to Muḥammad "until he mentioned their idols" and that then wealthy Quraysh from al-Ṭā'if took the lead in stirring up opposition to him. The "mention of idols" probably means the cancellation of the "satanic verses"; and it is conceivable that Meccans from al-Ṭā'if led the opposition because the rejection of the shrine of the goddess Allāt there somehow adversely affected their business interests. The "mention of the idols," however, was doubtless no more than the occasion for the development of oppressive measures, since the worship of the idols probably meant little to the materialistic merchants. The basic reasons for their opposition were the Qur'ānic critique of their attitudes and practices, and the threat to themselves from Muḥammad's increasing power. It was possibly also relevant to the growth of opposition that Muḥammad's followers were largely young men, some of them sons and younger brothers of the leading merchants.

The various ways in which life was made difficult for Muḥammad and the Muslims are illustrated in the pages of Ṭabarī. There was economic pressure on individuals, and finally on the whole clan of Hāshim. There were insulting words and actions. There were repressive measures involving physical coercion. The last happened within the clan or even family, since peace was maintained in Mecca, as elsewhere in Arabia, by the *lex talionis,* (law of retaliation). Each individual was normally "protected" by his clan in the sense that, if he were to be injured, honor would demand that his clan should exact "an eye for an eye," and so on. Muḥammad himself suffered little other than petty annoyances because his uncle Abū Ṭālib, as chief of Hāshim, refused to withdraw clan protection from him despite attempts of the opponents to entice or threaten him into changing his mind — he was not himself a Muslim.

When the level of prosecution became intolerable for some of the Muslims, Muḥammad encouraged them to emigrate to Abyssinia, a country with which Mecca had trading relations. The primary motive was to escape from persecution, but there may also have been secondary motives of various kinds, perhaps even the hope that the Christian emperor (or Negus) might become a Muslim. Two separate emigrations are sometimes spoken of, but this seems to be an unjustified deduction from the fact that Ibn Isḥāq has two separate lists. It is also said that some of the Emigrants came back when they heard that after the "satanic verses" the leading Meccans had joined Muḥammad in the prayer; they did not hear of the cancellation until they were near Mecca, but they then returned to Abyssinia. What seems likely is that there was a succession of small groups rather than two emigrations of large parties. Not all the Muslims in Mecca emigrated. Those who did nearly all belonged to a specific group of clans, and this was doubtless because these clans were more vigorous in persecuting their own members. Some of the Emigrants returned to Mecca before the hijrah, but others remained in Abyssinia until six years after that event, presumably making a good living as traders.

The culmination of the attempts of the opponents to deprive Muḥammad of the "protection" of his clan was an agreement by most of the clans of Mecca not to trade with the clan of Hāshim (and its associated clan of al-Muṭṭalib) and not to intermarry. This "boycott" is said to have lasted for about three years. It does not seem to have caused undue hardship to Hāshim, possibly because they were not dependent on the boycotting clans for the importing of food. Some of these clans eventually broke the boycott, perhaps feeling that they were losing more from it than they were gaining.

It was probably in the year 619 A.D. that the boycott ended, and shortly afterwards Muḥammad lost by death both his wife Khadījah and the uncle who had protected him, Abū Ṭālib. Abū Ṭālib was succeeded as chief of Hāshim by another uncle Abū Lahab, and the latter soon found an opportunity of depriving Muḥammad of clan protection without loss of face; the reason given is said to have been that Muḥammad had alleged their common ancestor ʿAbd al-Muṭṭalib to be in Hell.

The final years at Mecca and the Hijrah (1199–1245)

Soon after these events Muḥammad made a journey to al-Ṭā'if, doubtless because he had lost, or was about to lose, his "protection" in Mecca. He may have hoped to find some support for his religion there, because al-Ṭā'if, a trade rival of Mecca, had been forcibly brought under the control of its stronger neighbor. When he reached al-Ṭā'if, however, he found no one ready to support him and stand up for him, and he suffered badly at the hands of some of the local population. Before he returned to Mecca he had to obtain the "protection" of some man of importance. Two requests were rejected, but the third man he approached, the head of the clan of Nawfal, gave a positive answer, though he probably imposed conditions, such as not preaching, of which we are not informed.

The impossibility of spreading Islam further in Mecca made Muḥammad look for potential followers elsewhere. He approached some of the nomadic tribes when they were at Mecca for the annual pilgrimage, but found no response. Then, probably in 620, he met half a dozen men from al-Madīnah and was listened to with interest. Unlike Mecca, where there was no agriculture, al-Madīnah was an oasis growing dates and cereals; but for a long period it had been plagued with feuds of increasing intensity between rival clans and groups of clans. Most recently, at the battle of Bu'āth about 617, nearly all the clans of al-Madīnah had been involved on one side or the other. Peace had been restored but it was still fragile, and many people in al-Madīnah were attracted by the prospect of having someone with an authority such as Muḥammad's, who might be able to settle their disputes.

A more representative group of twelve came to the pilgrimage of 621 and took the first pledge of al-'Aqabah, which was tantamount to accepting Islam. Muḥammad sent an agent to al-Madīnah with them, ostensibly to teach them Islam, but probably also to gain detailed information about political trends in al-Madīnah and to avoid a repetition of the fiasco at al-Ṭā'if. A year later, at the pilgrimage of 622, over seventy men and one or two women made the second pledge of al-'Aqabah, the pledge of war, by which they not only accepted Islam but also undertook to "protect" Muḥammad in al-Madīnah as they would one of their nearest kinsmen.

This pledge made it possible for Muḥammad and the community of Muslims to "emigrate" to al-Madīnah. Muḥammad encouraged those who wanted to go to make the journey in small groups. After about two months, over seventy men with their wives and families had reached al-Madīnah. Some Muslims chose to remain in Mecca, but it is difficult to know how many. The leading opponents apparently had some awareness of what was happening, and realized that it could create problems for themselves, though, despite some of their alleged remarks, they could hardly have anticipated the precise nature of their problems. There may well have been a plot to kill Muḥammad of the kind described by Ṭabarī.

So long as he remained in Mecca Muḥammad was presumably still under the "protection" of the clan of Nawfal. On leaving Mecca, however, he would have no "protection" until he reached al-Madīnah. This was the reason for the secrecy of his departure, for his hiding in the cave, and then following an unusual route to al-Madīnah. His precautions were effective, and he reached al-Madīnah safely on 24 September 622.

Questions of chronology (1245–56)

The various statements about the length of Muḥammad's prophetic career in Mecca support the view adopted above that there were two points, about three years apart, at each of which an important step forward was taken. The second was almost certainly the beginning of the public proclamation of the message. The first is not so clear, but was probably not the beginning of verbal revelation, that is, of the Qur'ān. If, as some of the sources seem to indicate, the period of public preaching at Mecca was ten years, then it must have begun about 612, and the earlier stage about 609; but these dates are admittedly only approximate.

The establishment of the Islamic era was almost certainly the work of the caliph 'Umar (634–44). The matter could hardly have been of concern to Muḥammad while the Islamic polity was still at the embryonic stage. The distinctive character of the Islamic year, of course, was fixed shortly before Muḥammad's death by the Qur'ānic rejection of intercalation.[48] The choice of the hijrah for the beginning of the Islamic era was doubtless made because it was the effective beginning of the Islamic state, and for the practical reason that there was little chronological material before the hijrah and a large amount afterwards.

The Islamic era was fixed to begin with the first month of the Arab year during which Muḥammad made the hijrah, and it was decided, by working backwards, that Muḥarram 1, A.H. 1 was equivalent to July 16, A.D. 622 This was based, however, on the assumption that no intercalary months were observed after the hijrah, though it is unlikely that this was so. This may explain why the sources say that Muḥammad arrived in al-Madīnah on a Monday, whereas according to the standard calendar the day was a Friday.

W. Montgomery Watt

48. Qur'ān 9:36f. See also n. 74 to the text.

The Lineage of the Messenger of God [1073]

ʿAbdallāh (His Father)

The name of the Messenger of God was Muḥammad, and he was the son of ʿAbdallāh b. ʿAbd al-Muṭṭalib. ʿAbdallāh, the father of the Messenger of God, was his father's youngest son. ʿAbdallāh, al-Zubayr, and ʿAbd Manāf, who is Abū Ṭālib, were sons of ʿAbd al-Muṭṭalib by the same mother, Fāṭimah bt. ʿAmr b. ʿĀʾidh b. ʿImrān b. Makhzūm. This information was given to us by Ibn Ḥumayd—Salamah b. al-Faḍl—Ibn Isḥāq.

Hishām b. Muḥammad—his father: ʿAbdallāh b. ʿAbd al-Muṭṭalib, the father of the Messenger of God, Abū Ṭālib, whose name was ʿAbd Manāf, al-Zubayr, ʿAbd al-Kaʿbah, ʿĀtikah, Barrah and Umaymah, the children of ʿAbd al-Muṭṭalib, were full brothers and sisters, their mother being Fāṭimah bt. ʿAmr b. ʿĀʾidh b. ʿImrān b. Makhzūm b. Yaqaẓah.

Yūnus b. ʿAbd al-Aʿlā—Ibn Wahb—Yūnus b. Yazīd—Ibn Shihāb—Qubayṣah b. Dhuʾayb: A woman had sworn to sacrifice her son at the Kaʿbah if she achieved a certain matter; she did (in fact) achieve it and then she came to al-Madīnah to seek a legal opinion on her oath.[1] She went to ʿAbdallāh b. ʿUmar, who said, "I do not know that God has given any command concerning oaths other other than that one should be faithful to them." "Am I to sacrifice

1. This incident probably occurred a few years after A.D. 661 when the seat of the caliphate had been moved to Damascus. Among the religious authorities remaining in al-Madinah were ʿAbdallāh b. ʿUmar, son of the caliph ʿUmar, and ʿAbdallāh b. ʿAbbās, son of Muḥammad's uncle al-ʿAbbās.

my son, then?" she asked. ʿAbdallāh replied, "God has forbidden you to kill one another," and said no more to her than that. Then she went to ʿAbdallāh b. ʿAbbās and asked his opinion . He replied, "God has commanded you to be faithful to your oaths and has for-
[1074] bidden you to kill one another. ʿAbd al-Muṭṭalib b. Hāshim vowed that if ten of his sons grew to manhood he would sacrifice one of them. He cast lots among them, and the lot fell on ʿAbdallāh b. ʿAbd al-Muṭṭalib, whom he loved more than any other. Then he said, 'O God, shall I sacrifice him or a hundred camels?' He cast lots between him and the camels, and the lot fell on the hundred camels." Then Ibn ʿAbbās said to the woman, "My opinion is that you should sacrifice a hundred camels in place of your son."

Finally the matter came to the attention of Marwān,[2] who was governor of al-Madīnah at that time, and he said, "I do not think that either Ibn ʿUmar or Ibn ʿAbbās has given a correct opinion; no vow which contravenes God's commands can be binding. Ask God's forgiveness, repent, give alms, and perform such charitable actions as you are able. As for sacrificing your son, God has forbidden you to do that." The people were delighted and lost in admiration at this verdict, and concluded that Marwān's opinion was the correct one; from that time on they adopted the opinion that no vow which contravenes God's commands can be binding.

Ibn Isḥāq gives a fuller account of this matter of ʿAbd al-Muṭṭalib's vow than one given above.[3] Ibn Ḥumayd—Salamah b. al-Faḍl—Muḥammad b. Isḥāq: ʿAbd al-Muṭṭalib b. Ḥāshim, so it is said—and God knows best—had vowed, when Quraysh made difficulties for him about the digging of Zamzam, that if ten sons were born to him and reached maturity so that they could protect him, he would sacrifice one of them to God at the Kaʿbah.[4] When he had ten sons grown to maturity and he knew that they

2. Marwān b. al-Ḥakam, of the clan of Umayyah, became Caliph in 684 and died in 685. The story puts the Umayyads in a favorable light.

3. Ibn Hishām, *Sīrah*, 97-101.

4. The name Allāh has throughout been translated as "God." It should be kept in mind, however, that in the pre-Islamic period it does not necessarily mean "God" in a monotheistic sense. It is known from the Qur'ān (29:61-5; 39:38; etc.) that many pre-Islamic Arabs believed in Allāh as a high or supreme god superior to the other gods whom they also recognized. See: Watt, "Belief in a 'high god' in pre-Islamic Mecca," *Journal of Semitic Studies*, xvi (1971):35-40; "The Qurān and Belief in a 'High God,'" *Der Islam*, lvi (1979),: 205-11. This explains how it was possible for ʿAbd al-Muṭṭalib to stand beside Hubal while praying to Allāh, as

would protect him, he brought them together, told them of his vow, and called on them to keep faith with God in this matter. They expressed their obedience, and asked what they should do. [1075] He replied, "Let every one of you take an arrow, write his name on it, and bring it to me." They did this, and he went into the presence of Hubal in the interior of the Kaʿbah. Hubal was the greatest of the idols of Quraysh in Mecca, and stood by a well inside the Kaʿbah in which were gathered the offerings made to the Kaʿbah.

Beside Hubal there were seven arrows, on each of which there was writing. On one was written, "the blood money"; when a dispute arose as to which of them was responsible for paying blood money, they cast lots with the seven arrows to settle the matter. On another arrow was written "yes"; when they were considering some course of action, they cast lots, and if the "yes" arrow came out they acted on it. Another arrow had "no," and if that came out they did not proceed with their course of action. On the other arrows was written "of you", "attached",[5] "not of you," and "Water." When they wanted to dig for water they cast lots with the arrows, including this last one, and wherever it fell they started digging. Whenever they wanted to circumcise a boy, arrange a marriage, or bury someone who had died, or when they were in doubt as to the descent of one of them, they took him to Hubal together with a hundred dirhams and a slaughtering-camel which they would give to the custodian who used to cast lots with the arrows. Then they would bring forward the person about whom they wished to consult the oracle and would say, "O god of ours, this is so-and-so the son of so-and-so, about whom we wish to know such-and-such; so reveal the truth concerning him." Then they would say to the custodian of the arrows, "Cast!" The latter would cast them, and if "of you" fell to the person in question, that meant that he was a fellow tribesman; if it was "not of you," he was a confederate; and if it was "attached," he remained as he was, linked to them neither by descent nor alliance. In matters [1076] other than these, when "yes" came out they acted accordingly, and when "no" came out they deferred the matter until the following year , when they brought it up again. This recourse to the

described below.

5. Ar. *mulṣaq;* according to Ibn Manẓūr this means one who lives among a tribe but is not of them. See *Lisān* s.v. L-S-Q.

way the arrows fell was their ultimate method of deciding their affairs.

Accordingly, ʿAbd al-Muṭṭalib said to the custodian of the arrows, "Cast my sons' arrows to determine their fate," and told him of the vow which he had made. Each of them gave the custodian his arrow with name written on it. ʿAbdallāh b. ʿAbd al-Muṭṭalib was his father's youngest son and, it is claimed, the one he loved most, and ʿAbd al-Muṭṭalib thought that if the arrow missed (this son) he himself would be able to endure the outcome. ʿAbdallāh was the father of the Messenger of God. When the custodian of the arrows took the arrows to cast them, ʿAbd al-Muṭṭalib stood beside Hubal in the interior of the Kaʿbah, calling upon God. The custodian of the arrows cast, and the lot fell against ʿAbdallāh. ʿAbd al-Muṭṭalib took him by the hand, took a large knife, and went up to Isāf and Nāʾilah, two idols of Quraysh at which they used to slaughter their sacrifices, to sacrifice him. However, the Quraysh rose from their assemblies and came to him, saying, "What do you intend to do, ʿAbd al-Muṭṭalib?" He replied "To sacrifice him," but the Quraysh and ʿAbd al-Muṭṭalib's other sons said, "By God! You shall never sacrifice him but must get an excuse for not doing so. If you act thus men will never stop bringing their sons to sacrifice them, and how will the people survive in this way?" Then al-Mughīrah b. ʿAbdallāh b. ʿUmar b. Makhzūm, from whose tribe ʿAbdallāh's mother was, said, "By God! You shall never sacrifice him, but must get an excuse for not doing so. If it takes all we possess to ransom him, we shall do so."

The Quraysh and the other sons of ʿAbd al-Muṭṭalib then said, "Do not do this, but take him to the Ḥijāz. There is a sorceress there who has a familiar spirit; ask her, and you will know what
[1077] to do. If she commands you to sacrifice him, you will sacrifice him, and if she commands you to do something which offers relief to you and to him, you can accept it." They went to al-Madīnah where, it is claimed, they found that she was in Khaybar. They rode until they reached her and consulted her. ʿAbd Al-Muṭṭalib told her the story about himself and his son, what he had intended to do to him, and the vow which he had made, and she said to them, "Retire from me for today, until my familiar visits me and I can ask him."

They retired from her, and when they had left her presence

ʿAbd al-Muṭṭalib stood and prayed to God. On the following day they went back to her and she said, "Yes, news has come to me. How much is the blood-money among you?" They replied, "Ten camels," which it was. "Go back to your country, then," she said, "and bring forward the young man and ten camels, and cast the arrows. If they fall against the young man, add to the camels until your Lord is satisfied. If they fall against the camels, sacrifice them, and your Lord will be satisfied and the young man will be saved."

They left and returned to Mecca, and when they had all agreed on the matter, ʿAbd al-Muṭṭalib stood and prayed to God. Then they brought forward ʿAbdallāh and ten camels, while ʿAbd al-Muṭṭalib was in the interior of the Kaʿbah beside Hubal praying to God. The arrow fell against ʿAbdallāh, so they added ten camels, making twenty, while ʿAbd al-Muṭṭalib stood where he was praying to God. Then they cast again, and the arrow fell against ʿAbdallāh, so they added another ten camels, making thirty. They went on in this way, casting the arrows and adding ten camels every time the arrow fell against him, until they had cast ten times and the number of camels had reached a hundred, while ʿAbd al-Muṭṭalib continued to pray. Then they cast again, and the arrows fell against the camels. Then the Quraysh and those others present said, "Your Lord is satisfied at last, ʿAbd al-Muṭṭalib." They claim that he said, "No, by God, not until I cast the arrows against them [1078] three times." So they cast the arrows between the camels and ʿAbdallāh while ʿAbd al-Muṭṭalib prayed, and they fell against the camels; then they did it again, a second and a third time, with the same result. Then the camels were slaughtered and left there, and no man or wild beast was turned back from eating them.

ʿAbd al-Muṭṭalib left, taking his son ʿAbdallāh by the hand. It is alleged that he passed by a woman of the Banū Asad called Umm Qattāl bt. Nawfal b. Asad b. ʿAbd al-ʿUzzā, the sister of Waraqah b. Nawfal b. Asad; she was by the Kaʿbah. When she looked at his face she said, "Where are you going, ʿAbdallāh?" "With my father," he said. She said, "I have for you as many camels as were slaughtered for you, so sleep with me now." "My father is with me," he replied, "and I cannot oppose his wishes or leave him." ʿAbd al-Muṭṭalib took him away and brought him to Wahb b. ʿAbd Manāf b. Zuhrah, who was the leading man of the Banū Zuhrah in age and eminence at that time, and the latter married him to (his daughter) Āminah bt. Wahb, who was then the most excellent woman in Quraysh as regards genealogy and status. Her mother was Barrah bt. ʿAbd al-ʿUzzā b. ʿUthmān b. ʿAbd al-Dār b. Qusayy, Barrah's mother was Umm Ḥabīb bt. Asad b. ʿAbd al-ʿUzzā b. Qusayy, and Umm Ḥabīb's mother was Barrah bt. ʿAwf b. ʿAbīd b. ʿAwīj b. ʿAdī b. Kaʿb b. Lu'ayy.

It is alleged that he consummated his marriage to her there as soon as he married her, that he lay with her and that she conceived Muḥammad; then he left her presence and came to the woman who had propositioned him, and said to her, "Why do you not
[1079] make the same proposition to me today which you made to me yesterday?" She replied, "The light which was with you yesterday has left you, and I have no need of you today." She had heard (about this) from her brother Waraqah b. Nawfal, who was a Christian and had studied the scriptures; he had discovered that a prophet from the descendants of Ismāʿīl was to be (sent) to this people; this had been one of the purposes of his study.

Ibn Ḥumayd—Salamah—Muhammad b. Isḥāq—his father, Isḥāq b. Yasār: ʿAbdallāh paid a visit to a wife whom he had in addition to Āminah bt. Wahb b. ʿAbd Manāf b. Zuhrah. He had been working in clay[6] and traces of the clay were still on him, and when he invited her to lie with him she made him wait because of this. He went out, performed his ablutions, washed off the clay which was on him, and went to Āminah's quarters. He went in and lay with her, and she conceived Muḥammad. Then he passed by this other woman and said, "Do you wish to lie with me?" "No," she replied. "When you passed by me before you had a white blaze between your eyes. You invited me to lie with you and I refused, so you went to Āminah and she has taken it away."

They allege that this wife of his used to relate that when he passed by her he had between his eyes something like the white blaze on a horse's forehead, that she invited him in the hope that he would lie with her, but that he refused and went in to Āminah bt. Wahb and lay with her, as a result of which she conceived the Messenger of God.

6. R.B. Serjeant in his comments on Alfred Guillaume's translation of the *Sīrah* (*Bulletin of the School of Oriental and African Studies,* xxi[1958]:1-14 says this means a cultivated plot or field. There was, however, little cultivable land near Mecca.

ʿAlī b. Ḥarb al-Mawṣilī—Muhammad b. ʿUmārah al-Qurashī—al-Zanjī b. Khālid—Ibn Jurayj—ʿAṭā'—Ibn ʿAbbās: When ʿAbd al-Muṭṭalib was taking ʿAbdallāh to marry him to Āminah, they passed by a female soothsayer from the tribe of Khathʿam called Fāṭimah bt. Murr, a convert to Judaism from the people of Tabālah, who had read the scriptures and who saw light in his face. "Young man," she said, "would you like to lie with me now, and I will give you a hundred camels?" He replied,

As for unlawful relations, I would sooner die, [1080]
and as for lawful marriage, there can be none, as
I clearly recognize.
So how can that be which you desire?

Then he said, "I am with my father and I cannot leave him." His father took him and married him to Āminah bt. Wahb b. ʿAbd Manaf b. Zuhrah, and he stayed with her for three days. Then he left her, and when he passed by the Khathʿamī woman he felt a desire to accept the proposition which she had made, and he asked her, "Would you like what you wanted before?" "Young man," she said, "I am not, by God, a woman of questionable morals. I saw light in your face and wished it to be within me, but God willed that He should place it where He wished. What did you do after you left me?" He said, "My father married me to Āminah bt. Wahb and I stayed with her for three days." Then Fāṭimah bt. Murr recited the following verses:

I saw a sign which shone
and gleamed in the black rainclouds.
I comprehended it as light which illuminated
what was around it like the full moon.
I hoped to have it as a source of pride which
I might take back with me,
but not everyone who strikes a flint produces fire.
By God, no other Zuhrī woman has plundered
your person of that which Āminah has, and yet
she is unaware of it.

She also said:

Banū Hāshim, Āminah has left (bearing something) [1081]

from your brother,
    while there is a dispute over marriage,
Just as wicks leave the lamp behind when it goes out,
    having absorbed its oil.
Not all the fortune which the young man inherits
    comes from resolve, nor does that which escapes
    him come from remissness.
So if you desire something behave with restraint,
    for two grandfathers combined will ensure it for you.
Either a hand with fingers clenched
    or else a hand with fingers outstretched will ensure
    it for you.
When Āminah conceived that which she conceived
    from him, she conceived an incomparable glory.

Al-Ḥārith b. Muḥammad—Muḥammad b. Saʿd—Muḥammad b. ʿUmar—Maʿmar and others—al-Zuhrī: ʿAbdallāh b. ʿAbd al-Muṭṭalib was the handsomest of the men of Quraysh. They told Āminah bt. Wahb of his handsomeness and his appearance and asked if she would like to marry him, so she married him. He consummated his marriage to her, and she conceived the Messenger of God. ʿAbdallāh's father sent him to al-Madīnah for provisions, where he died. When he was late in returning, ʿAbd al-Muṭṭalib sent his son al-Ḥārith to look for him, but al-Ḥārith found that he had died.

Al-Wāqidī: This is an error. In our view the consensus of opinion concerning the marriage of ʿAbdallāh b. ʿAbd al-Muṭṭalib is that which is related to us by ʿAbdallāh b. Jaʿfar al-Zuhrī—Umm Bakr bt. al-Miswar who said: ʿAbd al-Muṭṭalib came with his son ʿAbdallāh, seeking a wife for himself and one for his son; they were married at the same time. ʿAbd al-Muṭṭalib married Hālah bt. Uhayb b. ʿAbd Manāf b. Zuhrah, and ʿAbdallāh b. ʿAbd al-Muṭṭalib married Āminah bt. Wahb b. ʿAbd Manāf b. Zuhrah.[7]

[1082] Al-Ḥārith—Ibn Saʿd—al-Wāqidī: In our opinion, the most trustworthy version about which there is no dispute among our fellow scholars, is that ʿAbdallāh b. ʿAbd al-Muṭṭalib came from Syria in a caravan belonging to Quraysh, stopped at al-Madīnah owing to ill-

7. Ibn Saʿd, *Ṭabaqāt*, 1:58, 3-17; the previous paragraph has not been found in Ibn Saʿd, but the following is in Ibn Saʿd, *Ṭabaqāt*, 1:61.

ness, and remained there until he died. He was buried in the house of al-Nābighah (or, some say, of al-Tābi'ah) in the small room on your left as you enter. There is no dispute about this among our fellow scholars.

'Abd al Muṭṭalib (His Grandfather)

'Abdallāh was the son of 'Abd al-Muṭṭalib, whose name was Shaybah. I was told on the authority of Hishām b. Muḥammad—his father—that he was given this name because his hair was white, (*shaybah* means white hair).

Ibn Ḥumayd—Salamah—Ibn Isḥāq; and Hishām b. Muḥammad —his father; and al-Ḥārith—Muḥammad b. Sa'd—Muḥammad b. 'Umar: Some of them narrate a version which overlaps that of others and some of them add to the versions of others: He was known as 'Abd al-Muṭṭalib for the following reason. His father Hāshim had set off for Syria on a commercial expedition taking the Madīnan route, and when he reached al-Madīnah he stayed with 'Amr b. Zayd b. Labīd al-Khazrajī. There he saw Salmā bt. 'Amr (Ibn Ḥumayd—Salamah—Ibn Isḥaq: Salmā bt. Zayd b. 'Amr)[8] b. Labīd b. Ḥarām b. Khiddash b. Jundub b. 'Adī b. al-Najjār, admired her, and asked her father 'Amr for her hand in marriage. The latter married her to him, stipulating that if she gave birth to any children it should be among her own family. Hāshim went on his way without consummating the marriage, consummating it instead on his way back from Syria while staying with [1083]
her family in Yathrib. She became pregnant, and he left for Mecca taking her with him. When she became heavy with child he took her back to her family, while he himself went on to Syria, and died there in Gaza. Salmā gave birth to his son 'Abd al-Muṭṭalib, who remained in Yathrib for seven or eight years. Then a man from the Banū al-Ḥārith b. 'Abd Manāt passed through Yathrib and saw some boys competing at archery. When Shaybah hit the mark he would say, "I am the son of Hāshim, I am the son of the Lord of the Valley?"[9] The Ḥārithī said, "Who are you?" and he replied, "I

8. Ibn Hishām, *Sīrah,* 88 has Salmā bt. Āmr; see Ibn Sa'd, *Tabaqāt,* Ṭabarī is not following either source exactly.

9. The word *baṭḥā'* (plural *biṭāḥ),* here translated "valley," is properly the bed of a torrent. The central part of Mecca round the Ka'bah was known as al-Biṭāḥ, in

am Shaybah b. Hāshim b. 'Abd Manāf." When the Ḥārithī arrived back in Mecca he said to al-Muṭṭalib (brother of Hāshim), who was sitting in the Ḥijr (a part of the Ka'bah), "Abū al-Ḥārith, do you know that in Yathrib I found some boys competing at archery and among them was a boy who, when he hit the mark, would say, 'I am the son of Hāshim, I am the son of the Lord of the Valley?' " Al-Muṭṭalib said, "By God, I shall not return to my family until I bring him here!" "My she-camel is here in the courtyard," said the Ḥārithī, "ride her!"

Al-Muṭṭalib mounted the camel, (eventually) arriving in Yathrib in the early evening. He went to the Banū 'Adī b. al-Najjār, and there he saw some boys playing football in the midst of an assembly. He recognized his brother's son and said to the people, "Is this Hāshim's son?" "Yes," they said, "this is your brother's son, and if you want to take him, do so now, before his mother finds out. If she does find out, she will not let him go, and we shall have to prevent you from taking him." So he called to him and said, "Nephew, I am you uncle, and I want to take you to your people." He made his camel kneel, and without hesitation the boy sat on its rear-quarters. Then he set off with him, and his mother did not find out about it until nightfall, when she was standing bewailing her son; then they told her that his uncle had taken him away.

Al-Muṭṭalib brought him into Mecca during the morning while the men were sitting in their assemblies. They began to say, "Who
[1084] is that sitting behind you?" and he replied, "My slave." Finally he brought him home and took him to his wife Khadījah bt. Sa'īd b. Sahm, who said, "Who is this?" "My slave," he replied. He then went out to al-Ḥazwarah and bought a robe with which he clothed Shaybah. In the evening he took him out to the assembly of the Banū 'Abd Manāf, and after that he led him round the streets of Mecca wearing the robe. People said, "This is al-Muṭṭalib's slave (*'abd al-Muṭṭalib*)," for when his people had asked him he had said, "This is my slave." Al-Muṭṭalib said:

I recognized Shaybah as the sons of al-Najjār
were around him competing at archery.

---

contrast to al-Ẓawāhir or outskirts, and the main clans of the Quraysh were called Quraysh al-Biṭāḥ. The Ḥijr (below) was a section of the courtyard immediately surrounding the Ka'bah; see *EI*², s.v. Ka'ba.

ʿAlī b. Ḥarb al-Mawṣilī—Abū Maʿn ʿĪsā, a descendant of Kaʿb b. Mālik[10] —Muḥammad b. Abī Bakr al-Anṣārī—the shaykhs of the Anṣār: Hāshim b. ʿAbd Manāf married a noblewoman from the Banū ʿAdī b. al-Najjār, accepting the condition imposed upon whoever sought her hand in marriage that she should remain in her family's settlement. She married Hāshim and bore him the praiseworthy Shaybah. He grew up among his maternal uncles, treated with respect. While he was competing with the boys of the Anṣār at archery, he hit the target and said, "I am the son of Hāshim!" A man who was passing through heard him, and when he came to Mecca he said to the boy's uncle al-Muṭṭalib b. ʿAbd Manāf, "I was passing by the settlement of the Banū Qaylah[11] and saw a boy of such-and-such a description competing with their boys at archery. He claimed to be your brother's son, and you should not leave such a fine boy to live among strangers."

Al-Muṭṭalib rode to al-Madīnah, and persuaded the boy to travel to Mecca. Then he spoke to the boy's mother, and did not leave her in peace until she gave him permission to take him. He mounted the boy behind him and took him to Mecca. Whenever people met him and said, "Who is this, Muṭṭalib?" he would say, "My slave." This is why he was called ʿAbd al-Muṭṭalib. When he arrived in Mecca, al-Muṭṭalib told the boy what his father's property consisted of and made it over to him. (Some time later) Nawfal b. ʿAbd Manāf opposed al-Muṭṭalib in respect of a courtyard which belonged to the latter and unlawfully seized it from him. ʿAbd [1085] al-Muṭṭalib then went to the men of his tribe and asked them to assist him against his uncle, but they said to him, "We cannot intervene between you and your uncle."[12] When he saw what their

10. Kaʿb b. Mālik of the clan of Salimah in al-Madīnah was one of the poets supporting Muḥammad; see. *EI*, s.v. Kaʿb b. Mālik.

11. The Banū Qaylah are all the Arabs of al-Madīnah, also known in Islamic times as the Anṣār. Qaylah was the mother of al-Aws and al-Khazraj, the ancestors of the two main tribes.

12. It is made clear later that this affair took place after the death of al-Muṭṭalib, when Nawfal was the only surviving son of ʿAbd Manāf. Since other descendants of ʿAbd Manāf would be much younger than Nawfal, they would not have felt able to oppose him. ʿAbd al-Muṭṭalib then appealed to a wider circle of the men of Quraysh, but it would have been against normal custom for them to interfere in a matter concerning only a single family. They could probably, however, had they so desired, have brought some moral pressure to bear on Nawfal; but many of the merchants of Mecca seem to have been unscrupulous in such matters. An

attitude was, he wrote to his maternal uncles telling them about the attitude of Nawfal. Included in his letter were the following lines:

Tell the Banū al-Najjār if you come to them
 that I am one of them, their son and their
 close associate.[13]
I think that they are a people who, if I come to them,
 love to meet me and to hear my voice.
My uncle Nawfal persists in an action from which even
 a base man would avert his eyes in disgust.

Abū Sa'd b. 'Udas al-Najjārī then led eighty riders to the valley,[14] and when 'Abd al-Muṭṭalib heard of this he went to meet him and said, "Come to my home, uncle!" "Not until I have met Nawfal," he replied. "I left him sitting in the Ḥijr among the shaykhs of Quraysh," said 'Abd al-Muṭṭalib. Then his uncle went and stood next to Nawfal, unsheathed his sword, and said, "By the Lord of this edifice, either you return his courtyard to my sister's son, or my sword will drink its fill of your blood!" "By the Lord of this edifice," said Nawfal, "I shall return his courtyard, and I call upon those present to witness this." Then Abū Sa'd said, "Let us go to your house, nephew." He stayed there for three days and performed the lesser pilgrimage (*'umrah*). On this occasion, 'Abd al-Muṭṭalib recited the following lines:

Māzin, the Banū 'Adī and Dīnār
 b. Taym al-Lāt refused to accept that I should be
 wronged,
As did the lords of Mālik;[15] and after this Nawfal
 withdrew his pretensions to my property

---

idea of the "wheeling and dealing" which was going on may be obtained from Watt, *Muhammad at Mecca*, 5-7. This story is also of interest as illustrating how matrilineal kinship was still strong in al-Madīnah, whereas in Mecca men were thinking mainly in terms of patrilineal kinship, even though some matrilineal usages continued there. This matter is a complex one. There is a collection of relevant material in Watt, *Muhammad at Medina*, 373-88. In a sense, 'Abd al-Muṭṭalib was here invoking the matrilineal system against unjust behavior by the patrilineal system.

13. The meaning of *wa-l-khamīs* is somewhat obscure.

14. *Al-abṭaḥ*, a variant of *baṭḥā'*, is the central district of Mecca; see n. 8 above.

15. According to the genealogists, Māzin, 'Adī, Dīnār, and Mālik were the four sons of al-Najjār and gave their names to the main subdivisions of the clan, which

Through them God returned my courtyard to me
though they were not as closely related to me as
my own tribe.

With regard to this matter, Samurah b. ʿUmayr Abū ʿAmr al-Kinānī said:

By my life, Shaybah's maternal uncles, despite
being less closely related,
are more dutiful and mindful of bloodties than
his closely related paternal uncles.
They responded to their newphew's appeal though they
were far away,
and were not deflected when Nawfal overstepped his
rights.
May God requite with good a band of Khazrajīs [1086]
who called upon one another to respect family duty;
he who does so is more virtuous.

Faced with this, Nawfal formed a confederacy with the whole of the Banū ʿAbd Shams against the Banū Hāshim.

Muḥammad b. Abī Bakr: I related this story to Mūsā b. ʿĪsā and he said to me, "Ibn Abī Bakr, this is something which the Anṣār relate in order to court our favor, since God has placed sovereignty in our hands.[16] ʿAbd al-Muṭṭalib was held too dear by his own people to need the Banū al-Najjār to ride to his aid from al-Madīnah." "May God make the amīr prosper," I said, "one who was better than ʿAbd al-Muṭṭalib needed their assistance." He had been reclining, but he sat up straight in anger and said, "Who is better than ʿAbd al-Muṭṭalib?" "Muḥammad, the Messenger of God," I replied. "You are right," he said and returned to his previous posture. Then he said to his sons, "Write down this anecdote from Ibn Abī Bakr."

The following anecdote concerning ʿAbd al-Muṭṭalib and his uncle Nawfal was related to me by Hishām b. Muḥammad—his father—Ziyād b. ʿIlāqah al-Taghlibī, who was born in the

was a large one. Al-Najjār was also known as Taym Allāt, which was later changed to Taym Allāh.

16. Mūsā b. ʿĪsā appears to be an ʿAbbāsid governor. Muḥammad b. Abī Bakr al-Anṣārī was a scholar, (d. 132/749); see Ibn Ḥajar *Tahdhīb,* ix:80

Jāhiliyyah: It was the confederacy between the Banū Hashim and Khuzā'ah, which led to the Messenger of God conquering Mecca and to saying "Let this cloud empty its rain in aid of the Banū Ka'b."[17] The reason for the beginning of this confederacy was that Nawfal b. 'Abd Manāf, who was the last surviving son of 'Abd Manāf, wrongfully deprived 'Abd al-Muṭṭalib b. Hāshim b. 'Abd Manāf of certain courtyards. 'Abd al-Muṭṭalib's mother was Salmā bt. 'Amr al-Najjāriyyah of (the tribe of) al- Khazraj. 'Abd al-Muṭṭalib asked for justice from his paternal uncle, but he did not treat him justly; so he wrote to his maternal uncles:

My night is made long by my sorrows and cares;
[1087] will anyone take a message to al-Najjār, my uncles,[18]
To inform 'Adī, Dīnār and Māzin
and Mālik, the protectors of their clients, of my circumstances?
When I was among you I did not fear any oppressor,
and I was respected, inviolable, and carefree.
But when I travelled to my own tribe, urged
to travel and leave that situation by my uncle al-Muṭṭalib,
Even though I lived a life of ease and joy when he was alive,
walking with a proud gait and trailing the hems of my garments,
Yet he was swallowed up by a gloomy grave
and Nawfal arose to deal unjustly with my property.
Was it because he saw a man bereft of paternal
and maternal uncles and without a protector,
That he attacked him and ignored the ties of blood?
When a man is among his paternal and maternal uncles, how immune to attack he is!
Call your men together for war, and defend your nephew against oppression;
do not abandon him, for you are not men to abandon others.
There is no clan like you among the sons of Qaḥṭān
to come to the aid of a client or to bestow favors.
You are mild to those who behave mildly to you

17. Banū Ka'b b. 'Amr was an important subdivision of the tribe of Khuzā'ah.
18. See n. 15.

and live at peace with you, and are poison[19] to the
haughty and overbearing.

Eighty of their riders came to him and made their camels kneel in the courtyard of the Ka'bah. When Nawfal b. 'Abd Manāf saw them he said, "Good morning," but they replied, "No good morning to you, man! Give our nephew redress from the injustice which you have inflicted upon him!" "I will do it," he said, "for the love and respect which I feel for you." Then he gave the courtyards back to his nephew and treated him justly, and they went back to their own country. [1088]

These events prompted 'Abd al-Muṭṭalib to form a confederation, and accordingly he summoned Busr b. 'Amr, Warqā b. 'Abd al-'Uzzā[20] and some of the leading men of Khuzā'ah, who entered the Ka'bah with him and drew up a contract of confederation.

After the death of his uncle al-Muṭṭalib b. 'Abd Manāf, 'Abd al-Muṭṭalib held the privilege of providing food and drink to the pilgrims which the sons of 'Abd Manāf had held before him. He was honored among his people and was a man of great importance among them, for not one of them was his equal. He it was who discovered Zamzam, the well of Ishmael, the son of Abraham, and brought out what was buried there, namely, two golden gazelles which Jurhum are said to have buried when they were evicted from Mecca, and Qal'ī[21] swords and coats of mail. He made the swords into a door for the Ka'bah and covered the door with the gazelles in the form of gold plate. This, it is said, is the first gold with which the Ka'bah was ornamented.

'Abd al-Muṭṭalib's patronymic *(kunyah)*[22] was Abū al-Ḥārith; he was so called because his eldest son was named al-Ḥarith; his own name was Shaybah.

---

19. Vocalized as *samām* in the Leiden edition, though *simām*, a pural of *samm* (poison), would also be possible. "Poison" is almost certainly the meaning here, though it is not given for *samām* in the dictionaries.

20. Following the correction in the Leiden edition.

21. A well-known type of sword, possibly of Indian origin, and apparently made of or incorporating tin of high quality; see *EI*^{2}, *s.v. Ḳal'ī.*

22. The *kunyah* was a patronymic or name of honor of the form Abū N or Umm N (father or mother of N). N was normally the eldest son; but a *kunyah* could be given even to childless persons such as Muḥammad's wife 'Ā'ishah.

Hāshim

ʿAbd al-Muṭṭalib was the son of Hāshim, whose name was ʿAmr; he was called Hāshim because he used to break up *(hashama)* bread for *tharīd*[23] for his people in Mecca and feed them with it. Matrūd b. Kaʿb al-Khuzāʿī—or Ibn al-Zibaʿrā, according to Ibn al-Kalbī—says of him:

[1089] ʿAmr who broke up bread for *tharīd* for his people
when the men of Mecca were drought-stricken and lean.

It is said that his people, Quraysh, were stricken by dearth and drought and that he travelled to Palestine and bought flour there. Then he returned to Mecca, gave orders for it to be baked into bread, slaughtered a camel, and made *tharīd* with the bread. It is also said that he was the first to institute the two yearly caravans, those of winter and summer, for Quraysh.[24]

Hishām b. Muḥammad—his father: ʿAbd Manāf's sons were Hāshim, ʿAbd Shams, the eldest, al-Muṭṭalib, the youngest, the mother of these being ʿĀtikah bt. Murrah al-Sulamiyyah, and Nawfal, whose mother was Wāqidah. They succeeded jointly to their father's authority, and were called "those who make mighty" (*al-mujabbirūn*) . Of them it was said:

O man who is unfastening his saddle,
Why do yo not lodge with the sons of ʿAbd Manāf?

They were the first to obtain for Quraysh guarantees of immunity which allowed them to travel far and wide from the sacred precints of Mecca (Haram). Hāshim obtained for them a treaty with the Greek rulers of Syria and with Ghassān, ʿAbd Shams obtained for them a treaty with the Great Negus as a result of which they travelled regularly to Abyssinia, Nawfal obtained for them a treaty with the Persian emperors as a result of which they travelled regularly to Iraq and Persia, and al-Muṭṭalib obtained for them a treaty with the kings of Ḥimyar as a result of which they travelled regularly to the Yemen. By means of them God made

23. A kind of broth into which bread was crumbled.

24. The winter and summer caravans are referred to in Qurʾān 106:2. The winter caravan is said to have gone to the Yemen and Abyssinia, and the summer one to Syria. Ghassān was an Arab tribe on the southern border of the Byzantine empire in alliance with it; see *EI*^{2} , s.v.

Quraysh mighty, and they were called "those who make mighty" *(al-mujabbirūn).*

It is said that Hāshim and ʿAbd Shams were twins and that one was born before the other with one of his fingers stuck to his twin's forehead; when his finger was separated blood flowed; people regarded this as an omen and said, "There will be blood between them."

After his father's death Hāshim succeeded to the office of providing food and drink.

Al-Ḥārith—Muḥammad b. Saʿd—Hishām[25] b. Muḥammad— [1090] Maʿrūf b. al-Kharrabūdh al-Makkī—a man of the Āl ʿAdī b. al-Khiyār b. ʿAdī b. Nawfal b. ʿAbd Manāf—his father: Wahb b. ʿAbd Qusayy spoke the following lines on Hāshim's feeding his people with *tharīd:*

Hāshim took upon himself the responsibility
 which no other mortal was able to undertake.
He brought them sacks from Syria
 full of winnowed wheat
And gave the people of Mecca their fill of broken bread,
 mixing the bread with fresh meat.
The people were surrounded by wooden bowls piled high
 whose contents were overflowing.

Umayyah b. ʿAbd Shams b. ʿAbd Manāf, who was a man of wealth, was envious of Hāshim and unwillingly attempted to emulate him; but he could not do it, and some of the men of Quraysh gloated over his discomfiture. He was angry and maligned Hāshim, and challenged him to a contest before an arbiter as to which of them was nobler *(manāfarah).* Hāshim did not wish to accept this because of his age and standing, but the Quraysh would not allow him to refuse, and they finally irritated him so much that he said, "I accept this challenge, on condition that the loser slaughters fifty black-eyed camels in the valley of Mecca and leaves Mecca for ten years." Umayyah accepted this, and they chose a Khuzāʿī soothsayer to judge between them. The soothsayer awarded the victory to Hāshim, who took the camels, slaughtered them, and fed those present (at the event). Umayyah

25. Ibn Saʿd, Ṭabaqāt, I:43,24-44,11.

then left for Syria and stayed there for ten years. This was the first occasion on which enmity broke out between the families of Hāshim and Umayyah.[26]

[1091] Al-Ḥārith—Muḥammad b. Sa'd—Hishām b. Muḥammad—a man of the Banū Kinānah called Ibn Abī Ṣāliḥ and a man from Raqqah, a *mawlā* of the Banū Asad who was a scholar: 'Abd al-Muṭṭalib b. Hāshim and Ḥarb b. Umayyah asked the Negus of Abyssinia to judge which of them was the nobler, but he refused. So they asked Nufayl b. 'Abd al-'Uzzā b. Riyāḥ b. 'Abdallāh b. Qurṭ b. Rizāḥ b. 'Adī b. Ka'b to judge between them. He said to Ḥarb, "Abū 'Amr, do you challenge a man who is greater than you in height, larger than you in the size of his head, more beautiful of face, more highly born, who has more sons than you, gives more abundant gifts, and is a more influential speaker?" Then he gave the victory to 'Abd al-Muṭṭalib and Ḥarb said, "It is a sign of the degeneration of the times that we made you an arbiter!"

The first of the sons of 'Abd Manāf to die was Hāshim, who died in Gaza in Syria. He was followed by 'Abd Shams, who died in Mecca and was buried in Ajyād. Then Nawfal died at Salmān on the road to Iraq, and finally al-Muṭṭalib died at Radmān in the Yemen.[27] After Hāshim's death the office of feeding and watering the pilgrims passed to his brother al-Muṭṭalib.

'Abd Manāf

Hāshim was the son of 'Abd Manāf, whose name was al-Mughīrah; he was (also) called "al-Qamar" (the moon) on account of his beauty. They claim that Quṣayy used to say, "I have four sons; I named two of them after my idols, one after my settlement and one after myself." These were, respectively, 'Abd Manāf, 'Abd al-'Uzzā, who was the father of Asad, 'Abd al-Dār, and 'Abd Quṣayy, who died childless. All of these, together with his daughter Barrah, were by Ḥubbā bt. Ḥulayl b. Ḥubshiyah b.Salūl b. Ka'b b. 'Amr b. Khuzā'ah.

26. Umayyah is the ancestor of the Umayyad dynasty, as Hāshim is of the 'Abbāsids. The following paragraph appears to be another version of the same story placed a generation later; see Ibn Sa'd, *Ṭabaqāt*, I:5212-20.

27. According to what was said on pp. 1086, and 1087, Nawfal survived al-Muṭṭalib and, after the latter's death, seized property belonging to 'Abd al-Muṭṭalib; see n. 12.

Hishām b. Muḥammad—his father: ʿAbd Manāf was called "al-Qamar," but his name was al-Mughīrah, and he was generally known as ʿAbd Manāf because his mother Ḥubbā offered him to Manāf, the greatest of the idols of Mecca, to show her devotion to it. Of ʿAbd Manāf it was said: [1092]

Quraysh was an egg, and it split open;
the choicest part belongs to ʿAbd Manāf alone.

Quṣayy

ʿAbd Manāf was the son of Quṣayy, whose name was Zayd. He was called Quṣayy for the following reason. His father Kilāb b. Murrah married his mother Fāṭimah bt. Saʿd b. Sayal (whose name was Khayr) b. Ḥamālah b. ʿAwf b. Ghanm b. ʿĀmir al-Jādir b. ʿAmr b. Juʿthumah b. Yashkur of the Azd Shanū'ah; they lived as confederates among the Banū al-Dīl.[28] Fāṭimah bore Zuhrah and Zayd to Kilāb, who died while Zayd was still a child. Zuhrah had grown up and had reached adulthood. Rabīʿah b. Ḥarām b. Ḍinnah b. ʿAbd b. Kabīr b. ʿUdhrah b. Saʿd b. Zayd, one of the Quḍāʿah, then came to Mecca and married Fāṭimah, the mother of Zuhrah and Quṣayy, according to Ibn Ḥumayd—Salamah—Ibn Isḥāq. This tradition is also related by Hishām b. Muḥammad—his father. Zuhrah had grown up and was a man, while Quṣayy had not long been weaned, so when Rabīʿah took Fāṭimah to the territory of the Banū ʿUdhrah in the Syrian highlands she took Quṣayy with her because he was so young, whereas Zuhrah stayed among his own tribe. After this Faṭimah bore Rizāḥ b. Rabīʿah to Rabīʿah, so that Rizāḥ was Quṣayy's half-brother on his mother's side. Rabīʿah had three other sons by another wife, Ḥunn, Maḥmūd, and Julhumah. Zayd [1093] grew up under Rabīʿah's guardianship, and was called Quṣayy (the little distant one) because he lived so far from his tribe. Zuhrah continued to live in Mecca, but while Quṣayy b. Kilāb was in the territory of Quḍāʿah, it is asserted, he regarded himself as being a full member of Rabīʿah b. Ḥarām's family. One day, when Quṣayy had grown up and was a young man, there was some kind of dis-

28. Also called Banū al-Du'il, which is perhaps the original form; see al-Qalqashandī, *Nihāyat al-Arab fī Ansāb al-ʿArab,* Cairo 1959, p.54. Most of the material about Quṣayy is not in Ibn Hishām, *Sīrah;* see 75f., 79-81.

pute between him and a man of Quḍāʿah. The Quḍāʿī reproached him for being a stranger, and said, "Do not swear by your tribe and your descent, for you are not one of us." Quṣayy went back to his mother, pained at what the man had said, and asked her about it. "By God," she answered, "you are nobler than he and have a nobler father, my son. You are the son of Kilāb b. Murrah b. Kaʿb b. Lu'ayy b. Ghālib b. Fihr b. Mālik b. al-Naḍr b. Kinānah al-Qurashī. Your tribe live in Mecca by the Kaʿbah and in its neighborhood."

Quṣayy decided to go to his people and to join them, for he hated being a stranger in the territory of the Quḍāʿah. His mother said to him, "My son, do not be in too much of a hurry. Wait for the sacred month and go with the pilgrimage, for I am afraid that some misfortune may befall you." Quṣayy waited until the sacred month arrived and the pilgrims from the Quḍāʿah set out, and went with them. When he reached Mecca and had completed the pilgrimage, he remained there. He was a strong man of good lineage, and when he asked Ḥulayl b. Ḥubshiyyah al-Khuzāʿī for the hand of his daughter Ḥubbā, Ḥulayl, recognising his lineage and regarding him as a desirable match, gave his consent and married her to him. At that time, it is claimed, Ḥulayl was in charge of the Kaʿbah and ruled in Mecca.

Ibn Isḥāq: Quṣayy stayed with him (i.e. Ḥulayl) and Ḥubbā bore him ʿAbd al-Dār, ʿAbd Manāf, ʿAbd al'Uzzā and ʿAbd. His progeny
[1094] increased, his wealth multiplied and he became greatly honoured, and when Ḥulayl b. Ḥubshiyyah died Quṣayy thought that he had a better right to the Kaʿbah and to rule over Mecca than the Khuzāʿah and the Banū Bakr, since the Quraysh were the noblest and purest of the descendants of Ishmael, son of Abraham. He spoke to some men of the Quraysh and the Banū Kinānah and called upon them to expel the Khuzāʿah and the Banū Bakr from Mecca. They accepted his proposal and swore an oath of allegiance to him to do this. Then he wrote to his half-brother Rizāḥ b. Rabīʿah b. Ḥarām, who was in his tribal lands, asking him to come to his assistance and fight along with him. Rizāḥ b. Rabīʿah stood up among the Quḍāʿah and called upon them to come to the assistance of his brother and to march with him, and they answered his call.

Hishām: Quṣayy went to his brother Zuhrah and his people, and before long became their chief. The Khuzāʿah were more numerous than the descendants of al-Naḍr[29] in Mecca, so Quṣayy asked his brother Rizāḥ for assistance. Rizāḥ had three brothers on his father's side by a different wife, and he came with them and those clans of the Quḍā'ah who answered his summons. Quṣayy had with him his tribe, the Banū al-Naḍr, and together they expelled Khuzā'ah.

Quṣayy had married Ḥubbā bt. Ḥulayl b. Ḥubshiyyah, a Khuzā'ī woman, and she had borne him four sons. Ḥulayl was the last (member of Khuzā'ah) to be the custodian of the Ka'bah, and when he became too old for the task he handed it over to his daughter Ḥubbā. She said,"You know that I am not strong enough to open and shut the door," so he said, "I will give the task of opening and shutting the door to a man who will do it for you." He gave the task to Abū Ghubshān, whose name was Sulaym b. 'Amr b. Buwayy b. Milkān b. Afṣā, and Quṣayy purchased the custodianship of the Ka'bah from him for a skin full of wine and a lute. When the Khuzā'ah saw this, they gathered against him, so he asked his brother for assistance and fought the Khuzā'ah.

I have heard, and God knows best, that the Khuzā'ah were seized by an outbreak of pustules which was likely to wipe them out and that, seeing this, they abandoned Mecca. Some of them gave their houses away, some sold them, and some leased them. Quṣayy [1095]
took charge of the House (the Ka'bah) and the lordship of Mecca.[30] He gathered together the clans of Quraysh and settled them in the valley of Mecca, while some remained in the ravines and hilltops.[31] To each (clan) he allotted their settlements. (Because he thus gathered together and settled the Quraysh) he was called "gatherer" (*mujammi'*). Of him Maṭrūd—some say Ḥudhāfah b. Ghānim—said:

29. The Banū al-Naḍr (a section of the tribe of Kinānah) were the effective clan (or tribe) to which Quṣayy belonged. They included more than the group known as Quraysh, since these were usually reckoned to be the descendants of Fihr, the grandson of al-Naḍr.

30. The Arabic here is somewhat vague: *wallā Quṣayy al-bayt wa-amr Makkah wa-l-ḥukm bi-hā; amr* may mean either "rule" or "affairs," while *hukm* may refer to the giving of decisions in accordance with custom. It is not clear how much is involved in the kingship or supreme rule attributed to him in what follows, but he was certainly the man in Mecca with supreme authority.

31. This is the distinction mentioned in notes 8 and 14. Those in the "valley" (here *abṭaḥ)* are Quraysh al-Biṭāḥ, and the others Quraysh al-Ẓawāhir.

Your father Quṣayy was called *mujammiʿ*;
through him God gathered the clans of Fihr.

The tribe made him their king over them.

Ibn Isḥāq: Rizāḥ answered Quṣayy's call to come to his aid and went with his three brothers and those men of the Quḍāʿah who followed him to Mecca on the pilgrimage, determined to come to Quṣayy's aid and to fight on his side. Khuzāʿah claim that Ḥulayl b. Ḥubshiyyah made his position over to Quṣayy and commanded him to accept it when the latter's sons by (Ḥulayl's) daughter increased, saying, "You are more worthy of the Kaʿbah and its custodianship, and of ruling Mecca, than the Khuzāʿah." Thereupon Quṣayy made his request for assistance. The pilgrims gathered in Mecca, went out to the *mawqif*[32] completed the pilgrimage and went to Minā. Quṣayy and his followers from his own tribe of the Quraysh and the Banū Kinānah, together with those Quḍāʿah who supported him, had decided upon their course of action; nothing now remained of the ritual of the pilgrimage but the dispersal from Minā.

The Ṣūfah[33] used to drive the people away from ʿArafah and give them permission to depart when they dispersed from Minā. On the day of dispersal they went to stone the *jimār*,[34] and a man of the Ṣūfah used to throw stones for the pilgrims, none throwing until he had thrown. Those who had urgent matters to attend to would come to him and say, "Get up and throw, so that we can throw with you," but he would say, "No, by God, not until the
[1096] sun begins to set." Then those who had matters to attend to and wanted to hasten the proceedings would throw stones at him in an attempt to hurry him up, and say, "Get up and throw, for heaven's sake!" But he would refuse until the sun began to set; then he

32. The *mawqif* or "place of standing" is the plain of ʿArafāt, about 24 km east of Mecca. The "standing" here between midday and sunset on the appointed day is one of the most important rites of the *ḥajj* or pilgrimage. This was followed by the *ifāḍah* or "dispersal" (with a suggestion of haste) to Minā, rather more than half way back to Mecca. Ṭabarī uses *nafr* for "dispersal" instead of the more usual *ifāḍah*, and also has the singular ʿArafah instead of the plural. See *EI* ^{2}, s.v. Ḥadjdj, sect. 1.

33. Ṣūfah was a small clan or group of kinsmen; see Ibn Hishām, *Sīrah*, 76f.; also Ibn Ḥabīb, *K. al-Munammaq*, 14.

34. The *jimār* were three erections or heaps of stones, at which stones or pebbles were thrown. In Islam, they were held to represent the devil. See *EI* ^{2}, s.v. Djamra.

would throw and the pilgrims would throw with him.

Ibn Humayd—Salamah—Ibn Isḥāq—Yahyā b. ʿAbbād b. ʿAbdallāh b. al-Ẓubayr—his father ʿAbbād: When they had finished stoning the *jimār* and wanted to disperse from Minā, the Ṣūfah would occupy both sides of the pass of al-ʿAqabah and detain the pilgrims. The pilgrims would say, "Give the permission to depart, Ṣūfah!" Nobody left until the Ṣūfah passed through; when they had dispersed and left, the other pilgrims were free to go, and set out after them.

This year the Ṣūfah acted as usual. The Arabs recognized their right to do this, since they regarded it as a religious duty during the rule of the Jurhum and the Khuzāʿah. Quṣayy b. Kilāb, accompanied by his followers from his own tribe of Quraysh, from the Kinānah and from Quḍāʿah, came to the Ṣūfah at al-ʿAqabah and said, "We have a better right to this than you." At that they opposed one another and began to fight. A fierce battle broke out, as a result of which the Ṣūfah were put to flight, and Quṣayy wrested from them the privileges which had been in their hands, thus denying them.

When this happened the Khuzāʿah and the Banū Bakr drew back from Quṣayy b. Kilāb, knowing he would impose prohibitions upon them as he had on the Ṣūfah, and that he would exclude them from the Kaʿbah and control of Mecca. When they drew back from him, Quṣayy revealed his enmity to them openly and resolved to do battle with them. His brother Rizāḥ b. Rabīʿah with his fellow-tribesmen from the Quḍāʿah stood firm beside him while the Khuzāʿah and the Banū Bakr took the field against them and prepared for battle. The forces met and a fierce battle took place. There were many dead and wounded on both sides. Finally, both sides called for peace and for the appointment of one of the Arabs to arbitrate between them on their differences. [1097]
They appointed Yaʿmar b. ʿAwf b. Kaʿb b. Layth b. Bakr b. ʿAbd Manāt b. Kinānah, whose verdict was that Quṣayy had a better right to the Kaʿbah and to rule Mecca than the Khuzāʿah, that all injuries inflicted by Quṣayy upon the Khuzāʿah and the Banū Bakr were remitted and trampled beneath his feet, while all injuries inflicted by the Khuzāʿah and the Banū Bakr upon the Quraysh, the Banū Kinānah, and Quḍāʿah should be compensated for by blood money. He added that Quṣayy b. Kilāb should be allowed to con-

trol the Ka'bah and Mecca. On that day Ya'mar b. 'Awf was given the name al-Shaddākh, because of the blood money which he remitted and trampled underfoot *(shadakha)*. Quṣayy took control of the Ka'bah and rule over Mecca, and gathered together his tribe from their dwellings and settled them there. He assumed rule over his tribe and the people of Mecca, and they accepted him as their king. Quṣayy was the first of the descendants of Ka'b b. Lu'ayy to attain rule acknowledged by his tribe. He held the privileges of being doorkeeper of the Ka'bah, providing the pilgrims with food and drink, presiding over the assembly, and appointing standard bearers, thus taking all the honors of Mecca for himself. He also divided Mecca into quarters for his tribe, settling every clan of the Quraysh in the dwelling places assigned to them in Mecca.

Ibn Ḥumayd—Salamah—Ibn Isḥāq: People allege that the Quraysh were afraid to cut down the trees of the Ḥaram in their settlements, and that Quṣayy thus cut them down with his own hands, and that they then helped him. The Arabs called him "Gatherer" *(mujammi')* because of his gathering them, and they regarded his rule as a good omen. No woman or man of Quraysh was married anywhere but in the house of Quṣayy b. Kilāb, nor did Quraysh consult together about any matter affecting them anywhere but in his house. When they were about to fight another tribe, banners were tied only in his house, where one of his own sons would hand the banner over. Whenever a girl of Quraysh came of age to put on her shift, she would do so only in his house; there her shift would be split over her, and she would put it on and be taken to her family. His authority among his tribe of Quraysh,
[1098] in his lifetime and after his death, was like a religion which people followed; they always acted in accordance with it, regarding it as filled with good omens and recognizing his superiority and nobility. He took for himself the assembly house and made the door which (later) led from it to the mosque of the Ka'bah, The Quraysh used to decide their affairs in that house.

Ibn Ḥumayd—Salamah—Muḥammad b. Isḥāq—'Abd al-Malik b. Rāshid—his father—al-Sā'ib b. Khabbāb, the author of *al-Maqṣūrah:* I heard a man telling 'Umar b. al-Khaṭṭāb, when he was Caliph, this story of Quṣayy b. Kilāb, that is, how he gathered his own tribe together, expelled the Khuzā'ah and the Banū Bakr from Mecca, and gained control of the Ka'bah and rule over

Mecca; ʿUmar did not reject it or disavow it.

Quṣayy remained in Mecca, held in honor and high esteem by his tribe, and not opposed in his rule of Mecca in any way. As regards the pilgrimage, he confirmed the rights of the Arabs to continue their previous customs. This is because he considered these to be a religious duty which he should not change. The Ṣūfah thus continued as they had before, (and did so) until they died out, their rights then passing by inheritance to the family of Ṣafwān b. al-Ḥārith b. Shijnah; the ʿAdwān also continued as they had, and likewise the intercalators from the Banū Mālik b. Kinānah and Murrah b. ʿAwf. No changes occurred until Islam, and God thereby did away with all these functions. Quṣayy had a house built in Mecca, which was the house of assembly, in which the Quraysh used to decide their affairs.

At last Quṣayy grew old and feeble; ʿAbd al-Dār, his first-born and his eldest son, was, it is claimed, a weakling, while ʿAbd Manāf was held in honor during his father's lifetime, and managed everything with his brothers ʿAbd al-ʿUzzā and ʿAbd. It is claimed that Quṣayy said to ʿAbd al-Dār, 'By God, I shall make you the equal of the others, even though they have been raised in dignity [1099]
over you. No man of them shall enter the Kaʿbah until you have opened it, no banner shall be tied for the Quraysh to go to battle except by your hand, no man shall drink water in Mecca except that which you have provided, no man shall eat food in the pilgrimage season other than your food, and the Quraysh shall not decide their affairs anywhere but in your house.' Then he gave him his own house, the assembly house, in which Quraysh always made their decisions, and gave him the offices of being doorkeeper, tying the banners, presiding over the assembly, and the *rifādah*. The *rifādah* was a tax which was levied in every pilgrimage season by the Quraysh according to their wealth and handed over to Quṣayy b. Kilāb. He used it to prepare food to be eaten by those pilgrims attending the pilgrimage who had neither means nor provisions. It was imposed on the Quraysh by Quṣayy, who said to them when he commanded them to pay it, "Quraysh, you are neighbors of God, people of his Kaʿbah and people of the sacred precincts (Ḥaram). the pilgrims are guests of God and visitors to his House, and are the most deserving of all guests of honorable treatment. Give them food and drink during the days of the pil-

grimage, until they depart from you." They did so, and every year they levied a tax on their property and paid it to him, and he would use it to prepare food for the pilgrims during the days of Minā. This institution of his became current among the Quraysh during the whole of the Jāhiliyyah up to the appearance of Islam, and then became current in Islam, continuing to this day. This is the food which the government supplies to the pilgrims every year at Minā until the pilgrimage is completed.

Ibn Ḥumayd—Salamah: This story of Quṣayy b. Kilāb and what he said to ʿAbd al-Dār concerning the offices which he handed over to him was told to me by Ibn Isḥāq b. Yasār—his father—al-Ḥasan b. Muḥammad b. ʿAlī b. Abī Ṭalib. Yasār said, "I heard al-Ḥasan b. Muḥammad saying this to a man of the Banū ʿAbd al-Dār called Nubayh b. Wahb b. ʿAmir b. ʿIkrimah b. Hāshim b. ʿAbd Manāf b. ʿAbd al-Dār. He said, 'Quṣayy made over to him all the authority which he had over his tribe. Quṣayy's commands
[1100] were never disobeyed and nothing he did was ever opposed. Then Quṣayy died and his sons assumed his authority over his tribe.'"

Kilāb

Quṣayy was the son of Kilāb. It is said that Kilāb's mother was Hind bt. Surayr b. Thaʿlabah b. al-Ḥārith b. Fihr b. Mālik b. al-Naḍr b. Kinānah. He had two half brothers by a different mother, Taym and Yaqaẓah, whose mother, according to Hishām b. al-Kalbī, was Asmāʾ bt. ʿAdī b. Ḥārithah b. ʿAmr b. ʿĀmir b. Bāriq. As for Ibn Isḥāq, he says that their mother was Hind bt. Ḥārithah al-Bāriqiyyah.[35] Some people say that Yaqaẓah's mother was Hind bt. Surayr, Kilāb's mother.

Murrah

Kilāb was the son of Murrah, whose mother was Waḥshiyyah bt. Shaybān b. Muḥārib b. Fihr b. Mālik b. al-Naḍr b. Kinānah. Murrah's two full brothers were ʿAdī and Huṣayṣ. Some say that the mother of these three was Makhshiyyah, others say that the mother of Murrah and Huṣayṣ was Makhshiyyah bt. Shaybān b.

35. The standard text of Ibn Isḥāq (Ibn Hishām, *Sīrah*, 67) has Hind bt. Surayr.

Muḥārib b. Fihr, and that ʿAdī's mother was Raqāsh bt. Rukbah b. Nā'ilah b. Kaʿb b. Ḥarb b. Taym b. Saʿd b. Fahm b. ʿAmr b. Qays b. ʿAylān.

Kaʿb

Murrah was the son of Kaʿb, whose mother, according to Ibn Isḥāq and Ibn al-Kalbī, was Māwiyyah bt. Kaʿb b. al-Qayn b. Jasr b. Shayʿ Allāh b. Asad b. Wabrah b. Taghlib b. Ḥulwān b. ʿImrān b. al-Ḥāf b. Quḍāʿah. He had two full brothers, ʿĀmir and Sāmah; the three of [1101] them were known as the Banū Nājiyah.[36] They also had a paternal half brother whose descendants regarded themselves as belonging to Ghaṭafān and became a part of them. He was called ʿAwf, and his mother was al-Bāridah bt. ʿAwf b. Ghanm b. ʿAbd Allāh b. Ghaṭafān. It is said that when Lu'ayy b. Ghālib died she went back with her son to her own people and married Saʿd b. Dhubyān b. Baghīḍ, who adopted ʿAwf; of him Fazārah b. Dhubyān is reported to have said:

Son of Lu'ayy, turn your camel aside to me;
 your own people have abandoned you, and you have
 no dwelling place.

Kaʿb had also two other paternal half brothers. One of these was Khuzaymah, who was known as ʿĀ'idhat Quraysh after his mother, ʿĀ'idhah bt. al-Khims b. Quḥāfah b. Khathʿam, and the other was Saʿd. The descendants of Saʿd are known as Bunānah, Bunānah being Saʿd's mother. Their nomadic kinsmen are now said to be part of the Banū Asʿad b. Hammām, a branch of the Banū Shaybān b. Thaʿlabah, while their settled section trace their descent back to Quraysh.

Lu'ayy

Kaʿb was the son of Lu'ayy, whose mother, according to Hishām was ʿĀtikah bt. Yakhlud b. al-Naḍr b. Kinānah. She was the first of the ʿĀtikahs of the tribe of Quraysh who were female ancestors of the Messenger of God. Lu'ayy had two full brothers; one of

36. Nājiyah appears to be a scribal error for Māwiyyah.

them was called Taym, and was known as Taym al-Adram. The name of al-Adram is derived from the word *daram,* which means "a deficiency in the chin"; it is said that he had a receding chin. The other was Qays; it is said that there are no living descendants of Qays the brother of Lu'ayy, and that the last of them was a man who died in the time of Khālid b. ʿAbdallāh al-Qasrī[37] and that his estate remained unclaimed, as nobody knew who had a right to
[1102] it. It is also said that the mother of Lu'ayy and his brothers was Salmā bt. ʿAmr b. Rabīʿah. Rabīʿah's name was Luhayy b. Ḥārithah b. ʿAmr Musayqiyā' b. ʿĀmir Mā' al-Samā' b. Khuzāʿah.

Ghālib

Lu'ayy was the son of Ghālib, whose mother was Laylā bt. al-Ḥārith b. Tamīm b. Saʿd b. Hudhayl b. Mudrikah, and his full brothers were al-Ḥārith, Muḥārib, Asad, ʿAwf, Jawn and Dhi'b. Muḥārib and al-Ḥārith belonged to the Quraysh al-Ẓawāhir, but al-Ḥārith came to live in the valley.[38]

Fihr

Ghālib was the son of Fihr. Hishām b. Muḥammad: He was the gatherer (*jammāʿ*) of Quraysh. His mother was Jandalah bt. ʿĀmir b. al-Ḥārith b. Muḍāḍ al-Jurhumī.

Ibn Ḥumayd—Salamah—Ibn Isḥāq: His mother was Jandalah bt. al-Ḥārith b. Muḍāḍ b. ʿAmr al-Jurhumī.

Abū ʿUbaydah Maʿmar b. al-Muthannā is reported to have said that his mother was Salmā bt. Udd b. Ṭābikhah b. Ilyās b. Muḍar. It is also said that his mother was Jamīlah bt. ʿAdwān of Bāriq of Azd. In his time, Fihr was the chief of the Meccans, according to Ibn Ḥumayd—Salamah—Ibn Isḥāq,[39] in their war against Ḥassān b. ʿAbd Kalāl b. Mathūb Dhū Ḥurath al-Ḥimyarī. It is said that Ḥassān advanced from the Yemen with Ḥimyar and a great many other Yemenite tribes. His intention was to transport the stones of

37. Umayyad governor of Iraq from about 724 to 738; see *EI* ^{2}, s.v. Khālid b. ʿAbdallāh al-Ḳasrī.

38. See n. 8 above.

39. This paragraph is not found in Ibn Hishām's recension of Ibn Isḥāq (IH, 61); see Guillaume's translation, p.41.

the Kaʿbah from Mecca to the Yemen, and so to divert the pilgrimage associated with the Kaʿbah to his own country. He advanced as far as Nakhlah, raided the Meccan herds, and blocked the road, but was afraid to enter Mecca. When Quraysh, the tribes of Kinānah, Khuzaymah, Asad, and Judhām, and fragmentary groups belong to Muḍar who were with them, saw this, they went out to meet Ḥassān in battle, under the leadership of Fihr b. Mālik. A fierce [1103]
battle ensued, the Ḥimyar were put to flight, and Ḥassan b. ʿAbd Kalāl, the king of the Ḥimyar, was taken captive by al-Ḥārith b. Fihr. Among those who were killed in the battle was Fihr's grandson, Qays b. Ghālib b. Fihr. Ḥassān was held captive in Mecca for three years, but finally ransomed himself from them. He was taken back to Yemen from Mecca but died on the way.

Mālik

Fihr was the son of Mālik, whose mother was ʿIkrishah bt. ʿAdwān. ʿAdwān was al-Ḥārith b. ʿAmr b. ʿAylān, according to Hishām.

Ibn Isḥāq: His mother was ʿĀtikah bt. ʿAdwān b. ʿAmr b. Qays b. ʿAylān.[40] It is said that ʿIkrishah was her nickname and that her real name was ʿĀtikah. It is also said that his mother was Hind bt. Fahm b. ʿAmr b. Qays b. ʿAylān. Mālik had two brothers; one was called Yakhlud, and his descendants became part of the Banū ʿAmr b. al-Ḥārith b. Mālik b. Kinānah and ceased to belong to the Quraysh; the other was called al-Ṣalt, but none of his descendants survive. It is said that the Quraysh were so called after Quraysh b. Badr b. Yakhlud b. al-Ḥārith b. Yakhlud b. al-Naḍr b. Kinānah. This is because when the caravan of the Banū al-Naḍr arrived the Arabs used to say, "The Caravan of Quraysh has arrived". They say that this Quraysh was the guide of the Banū al-Naḍr in their travels and was responsible for provisioning them. He had a son named Badr who dug the well at Badr, and the well called Badr is named after him.

Ibn al-Kalbī: Quraysh is a collective name, and cannot be traced back to a father or mother, or to a male or female guardian.

Others say that the descendants of al-Naḍr b. Kinānah were

40. Only this sentence is found in the standard text of Ibn Isḥāq (Ibn Hishām, *Sīrah*, 61).

[1104] called Quraysh because al-Naḍr b. Kinānah came out one day to his tribal assembly and they said to one another, "Look at al-Naḍr! he is like a *quraysh* [41] camel!" Others say that Quraysh were so called after a creature which lives in the sea and eats other sea creatures, namely, the shark (*qirsh*). The descendants of al-Naḍr b. Kinānah were named after the *qirsh* because it is the most powerful of sea creatures. Another account is that al-Naḍr b. Kinānah used to inquire after *qarrasha)* the needs of his people and to satisfy them with his wealth; the word *qarsh*, it is alleged, means "inquiry": his sons used to inquire after the needs of the pilgrims and to satisfy them fully. The following verse is quoted as evidence that the word *taqriīsh* means "inquiry";

You who are speaking and inquiring (*muqarrish*) about us
from ʿAmr, will they ever desist?[42]

Some say that al-Naḍr b. Kinānah was himself called Quraysh, while others deny this and maintain that al-Naḍr's descendants continued to be called the Banū al-Naḍr until Quṣayy b. Kilāb gathered them together; they were then called Quraysh because they had been gathered together, which is the meaning of the verb *taqarrasha*. The Arabs used to say, "*taqarrasha Banū al-Naḍr*" which means that they were gathered together. Yet another account is that they were called Quraysh because they made a profit (*taqarrasha)* from raiding.

Al-Ḥārith—Muḥammad b. Saʿd—Muḥammad b. ʿUmar (al-Wāqidī)—Abū Bakr b. ʿAbd Allāh b. Abī Sabrah—Saʿīd b. Muḥammad b. Jubayr b. Muṭʿim: ʿAbd al-Malik b. Marwān[43] asked Muḥammad b. Jubayr when the Quraysh were first called Quraysh. He replied "When they were gathered into the sacred precincts (Ḥaram) from their dispersion. This gathering together is *taqarrush*." ʿAbd al-Malik said, "I have not heard this, but I have heard that Quṣayy was called al-Qurashī and that the name

41. None of the works we have consulted gives a reasonable meaning for *quraysh* in this context.

42. This verse is from the *Muʿallaqah* of al-Ḥārith b. Ḥillizah, line 64 in al-Tibrīzī's recension, but the form there is different and does not include the word *muqarrish*. Ibn Manẓūr, *Lisān*, quotes the verse in a form closer to that of Ṭabarī, but explains *muqarrish* as "slandering and instigating" (s.v. *q-r-sh)*.

43. Umayyad caliph who ruled from 685 to 705. This and the following paragraphs are found in Ibn Saʿd, *Ṭabaqāt*, I:40.17-28; 41.10-15.

Quraysh was not used before him."

Al-Ḥārith—Muḥammad b. Sa'd—Muḥammad b. 'Umar—Abū Bakr b. 'Abdallāh b. Abī Sabrah—'Abd al-Majīd b. Suhayl b. 'Abd al-Raḥman b. 'Awf—Abū Salamah b. 'Abd al-Raḥmān b. 'Awf: When Quṣayy settled in the sacred precincts and became master of them, he performed fine deeds and was called al-Qurashī; he was the first to be called this. [1105]

Al-Ḥārith—Muḥammad b. Sa'd—Muḥammad b. 'Umar—Abū Bakr b. Abī Sabrah—Abū Bakr b. 'Ubaydallāh b. Abī Jahm: Al-Naḍr b. Kinānah was called al-Qurashī.

Al-Ḥārith—Muḥammad b. Sa'd—Muḥammad b. 'Umar: Quṣayy instituted the lighting of the fire at al-Muzdalifah when the *wuqūf* (standing) took place there,[44] so that those being driven away from 'Arafah could see it. This fire continued to be lit in this place throughout the Jāhiliyyah.

Al-Ḥārith—Muḥammad b. Sa'd—Muḥammad b. 'Umar and Kathīr b. 'Abdallāh al-Muzanī—Nāfi'—('Abdallāh) Ibn 'Umar: This fire was lit in the time of the Messenger of God, and of Abū Bakr, 'Umar and 'Uthmān.

Muḥammad b. 'Umar (al-Wāqidī): It is lit to this day.

Al-Naḍr

Mālik was the son of al-Naḍr, whose name was Qays and whose mother was Barrah bt. Murr b. Udd b. Ṭābikhah. His full brothers were Nuḍayr, Mālik, Milkān, 'Āmir, al-Ḥārith, 'Amr, Sa'd, 'Awf, Ghanm, Makhramah, Jarwal, Ghazwān, and Ḥudāl. Their paternal half brother was 'Abd Manāt, whose mother was Fukayhah— [1106]
according to others, Fakhah—whose name was al-Dhafrā' bt. Hanī b. Balī b. 'Amr b. al-Ḥāf b. Quḍā'ah. 'Abd Manāt had a maternal half brother called 'Alī b. Mas'ūd b. Māzin b. Dhī'b b. 'Adī b. 'Amr b. Māzin al-Ghassānī. 'Abd Manāt b. Kinānah married Hind bt. Bakr b. Wā'il, who bore him children. Then he died, and his maternal half brother 'Alī b. Mas'ūd married her, and she had children by him. He became the guardian of his brother's children, and they regarded themselves as being descended from him, so that the Banū 'Abd Manāt were called the Banū 'Alī. It is to them

44. Al-Muzdalifah is between 'Arafāt and Minā; "standing" here was one of the pilgrimage rites.

that the poet refers when he says:

How excellent are the Banū ʿAlī
the celibate and the married.

Kaʿb b. Zuhayr also refers to them when he says:

They clashed with ʿAlī on the day of Badr
and after that ʿAlī were subject to Nizār.[45]

Afterwards Mālik b. Kinānah fell upon ʿAlī b. Masʿūd and killed him, and Asad b. Khuzaymah paid his blood money.

Kinānah

Al-Naḍr was the son of Kinānah, whose mother was ʿAwānah bt. Saʿd b. Qays b. ʿAylān. It is also said that his mother was Hind bt. ʿAmr b. Qays. His paternal half brothers were Asad, Asadah—some say that he was Abū Judhām—and al-Hūn; their mother was Barrah bt. Murr b. Udd b. Ṭābikhah. She was also the mother of al-Naḍr b. Kinānah, as Kinānah married her after his father died.

Khuzaymah

Kinānah was the son of Khuzaymah, whose mother was Salmā bt. Aslum b. al-Ḥāf b. Quḍāʿah. His full brother was Hudhayl, and their maternal half brother was Taghlib b. Ḥulwān b. ʿImrān b. al-
[1107] Ḥāf b. Quḍāʿah. It is also said that the mother of Khuzaymah and Hudhayl was Salmā bt. Asad b. Rabīʿah.

Mudrikah

Khuzaymah was the son of Mudrikah, whose name was ʿAmr and whose mother was Khindif. Her real name was Laylā bt. Ḥulwān b. ʿImrān b. al-Ḥāf b. Quḍāʿah; her mother was Ḍariyyah bt. Rabīʿah b. Nizār, after whom, it is said, the Ḥimā Ḍariyyah was named. Mudrikah's full brothers were ʿĀmir, who was Ṭābikhah,

45. According to the genealogists, Nizār is the father of Muḍar, and the name includes a large number of "northern" tribes; see p. 1111 below. Banū ʿAlī had become assimilated to the tribe of ʿAlī b. Masʿūd which was Ghassān and was reckoned as "southern" or Yemenite.

and ʿUmayr, who was Qamaʿah, and is said to be the father of Khuzāʿah.

Ibn Ḥumayd—Salamah—Ibn Isḥāq: The mother of the sons of Ilyās was Khindif, who was a woman from the Yemen. Her name prevailed in her sons' genealogy, and they were known as the Banū Khindif. Mudrikah's name was ʿĀmir, and Ṭābikhah's name was ʿAmr. They claim that while the two of them were among camels which they were herding they caught some game. As they were sitting down cooking it a hostile raiding party attacked their camels, and ʿĀmir said to ʿAmr,"Will you catch up with the camels or cook this game?" ʿAmr said, "I will cook the game." So ʿĀmir caught up with the camels and brought them back. When they returned to their father and told him what had happened, he said to ʿĀmir, "You are the overtaker (*mudrikah*)" and he said to ʿAmr "You are the cook (*ṭābikhah*)."

Hishām b. Muḥammad: It is said that Ilyās took his herds out to look for pasture, and his camels ran away from a hare. ʿAmr went after them and overtook them, and so was called Mudrikah. ʿĀmir took the hare and cooked it, and so was called Ṭābikhah. ʿUmayr slunk *inqamaʿa* into the tents and did not come out, and so was called Qamaʿah. Their mother came walking out, and Ilyās said to her, "Where are you hurrying to (*tukhandifīn*)?" So she was called Khindif. The word *khandafah* means a certain kind of walking.

Qusayy b. Kilāb said:

My mother is Khindif and Ilyās is my father.

Ilyās said to his son ʿAmr: [1108]

What you sought you have overtaken (*adrakta*)

and to ʿĀmir:

What you cooked (*ṭabakhta*) you have done to a turn

and to ʿUmayr:

You have done badly and have slunk away.

Ilyās

Mudrikah was the son of Ilyās, whose mother was al-Rabāb bt.

Ḥaydah b. Ma'add and whose full brother was al-Nās, who was 'Aylān. He is said to have been called 'Aylān because people used to remonstrate with him over his generosity, and say, "You will be overcome by destitution *('aylah)*, 'Aylān." So this name stuck to him. Others say that he was called this because he was born on a mountain called 'Aylān, while yet others say that he was called this because he was raised by a slave of Muḍar called 'Aylān.

Muḍar

Ilyās was the son of Muḍar, whose mother was Sawdah bt. 'Akk and whose full brother was Iyād. They had two paternal half brothers, Rabī'ah and Anmār, whose mother was Jaddālah bt. Wa'lān b. Jawsham b. Julhumah b. 'Amr of Jurhum. Some say that when Nizār b. Ma'add was on the point of death he made his will and divided his wealth among his sons. He said, "This leather tent—it was a tent of red leather—and that of my wealth which resembles it go to Muḍar [as a result, Muḍar was called al-Ḥamrā', the red]; this black hair tent and that of my wealth which resembles
[1109] it go to Rabī'ah. [He left black horses, and Rabī'ah was called al-Faras, the horse.] This female servant and that of my wealth which resembles her go to Iyād. [She was grey-haired, so he took the piebald horses and the small sheep and goats]; and this purse full of dirhams and this place of assembly go to Anmār so that he can sit in it [and Anmār took what he had been given]. If you have any problems about this and you differ about the division, then betake yourselves to al-Af'ā al-Jurhumī."

They did differ about the division, so they set off for al-Af'ā. While they were on their way, Muḍar saw pasturage which had been grazed over, and said, "The camel which has been grazing this pasturage is one-eyed." Rabī'ah said, "It is crooked." Iyād said, "It is dock-tailed," and Anmār said, "It is a stray." They had not gone much farther before they were met by a man whose riding camel was carrying him along at a gentle pace. He asked them about the camel, and Muḍar said, "Is it one-eyed?" The man said, "Yes." Then Rabī'ah said, "Is it crooked?" The man said, "Yes." Then Iyād said, "Is it dock-tailed?" The man said, "Yes." Finally Anmār said, "Is it a stray?" The man said, "Yes." Then he said, "This is the description of my camel. Show me where it is." They swore to him that they had never seen it, but he clung to them and said, "How can I believe you, when you have described my camel just as it is?" So they all went on together, and finally reached Najrān. They halted at the dwelling of al-Afʿā al-Jurhumī, and the owner of the camel cried out, "These people have my camel. They described it to me just as it is, and then said, 'We have never seen it.'" The Jurhumī said, "How could you describe it when you have never seen it?" Muḍar said, "I saw that it had grazed on one side and left the other side alone, so I knew that it was one-eyed." Rabīʿah said "I saw that one of its feet had left a firm imprint while the other had left a weak one, so I knew that this was because it leaned heavily to one side owing to its crookedness." Iyād said, "I knew that it was dock-tailed because of the compactness of its dung. If it had had a long tail, it would have hit the dung with it." Anmār said, "I knew that it was a stray, because it had grazed an area with dense vegetation and had then left it for another area with thinner and poorer vegetation." Then the Jurhumī said, "They do not have your camel. Go and look for it." [1110]

Then he asked them who they were. They told him, and he welcomed them, saying, "Do you need me, when you are as perspicacious as I see you to be?" He called for food for them, and they and he ate and drank. Muḍar said, "I have never seen more excellent wine than this which we are drinking today, unless it has grown on a grave." Rabīʿah said, "I have never eaten meat more delicious, unless it has been fed on dog's milk." Iyād said, "I have never seen a man more generous than I have today, unless he be born of a father other than the one he claims." Anmār said, "I have never heard speech more profitable for our needs." The Jurhumī heard these words and marvelled at what they said. He went to his mother and questioned her, and she told him that she had been married to a king who could beget no children, and that, being unwilling that the kingship should depart, she had given a man who was staying with her the freedom to do with her as he would; so he lay with her, and she became pregnant by him. Next, he questioned his steward about the wine, and he said, "It comes from a trellised vine which I planted on your father's grave." Lastly, he went to his shepherd and asked him about the meat, and he said, "It is a sheep which I fed on the milk of a bitch, since no other sheep had been born in the flock."

He asked Muḍar, "How did you know that the wine had grown on a grave?" He replied, "Because I felt a severe thirst when I drank it." Then he asked Rabīʿah, "How did you recognize it?" and he told him. Then the Jurhumī came to them and said, "Describe to me the situation in which you find yourselves." So they told him the story of their father's will, and he awarded the red leather tent, the (gold) dinars, and the camels, which were red, to Muḍar, the black hair tent and the black horses to Rabīʿah, the female servant, who was grey-haired, and the piebald horses to Iyād and the (silver) dirhams to Anmār.

Nizār

[1111] Muḍar was the son of Nizār. It is said that Nizār had the patronymic (*kunyah*) Abū Iyād, and it is also said that on the contrary he was called Abū Rabīʿah. His mother was Muʿānah bt. Jawsham b. Julhumah b. ʿAmr, and his full brothers were Qunuṣ, Qunāṣah, Sinām,[46] Ḥaydān, Ḥaydah, Hayādah, Junayd, Junādah, al-Qaḥm, ʿUbayd al-Rammaḥ, al-ʿUrf, ʿAwf, Shakk, and Quḍāʿah. Maʿadd was called Abū Nizār after Nizār. The lines of many of these brothers have died out.

Maʿadd

Nizār was the son of Maʿadd. It is claimed by Hishām that Maʿadd's mother was Mahdad bt. al-Lihamm—according to others, al-Lahm—b. Jalḥab b. Jadīs or b. Ṭasm, or b. al-Ṭawsam, one of the descendants of Yaqshān the son of Abraham, the friend of the Compassionate.[47]

Al-Ḥārith b. Muḥammad—Muḥammad b. Saʿd—Hishām b. Muḥammad—Muḥammad b. ʿAbd al-Raḥmān al-ʿAjlānī: His full brothers were al-Dīth—it is said that al-Dīth was ʿAkk, and it is also said that ʿAkk was the son of al-Dīth b. ʿAdnān—ʿAdan b. ʿAdnān, of whom some genealogists claim that he was the Lord of

46. Vocalization unclear.

47. Abraham is often referred to in Arabic as the Friend of God, following Qurʾān 4:125, where it is said that "God took Abraham as a friend" (*khalīl*). The town of Hebron, which is associated with Abraham, is known in Arabic as al-Khalīl. Abraham is also called "friend of God" in the Bible: Isaiah 41:8; James 2:23.

Aden, which is named after him, and that its inhabitants were his descendants, but that they became extinct; Abyan, of whom they claim that he was Lord of Abyan, that it was named after him, and that its inhabitants were his descendants, but that they be- [1112] came extinct; al-Ḍaḥḥāk; and al-ʿAkk. The mother of all of them was Maʿadd's mother. Some genealogists say that ʿAkk departed for Samrān, in the Yemen, leaving his brother Maʿadd. This is because when the people of Ḥaḍūr killed Shuʿayb b. Dhī Mahdam al-Ḥaḍūrī God sent Nebuchadnezzar against them as a punishment. Armiyā and Barkhiyā went away taking Maʿadd with them, and when the warfare had died down they took him back to Mecca. Maʿadd then found that his brothers and uncles who were descended from ʿAdnān had joined the peoples of the Yemen and had intermarried with them; the Yemenites were sympathetic to them because they were descendants of Jurhum. They quote the following verses in proof of the above story:

We left our brothers, al-Dīth and ʿAkk
    on their way to Samrān, and they departed quickly.
They were of the Banū ʿAdnān,
    but they lost this descent irrevocably among themselves.

ʿAdnān[48]

Maʿadd was the son of ʿAdnān. ʿAdnān had two paternal half brothers, one called Nabt and the other ʿAmr. The genealogists do not differ concerning the descent of our Prophet Muḥammad as far as Maʿadd b. ʿAdnān, which is as I have expounded it.

Yūnus b. ʿAbd al-Aʿlā—Ibn Wahb—Ibn Lahīʿah—Abū al-Aswad and others: The lineage of the Messenger of God is as follows; Muḥammad b. ʿAbdallāh b. ʿAbd al-Muṭṭalib b. Hāshim b. ʿAbd Manāf b. Quṣayy b. Kilāb b. Murrah b. Kaʿb b. Luʾayy b. Ghālib b. Fihr b. Mālik b. al-Nadr b.Kinānah b. Khuzaymah b. Mudrikah b. Ilyās b. Muḍar b. Nizār b. Maʿadd b. ʿAdnān b. Udad; they differ [1113] concerning what comes after that.

48. According to the standard genealogical system, ʿAdnān is the ancestor of all the so-called northern Arabs. In the list of his sons above, ʿAyy of the text has been corrected to ʿAkk.

ʿAdnān's Descent from Ishmael, Abraham, and Adam[49]

Al-Zubayr b. Bakkār—Yaḥyā b. al-Miqdād al-Zamʿī—his paternal uncle Mūsā b. Yaʿqūb b. ʿAbdallāh b. Wahb b. Zamʿah—his maternal aunt Umm Salamah, the wife of the Prophet: I heard the Messenger of God say, "Maʿadd b. ʿAdnān b. Udad b. Zand b. Yarā b. Aʿrāq al-Tharā." Umm Salamah: Zand is al-Hamaysaʿ, Yarā is Nabt and Aʿrāq al-Tharā is Ishmael, son of Abraham.

Al-Ḥārith—Muḥammad b. Saʿd—Hishām b. Muḥammad—Muḥammad b. ʿAbd al-Rahmān al-ʿAjlānī—Mūsā b. Yaʿqūb al-Zamʿī—his paternal aunt—her grandmother Bint al-Miqdād b. al-Aswad al-Bahrānī: The Messenger of God said, "Maʿadd b. ʿAdnān b. Udad b. Yarā b. Aʿrāq al-Tharā."[50]

Ibn Ḥumayd—Salamah b. al-Faḍl—Ibn Isḥāq: ʿAdnān, as some genealogists assert, was the son of Udad b. Muqawwam b. Nāḥūr
[1114] b. Tayraḥ b. Yaʿrub b. Yashjub b. Nābit b. Ismāʿīl (Ishmael) b. Ibrāhīm (Abraham), while others say: ʿAdnān b. Udad b. Aytahab b. Ayyūb b. Qaydhar b. Ismāʿīl (Ishmael) b. Ibrāhīm (Abraham). Quṣayy b. Kilāb traces his descent back to Qaydhar in his poetry. Yet other genealogists say: ʿAdnān b. Maydaʿ b. Māniʿ b. Udad b. Kaʿb b. Yashjub b. Yaʿrub b. al-Hamaysaʿ b. Qaydhar b. Ismāʿīl (Ishmael) b. Ibrāhīm (Abraham). These differences arise because it is an old science, taken from the people of the first Book (the Old Testament).

Al-Ḥārith—Muḥammad b. Saʿd—Hishām (al-Kalbī): Someone told me on the authority of my father, Muḥammad b. al-Sāʾib al-Kalbī, although I did not hear this from him myself, that he traced the descent as follows; Maʿadd b. ʿAdnān b. Udad b. al-Hamaysaʿ b. Salāmān b. ʿAwṣ b. Būz b. Qamwāl b. Ubayy b. al-ʿAwwām b.

---

49. It is obvious to modern scholars that the lists of names between ʿAdnān and Adam have somehow or other been derived from those in the Bible. Most early Muslim scholars, however, were unwilling to admit to a Biblical source, and they often mentioned only their immediate source (as did Ibn Isḥāq in the standard text). In the material given by Ṭabarī we find both acknowledgement of the Biblical source and an attempt to provide an Arab source.

50. Ibn Saʿd, *Ṭabaqāt,* I:28.6-9; later passages are from I:28.20-29.19. There is no certainty about the vocalization of many of the names in the following lists. We have usually followed those given in the Leiden edition, which are partly based on the Hebrew parallels. It is also to be remembered that in some cases the names may be derived from a Syriac translation of the Hebrew. We have not called special attention to the Biblical parallels. In some names the diacritical points, and, therefore, the consonants, are uncertain.

Nāshid b. Ḥazā b. Bildās b. Yidlāf b. Ṭābakh b. Jāḥam b. Ṭāḥash b. Mākhā b. ʿAyfā b. ʿAbqar b. ʿUbayd b. al-Daʿā b. Ḥamdān b. Sanbar [1115]
b. Yathribī b. Yaḥzan b. Yalḥan b. Arʿawā b. ʿAyfā b. Dayshān b. ʿĪsar b. Aqnād b. Ayhām b. Muqṣir b. Nāḥath b. Rizāḥ b. Shammā b. Mizzā b. ʿAwṣ b. ʿArrām b. Qaydhar b. Ismāʿīl (Ishmael) b. Ibrāhīm (Abraham).

Al-Ḥārith—Muḥammad b. Saʿd—Hishām b. Muḥammad (al-Kalbī): There was a man from Tadmur whose patronymic (*kun-* [1116]
yah) was Abū Yaʿqūb. He was one of the children of Israel who had become a Muslim, who had read in their books and become deeply learned. He said that Barūkh b. Nāriyyā,[51] a scribe from Urmiyā, had established the lineage of Maʿadd b. ʿAdnān with him and had set it down in his writings. It was well known among the learned men of the People of the Book and set down in their books. It was close to the names given above, and perhaps the difference between them was owing to the language, since these names had been transliterated from the Hebrew.

Al-Ḥārith—Muḥammad b. Saʿd: Hishām (al-Kalbī) recited to me the following line of verse, which was related to him by his father:

I belong to no tribe which brought me up
 but that in which the descendants of Qaydhar and
 al-Nabīt took root.

By al-Nabīt, he meant Nabt b. Ismāʿīl (Ishmael).

Al-Zubayr b. Bakkār—ʿUmar b. Abī Bakr al-Muʿammalī—Zakariyyāʾ b. ʿĪsā—Ibn Shihāb: Maʿadd b. ʿAdnān b. Udad b. al-Hamaysaʿ b. Ashub b. Nabt b. Qaydhar b. Ismāʿīl (Ishmael).

Others relate: Maʿadd b. ʿAdnān b. Udad b. Umayn b. Shājab b. Thaʿlabah b. ʿAtr b. Yarbaḥ b. Muḥallam b. al-ʿAwwām b. Muḥtamil b. Rāʿimah b. al-ʿAyqān b. ʿAllah b. al-Shahdūd b. al- [1117]
Ẓarīb b. ʿAbqar b. Ibrāhīm (Abraham) b. Ismāʿīl b. Yazan b. Aʿwaj b. al-Muṭʿim b. al-Ṭamḥ b. al-Qasūr b. ʿAnūd b. Daʿdaʿ b. Maḥmūd b. al-Zāʾid b. Nadwān b. Atāmah b. Daws b. Ḥiṣn b. al-Nizāl b. al-Qumayr b. al-Mushajjir b. Muʿḍamir b. Ṣayfī b. Nabt b. Qaydhār b. Ismāʿīl (Ishmael) b. Ibrāhīm (Abraham), the Friend of the Compassionate.

Still others: Maʿadd b. ʿAdnān b. Udad b. Zayd b. Yaqdir b.

---

51. Baruch son of Neraiah was the secretary of Jeremiah.

Yaqdum b. Hamaysa' b. Nabt b. Qaydhar b. Ismā'īl (Ishmael) b. Ibrāhīm (Abraham).

Others: Ma'add b. 'Adnān b. Udad b. al-Hamaysa' b. Nabt b. Salmān, who is Salāmān, b. Ḥamal b. Nabt b. Qaydhar b. Ismā'īl (Ishmael) b. Ibrāhīm (Abraham).

Others: Ma'add b. 'Adnān b. Udad b. al-Muqawwam b. Nāḥūr b. Mishraḥ b. Yashjub b. Malik b. Ayman b. al-Nabīt b. Qaydhar
[1118] b. Ismā'īl (Ishmael) b. Ibrāhīm (Abraham).

Others: Ma'add b. 'Adnān b. Udd b. Udad b. al-Hamaysa' b. Asḥub b. Sa'd b. Yarbaḥ b. Naḍīr b. Ḥumayl b. Munaḥḥim b. Lāfath b. al-Ṣābūḥ b. Kinānah b. al-'Awwām b. Nabt b. Qaydar b. Ismā'īl (Ishmael).

A certain genealogist told me that he had found that some Arab scholars had memorized forty ancestors of Ma'add as far as Ismā'īl (Ishmael) in Arabic, quoting Arabic verses as evidence for this, and that he had collated the names they gave with what the People of the Book say and had found that the number agreed but that the actual names differed. He dictated these names to me and I wrote them down. They are as follows; Ma'add b. 'Adnān b. Udad b. Hamaysa' (Hamaysa' is Salmān, who is Umayn) b. Hamayta' (who is Hamayda', who is al-Shājab) b. Salāmān (who is Munjir Nabīt, so called, he claimed, because he fed the Arabs on milk and flour *anjara,* as the people lived well in his time. He quoted as evidence for this, the verse of Qa'nab b. 'Attāb al-Riyāḥī:

[1119] Ṭayy calls upon me, but Ṭayy is distant,
and reminds me of the *bālūdh* [52] of the times of Nabīt.)

Nabīt b. 'Awṣ (he is Tha'labah, to whom the Tha'labīs' descent is traced back) b. Būrā (who is Būz, who is 'Atr al-'Atā'ir, the first person to institute the custom of the *'atīrah* [53] for the Arabs) b. Shūḥā (who is Sa'd Rajab, the first person to institute the custom of the *rajabiyyah* for the Arabs) b. Ya'mānā (who is Qamwāl, who is Yarbaḥ al-Nāṣib, who lived in the time of Sulaymān b. Dāwūd

52. A sweetmeat, possibly a kind of blancmange, prepared from starch or flour, water, and honey, more usually *falūdh* or *falūdhaj* in Arabic. The word is originally Persian, *pālūda.*

53. A sacrificial lamb; the *rajabiyyah* mentioned below was a sheep or goat sacrificed by the Arabs in the month of Rajab in the Jāhiliyyah. The practice was forbidden in Islamic times. See Lane, p. 1034.

the prophet) b. Kasdānā (who is Muḥallam Dhū al-ʿAyn) b. Ḥazānā (who is al-ʿAwwām) b. Bildāsā (who is al-Muḥtamil) b. Badlānā (who is Yidlāf, who is Rāʿimah) b. Taḥbā (who is Ṭahab who is al-ʿAyqān) b. Jahmā (who is Jāham, who is ʿAllah) b. Maḥshā (who is Tāḥash. who is al-Shaḥdūd) b. Maʿjālā (who is Mākhā, who is al-Ẓarīb Khāṭim al-Nār b. ʿAqārā (who is ʿĀfā, who is ʿAbqar, the fa- [1120]
ther of the Jinn, to whom the garden of Abqar is ascribed) b. ʿAqārā (who is ʿĀqir, who is Ibrāhīm Jāmiʿ al-Shaml. He was called Jāmiʿ al-Shaml (settler of affairs) because every fearful person felt safe in his reign; he returned every outcast, and he attempted to make peace between all men) b. Bandāʿā (who is al-Daʿā, who is Ismāʿīl Dhū al-Maṭābikh (master of the kitchens), who was so called because during his reign he established a house for guests in every town of the Arabs) b. Abdāʿī (who is ʿUbayd, who is Yazan al-Ṭaʿʿān, the first man to fight with lances, which are ascribed to him) b. Hamādā (who is Ḥamdān, who is Ismāʿīl Dhū al-Aʿwaj; al-Aʿwaj was his horse, and the Aʿwajī breed of horses is ascribed to him) b. Bashmānī (who is Yashbīn, who is al-Muṭʿim fī al-Mahl) b. Bathrānī (who is Bathram, who is al-Ṭamḥ) b. Baḥrānī (who is Yaḥzan, who is al-Qasūr) b. Yalḥānī (who is Yalḥan, who is al-ʿAnūd) b. Raʿwānī (who is Raʿwā, who is al-Daʿdaʿ) b. ʿĀqārā (who [1121]
is ʿĀqir) b. Dāsān, (who is al-Zāʿid) b. ʿĀṣar (who is ʿĀṣir, who is al-Naydawān Dhū al-Andiyah; in his reign the sons of al-Qādhūr (who is al-Qādūr) were dispersed and the kingship departed from the descendants of al-Nabīt b. al-Qādūr and passed to the sons of Jāwān b. al-Qādūr, and then returned to them again) b. Qanādī (who is Qanār, who is Ayyāmah) b. Thāmār (who is Bahāmī, who is Daws al-ʿItq, Daws who, he asserts, was the most beautiful of mankind in his time. There is an Arab proverb, *aʿtaq min Daws,* which has two significations, either referring to his beauty (*ʿitq)* or to his antiquity (also *ʿitq),* that is, either "more beautiful than Daws" or "more ancient than Daws." In his reign Jurhum b. Fālij and Qatūrā were exterminated. This is because they acted wrongfully in the sacred precincts (Ḥaram), and Daws killed them. Tiny ants followed in the tracks of those of them who survived, penetrated into their ears, and destroyed them.) b. Muqṣir (who is Maqāṣirī, who is Ḥiṣn; he is also called Nāḥath, who is al-Nizāl) b. Zāriḥ (who is Qumayr) b. Sammī who is Sammā, who is al-Mujashshir, who was, he asserted, the most just king to succeed

to power and the best in managing his affairs; speaking of him, Umayyah b. Abī al-Ṣalt[54] said to Heraclius, the King of the Greeks:

[1122] Be like al-Mujashshir, of whom his subjects said
"al-Mujashshir was the most faithful of us in
fulfilling what he undertook.")

b. Marzā—or, some say, Marhar—b. Ṣanfa (who is al-Samr, who is al-Ṣafī, the most generous king to be seen on the face of the earth; of him Umayyah b. Abī al-Ṣalt said:

al-Ṣafī b. Nabīt, when he was king,
was loftier and more generous than Heraclius and Caesar.)

b. Ja'tham (who is 'Urām, who is al-Nabīt, who is Qaydhar; the interpretation of Qaydhar, he said, is "ruler", for he was the first of the descendants of Ismā'īl to be king) b. Ismā'īl (Ishmael), who was faithful to his promise, b. Ibrāhīm (Abraham), the Friend of the Compassionate, b. Tāriḥ (who is Āzar) b. Nāḥūr b. Sārū' b. Arghawā b. Bāligh (the interpretation of Bāligh is "the divider" as in Syriac; this is because it was he who divided the lands between the descendants of Adam, and he is Fālij) b. 'Ābar b. Shālikh b. Arfakhshad b. Sām (Shem) b. Nūḥ (Noah) b. Lamk b. Mattūshalakh b. Akhnūkh (he is the prophet Idrīs)[55] b. Yard (he is Yārid, in whose time idols were made) b. Mahlā'īl b. Qaynān b. Anūsh b. Shithth (who is Hibatallah) b. Ādam. Shithth (Seth) was the successor of his father after Hābīl (Abel) was killed; his father said, "A gift of God (*Hibatallāh*) in exchange for Hābil," and his name was de-
[1123] rived from this.

We have mentioned earlier in this work in a concise and abridged form a part of what we have been able to discover of the accounts of Ismā'īl (Ishmael) b. Ibrāhīm (Abraham) and his ancestors, male and female, back to Adam, and of the events of every age during this period of time, and we shall not repeat them here. Hishām b. Muḥammad: The Arabs used to say, "The flea has bit-

54. For Umayyah b. Abī al-Ṣalt, a poet from al-Ṭā'if, roughly contemporary with Muḥammad, see *EI*[1], s.v. and *GAL S*, I:55f. Heraclius is the well-known Byzantine emperor.

55. A prophet mentioned in the Qur'ān as "raised to high station" by God (19:56f.; see 21:85). He is usually identified with the Biblical Enoch (Akhnūkh) who "walked with God, and he was not, for God took Him" (Genesis 5:24). For other identifications see *EI*[2], s.v. Idrīs.

ten since our father Anūsh was born, and sin has been forbidden since our father Shithth was born." The Syriac name for Shithth is Shīth.

The Account of the Messenger of God and His Life

The Messenger of God Is Recognized by the Monk Baḥīrā

Ibn Humayd—Salamah—Muḥammad b. Isḥaq—ʿAbdallāh b. Abī Bakr.[56] ʿAbd al-Muṭṭalib died eight years after the Year of the Elephant. ʿAbd al-Muṭṭalib had entrusted the Messenger of God to the care of his paternal uncle Abū Ṭālib, because Abū Ṭālib and ʿAbdallāh, the father of the Messenger of God, had had the same mother. Abū Ṭālib assumed responsibility for the Messenger of God after the death of his grandfather and kept him with him. Once Abū Ṭālib was going on a trading expedition to Syria with a party of Quraysh, but when he had made his preparations and was ready to set out, the Messenger of God, as they allege, could not bear to be separated from him. Abū Ṭālib took pity on him and
[1124] said, "By God, I will take him with me, and we shall never part from one another," or words to that effect; and took him with him.

The caravan halted at Buṣra[57] in Syria, where there was a learned Christian monk named Baḥīrā in his cell. There had always been a monk in that cell, and their knowledge was passed on, it is alleged, by means of a book which was handed down from generation to generation. When the caravan halted at Baḥīrā's cell this year, he prepared a copious meal for them, because while he was

---

56. Ibn Hishām, *Sīrah,* 115–17; Ṭabarī omits some details given by Ibn Isḥāq. For Baḥīrā see *EI* ^{2}, s.v. Baḥīrā.

57. Bostra.

in his cell he had seen the Messenger of God shaded by a cloud which marked him out from among the company. Then they had come near, and, when they halted in the shade of a tree close to him, he observed the cloud covering the tree and bending down its branches over the Messenger of God until he was in the shade beneath it. When Baḥīrā saw this, he descended from his cell and sent the caravan a message inviting them all. When he saw the Messenger of God, he observed him very intently, noting features of his person whose description he had found in his book. After the company had finished the meal and dispersed, he asked the Messenger of God about certain matters which had taken place both when he was awake and when he was asleep. The Messenger of God told him, and he found that these things corresponded to the description which he had found in his book. Finally he looked at Muḥammad's back, and saw the seal of prophethood between his shoulders.

After this Baḥīrā asked Muḥammad's uncle, Abū Ṭālib, "What relation is this boy to you?" "My son," he replied. "He is not your son," said Baḥīrā. "This boy's father cannot be living." "He is my brother's son," said Abū Ṭālib. "What happened to his father?" he asked. "He died while the boy's mother was pregnant with him, " he replied. "You have spoken the truth," said Baḥīrā. "Take him back to your country, and be on your guard against the Jews, for, by God, if they see him and recognize what I have recognized in him, they will seek to do him harm. Great things lie ahead of him, [1125]
so take him back quickly to his country." His uncle then took him quickly back to Mecca.

Hishām b. Muḥammad: Abū Ṭālib took the Messenger of God to Buṣra in Syria when he was nine years old.

Al-ʿAbbās b. Muḥammad—Abū Nūḥ—Yūnus b. Abī Isḥāq—Abū Bakr b. Abī Mūsā—Abū Mūsā: Abū Ṭālib set off for Syria accompanied by the Messenger of God and a number of shaykhs of Quraysh. When they were above the monk's cell they went down and unloaded their camels. The monk came out to meet them, even though when they had passed by him previously he had not done so nor paid any attention to them. As they were encamped among their baggage he went among them, finally coming up and-taking hold of the hand of the Messenger of God. Then he said, "This is the Chief of the Worlds; this is the Messenger of the Lord of the Worlds: this person has been sent by God as a mercy to the Worlds." The shaykhs of the Quraysh said to him, "What is it that you know?" He replied, "I know that when you appeared at the top of the pass there was not a tree or a stone which did not prostrate itself in worship; and they only prostrate themselves to a prophet. I also recognize him by the seal of prophethood which is below the cartilage of his shoulders and which is like an apple." Then he returned and prepared a meal for them. When he brought it to them, the Messenger of God was tending the camels, so he said, "Send for him." He came with a cloud above him, and Baḥīrā said, "Look at him! There is a cloud above him which is shading him." When he approached the company he found that they had already occupied the shade of the tree; but when he sat down, the shade of the tree moved to cover him. Then Baḥīrā said, "Look at the shade of the tree! It has moved to cover him."

[1126] While he was standing by them beseeching them not to take the Messenger of God to the land of the Byzantines, since if these saw him they would recognize him by his description and would kill him, he turned around and suddenly beheld seven men advancing from the land of the Byzantines. He went up to meet them and said, "What brings you here?" They replied, "We have come because this prophet is appearing in this month. Men have been sent to every road, and we have been chosen as the best of men and sent to your road." "Have you left anyone behind you who is better than you?" he asked. "No," they said, "We have been chosen as the best of men for your road." He asked them, "Do you believe that something which God wishes to bring about can be prevented by any man?" "No," they said, and they followed him and remained with him. Then he went up to the members of the caravan and said to them, "I ask you in God's name, which of you is his guardian?" "Abū Ṭālib," they said. He did not cease to beseech Abū Ṭālib until he sent the Messenger of God back. Abū Bakr sent Bilāl to accompany him, and the monk supplied him with provisions of cakes and oil.

The Messenger of God Is Protected by God from Participating in Pagan Practices

Ibn Ḥumayd—Salamah—Muḥammad b. Isḥāq—Muḥammad b.

ʿAbdallāh b. Qays b. Makhramah—al-Hasan b. Muḥammad b. ʿAlī b. Abī Ṭalib—his father, Muḥammad b. ʿAlī—his grandfather, ʿAlī b. Abī Ṭālib: I heard the Messenger of God saying, "I was only tempted to take part in heathen practices on two occasions, and both times God prevented me from doing what I wanted. After that I was never tempted to evil, right up to the time when God honored me by making me his Messenger. One night I said to a lad from the Quraysh who was guarding flocks with me in the high ground of Mecca, ' Would you watch my flock for me so that I can go into Mecca and spend an evening there like other young men?' He agreed, so I set off with this object in mind. When I came to the first settlement in Mecca I heard the sound of tambourines and pipes, and I asked what was happening. They said that a wedding [1127] was taking place, so I sat down to watch them. But God prevented me from hearing, and I went to sleep and did not wake up until I felt the touch of the sun. Then I went back to my companion, who asked me what I had done. 'I did not do anything,' I replied, and then told him what had happened. Another night I made the same request, and he agreed, so I set out. When I reached Mecca I heard the same sound which I had heard on that earlier night, and I sat down to watch. Once again God prevented me from hearing and, by God, I only woke up when I felt the touch of the sun. I went back to my companion and told him what had happened. After that I was not tempted to evil, right up to the time when God honoured me by making me his Messenger."

The Prophet's Marriage to Khadījah[58]

Hishām b. Muḥammad: The Messenger of God married Khadījah when he was twenty-five years old. At that time, Khadījah was forty years of age.

Ibn Ḥumayd—Salamah—Ibn Isḥāq: Khadījah bt. Khuwaylid b. Asad b. ʿAbd al-ʿUzzā b. Quṣayy was a wealthy and respected merchant. She used to employ men to engage in trade with her prop-

58. Ibn Hishām, *Sīrāh,* 119–21; Ibn Saʿd, *Ṭabaqāt,* I:35.5-10. It is not clear how it was possible for Khadījah to trade on her own account, but the sources speak of at least one other Meccan woman who did so. Khadījah had previously been twice married, and the husbands were presumably now dead, so this may have had something to do with her special position.

erty and gave them a share in the profits, for Quraysh were a trading people. When she heard of the Messenger of God's truthfulness, reliability, and nobility of character, she sent for him and proposed to him that he should go to Syria and engage in trade with her property; she would give him more than she gave other men who traded for her and also a slave of hers called Maysarah. The Messenger of God accepted, and set out to trade with her property accompanied by her slave Maysarah. When he reached Syria he halted in the shade of a tree near a monk's cell. The monk
[1128] went up to Maysarah and said, "Who is this man who has halted beneath this tree?" Maysarah replied, "He is a man of Quraysh, one of the people of the sacred precinct (Ḥaram)." "No one has ever halted beneath this tree but a prophet," said the monk.

The Messenger of God sold the goods which he had brought with him, bought what he wanted to buy, and then set off back to Mecca accompanied by Maysarah. They assert that whenever the noonday heat grew intense Maysarah saw two angels shading him from the sun as he rode his camel. When he arrived in Mecca, he brought Khadījah her property, which she sold for twice the price or nearly so. Then Maysarah informed her of what the monk had said and how he himself had seen the two angels shading him. Khadījah was a resolute, intelligent and noble woman, and in addition to this God wished to ennoble her, so when Maysarah told her these things she sent for the Messenger of God and, it is reported, said to him, "Cousin, your kinship to me,[59] your standing among your people, your reliability, your good character and your truthfulness make you a desirable match." Then she offered herself to him in marriage. Khadījah was then the most distinguished of the women of Quraysh in lineage, the most highly honored, and the wealthiest, and all the men of her tribe would have been eager to accept this proposal had it been made to them. When she made this offer to the Messenger of God he told his uncles about it, and Ḥamzah b. ʿAbd al-Muṭṭalib went with him to Khuwaylid b. Asad and asked for (his daughter) Khadījah's hand on Muḥammad's behalf. Khuwaylid married Khadījah to the Messenger of God, and she bore all his children except for Ibrāhīm. They were Zaynab, Ruqayyah, Umm Kulthūm, Fāṭimah, al-Qāsim—

59. They were not closely related, but both were descendants of Quṣayy.

from whom he received his *kunyah* of Abū al-Qāsim—al-Ṭāhir, and al-Ṭayyib.[60] Al-Qāsim, al-Ṭahir, and al-Ṭayyib died during the Jāhiliyyah, while all of his daughters lived until Islam, became [1129]
Muslims, and emigrated with him to al-Madīnah.

Al-Ḥarith—Muḥammad b. Sa'd—Muḥammad b. 'Umar—Ma'mar and others—Ibn Shihāb al-Zuhrī: a similar report was given by other local scholars:[61] Khadījah hired only the Messenger of God and another man from Quraysh to go to the market of Ḥubāshah in Tihāmah. It was her father Khuwaylid who married her to Muḥammad, and the person who acted as an intermediary was a half-breed freedwoman from Mecca.

Al-Ḥārith—Muḥammad b. Sa'd—al-Wāqidī: All of this is an error.

Al-Wāqidī: They also say that Khadījah sent a message to the Messenger of God inviting him to take her, meaning that they should marry. She was a highly respected woman, and the whole of Quraysh would have been eager to marry her and would have spent much money to that end had they aspired to it. She called her father to her house, plied him with wine until he was drunk, slaughtered a cow, anointed him with perfume and clothed him in a striped robe; then she sent for the Messenger of God and his uncles and, when they came in, her father married him to her. When her father recovered from his intoxication, he said, "What is this meat, this perfume, and this garment?" She replied, "You have married me to Muḥammad b. 'Abdallāh." "I have not done so," he said. "Would I do this, when the greatest men of Mecca have asked for you and I have not agreed?"

Al-Wāqidī: This is also an error. In our opinion the trustworthy version is what is preserved in the account of Muḥammad b. 'Abdallāh b. Muslim—his father—Muḥammad b. Jubayr b. Muṭ'im; and in the account of Ibn Abī al-Zinād—Hishām b. Urwah—his father—'Ā'ishah; and in the account of Ibn Abī Ḥabībah—Dāūd b. al-Ḥuṣayn—'Ikrimah—Ibn 'Abbās: Her uncle 'Amr b. Asad married her to the Messenger of God. Her father died before the Sac- [1130]

60. Al-Ṭāhir is also said to have been called 'Abdallāh. Some critics have suggested that al-Ṭayyib is also an epithet applied to 'Abdallāh. None of the sources see anything unusual (or miraculous) in Khadījah having had seven children after the age of forty.

61. Literally, "the same was said by others than he of the people of the town," perhaps al-Madīnah or Damascus.

rilegious War (*al-fijār*).[62]

Abū Ja'far (al-Ṭabarī): Khadījah's house at that time was the house which is still known today and called Khadījah's House. It is related that Mu'āwiyah[63] bought it and turned it into a mosque in which people could pray. He rebuilt it in the form in which it exists today without alteration. The stone which is at the door of the house to the left as you go in is the stone beneath which the Messenger of God used to sit to shelter himself when people threw stones at him from the houses of Abū Lahab[64] and 'Adī b. Ḥamrā' al-Thaqafī, behind the house of Ibn 'Alqamah. The stone measures a cubit (*dhirā'*) and a span (*shibr*) one way, and a cubit the other way.

62. This was a war in which Quraysh supported by Kinānah fought against the tribe of Qays 'Aylān during the sacred month. It is said to have occurred when Muḥammad was twenty, that is, in A.D. 590; and he did not marry Khadījah until five years later. See *EI* ², s.v. Fidjār.

63. Umayyad caliph who reigned from A.D. 661 to 680. Abū Lahab (below) was the uncle of Muḥammad who succeeded Abū Ṭālib as chief of Hāshim and turned against Muḥammad.

64. Ibn Hishām, *Sīrah*, 122–26.

Events of the Life of the Messenger of God

The Rebuilding of the Ka'bah[65]

Abū Ja'far (al-Ṭabarī): We have mentioned previously the circumstances of the Prophet's marriage to Khadījah, the various conflicting reports about it, and the date of its occurence. Ten years after the marriage of the Messenger of God to Khadījah, Quraysh demolished the Ka'bah and then rebuilt it. According to Ibn Isḥāq, this was in the Messenger of God's thirty-fifth year.

Ibn Ḥumayad—Salamah—Ibn Isḥāq: The reason for their demolition of the Ka'bah was that at this time it consisted of loose stones rising to somewhat above a man's height, and they wished to make it higher and roof it over, since some men, Qurashites and others, had stolen the treasure of the Ka'bah, which was kept in a well in its interior.

History of the Ka'bah

Hisham b. Muḥammad—his father: The story of the two gazelles of the Ka'bah is as follows. The Ka'bah had been destroyed when the people of Noah were drowned, and God commanded his friend
Abraham and Abraham's son Ishmael to rebuild it on its original [1131]
foundations. This they did, as is stated in the Qur'ān:[66] And when Abraham and Ishmael were raising the foundations of the House

65. Ibn Hishām, *Sīrah*, (vol):122–26. There is nothing in the Qur'ān to connect Noah with the Ka'bah, so this must be a deduction by later Muslim scholars from the statement that the whole world was destroyed by the flood in the time of Noah.

66. 2:127.

(Abraham prayed) : Our Lord! Accept from us (this duty). Only You are the Hearer, the Knower.

It had not had any custodians since its destruction in the time of Noah. Then God commanded Abraham to settle his son by the Kaʿbah, wishing thereby to show a mark of esteem to one whom he later ennobled by means of his Prophet Muḥammad. Abraham, the Friend of the Compassionate, and his son Ishmael were custodians of the Kaʿbah after the time of Noah. At that time, Mecca was uninhabited, and the surrounding country was inhabited by the Jurhum and ʿAmāliqah.[67] Ishmael married a woman of the Jurhum. On this subject, ʿAmr b. al-Ḥārith b. Muḍāḍ said:

We allied ourselves by marriage to a man with the
noblest of fathers;
his sons are of us, and we are his brothers-in-law.

After Abraham, Ishmael became the custodian of the Kaʿbah, and after him, Nabt and his Jurhumī mother. When Nabt died, since Ishmael's sons were not numerous, Jurhum seized the custodianship. ʿAmr b. al-Ḥārith b. Muḍāḍ said:

We were the custodians of the Kaʿbah after Nābit;
we circumambulated it and good was manifest.

The first of the Jurhum to be custodian of the Kaʿbah was Muḍāḍ, followed by his descendants, generation after generation. Eventually the Jurhum acted wrongfully in Mecca, held lawful that which was forbidden, misappropriated the wealth which had been presented to the Kaʿbah, and oppressed those who came to Mecca. Their behavior became so unrestrained that when one of them could not find a place in which to fornicate he would go into the Kaʿbah and do it there. It is asserted that Isāf fornicated with Nā'ilah in the interior of the Kaʿbah and that they were transformed into two stones. During the Jāhiliyyah, any person who
[1132] acted wrongfully or oppresively in Mecca, or any king who held lawful what was forbidden there, perished on the spot. Mecca was called al-Nāssah, and was also called Bakkah, because it used to break *(tabukk)* the necks of evildoers and tyrants when they acted

67. These are the Amalekites of the Bible, but in the traditional history of pre-Islamic Arabia there is much non-Biblical material about them. See *EI* ², s.v. ʿAmālīḳ.

wrongfully there.

The Jurhum did not desist from their wickedness. When the Banū ʿAmr b. ʿĀmir dispersed from the Yemen,[68] the Banū Ḥārithah b. ʿAmr split off *(inkhazaʿa)* from them, settled in Tihāmah, and became known as Khuzāʿah.[69] Khuzāʿah consists of the Banū ʿAmr b. Rabīʿah b. Ḥārithah together with the clans of Aslam, Mālik, and Milkān, sons of Afṣā b. Ḥārithah. God sent a bleeding of the nose and a plague of ants[70] against the Jurhum and destroyed them, while Khuzāʿah joined together to expel those of them who survived. The chief of Khuzāʿah at that time was ʿAmr b. Rabīʿah b. Ḥārithah, whose mother was Fuhayrah bt. ʿĀmir b. al-Ḥārith b. Muḍāḍ. A battle took place, and when ʿĀmir b. al-Ḥārith[71] felt that he would be defeated, he brought out the two gazelles of the Kaʿbah and the stone of the *rukn,*[72] seeking forgiveness, and recited:

O God, Jurhum are your servants;
    our enemies are newcomers, while we are your
    hereditary servants,
Through whom your dwelling has flourished of old.

However his repentance was not accepted (by the opponents), so he flung the two gazelles of the Kaʿbah and the stone of the *rukn* into Zamzam, buried them and left with the remnants of the Jurhum for part of the territory of Juhaynah. There a sudden torrent overtook them and swept them away. On this subject Umayyah b. Abī al-Ṣalt said:

---

68. The reference is to ʿAmr Muzayqiyāʾ, who led the migration of several tribes from the Yemen at the time of the breaking of the dam of Maʾrib; he had sons called Ḥārithah and Afṣā.

69. The name Khuzāʿah is here explained as indicating that they have split off *(inkhazaʿa)* from the main tribe. The following sentence suggests that Khuzāʿah was at first a group of small related clans rather than being all descendants of a single ancestor.

70. The ants are mentioned on p. 1121.

71. There is some doubt about whether the name should be ʿĀmir or ʿAmr. ʿĀmir b. al-Ḥārith was the father of Fuhayrah, just mentioned.

72. The phrase *ḥajar al-rukn* is unusual. Each of the corners or angles of the Kaʿbah is called a *rukn,* but the English word "cornerstone" has misleading associations. It is possible that the stone here is the sacred Black Stone, which is now built into one *rukn* of the Kaʿbah and kissed or touched by pilgrims. Near the Black Stone is another stone, "the lucky stone" *(al-ḥajar al-asʿad),* which is touched but not kissed, and this might be what is meant here.

Jurhum blackened Tihāmah with the dung of their cattle
for a while,
and then Iḍam was awash with them all.

[1133] The custodianship was taken over by ʿAmr b. Rabīʿah, or, according to the descendants of Quṣayy, by ʿAmr b. al-Ḥārith al-Ghubshānī. He it is who says:

We became custodians of the Kaʿbah after Jurhum
that we might keep it prosperous, free from every
wrongdoer and unbeliever.

He also said:

A valley whose birds and wild animals may not be
touched.
We are its custodians and we do not discharge our
duties dishonestly.

and:

It is as though there had never been a close friend
between al-Ḥajūn and al-Ṣafā
and no companion had engaged in evening conversation
in Mecca.
Nay! We were its people, but we were destroyed
by the vicissitudes of time and stumbling fate.[73]

and:

Travel, men, for it would be negligence on your part
for you not to be travelling one day.
We were men like you, but fate changed our condition,
and you shall be as we were.
Urge on your mounts and slacken your reins
before you die, and perform your duties.

What he means is, "Strive for the hereafter and abandon the concerns of this world."

---

73. These two lines are quoted by Ibn Isḥāq (Ibn Hishām, *Sīrah,* 73) as part of a longer poem which he attributes to ʿAmr b. al-Ḥārith b. Muḍāḍ al-Jurhumī. It is virtually impossible to clear up the confusion of names here. Al-Hajūn is a mountain above Mecca, and al-Ṣafā is the point near the Kaʿbah from which the pilgrims begin to run to al-Marwah.

The Kaʿbah was taken over by the Khuzāʿah, except that there were three functions which were in the hands of tribes of (the group called) Muḍar. The first of these was the *ijāzah,* the giving of permission to the pilgrims to leave ʿArafah. This was in the hands of al-Ghawth b. Murr, who was (of the clan of) Ṣūfah. When it was time for the permission to be given the Arabs would say, "Give permission, Ṣūfah." The second function was the *ifāḍah,* the permission for the pilgrims to disperse to Minā on the morning of the sacrifice. This was in the hands of the Banū Zayd b. ʿAdwān; the last of them to hold this position was Abū Sayyārah ʿUmaylah b. al-Aʿzal b. Khālid b. Saʿd b. al-Ḥārith b. Wābish b. Zayd. The third function was the *nasī',* the delaying or postponement of the sacred month (by intercalation).[74] The right to decide this was in the hands of al-Qalammas, who was Ḥudhayfah b. Fuqaym b. ʿAdī, of the Banū Mālik b. Kinānah. After him, it passed to his descendants, down to the last of them, Abū Thumāmah, who was Junādah b. ʿAwf b. Umayyah b. Qalaʿ b. Hudhayfah. When Islam came, the sacred months had returned to their original times, and God established them firmly and abolished the *nasī'.* [1134]

When Maʿadd became numerous, they scattered, as Muhalhil says:

Our abode was in Tihāmah for a time,
and the descendants of Maʿadd dwelt there.

As for Quraysh, they did not leave Mecca.

When ʿAbd al-Muttalib dug (the well of) Zamzam, he found the two gazelles of the Kaʿbah which Jurhum had buried in it and brought them out. We have already mentioned the story of ʿAbd al-Muṭṭalib and the two gazelles in the appropriate place earlier

74. The Arabs observed lunar months, but, in order to keep their lunar year in line with the solar year, they occasionally intercalated an extra month; this is what is known as the *nasī',* the delaying or postponing of the sacred months. There is no mention of any fixed system of intercalation, and so it may have been carried out in haphazard fashion, and perhaps even in ways which were of personal advantage to those making the decision. This is presumably why it was forbidden by the Qur'ān (9:36f.). Muḥammad is said to have made these verses public at the Pilgrimage of Farewell (March 632). This committed the Muslims to a lunar year of 354 days, and thus caused difficulties for those engaged in agriculture who followed the solar calendar. It is difficult to give a reasonable sense to the phrase "had returned to their original times."

in this book.[75]

The Rebuilding of the Kaʿbah (Continued)

Returning to the narrative of Ibn Isḥāq:[76] The person in whose house the treasure of the Kaʿbah was found was Duwayk, a *mawlā* of the Banū Mulayḥ b. ʿAmr of Khuzāʿah, and they cut off his hand publicly. Among those who were suspected in this matter were al-
[1135] Ḥārith b. ʿĀmir b. Nawfal, Abū Ihāb b. ʿAzīz b. Qays b. Suwayd al-Tamīmī, who was a half brother of al-Ḥārith b. ʿĀmir b. Nawfal b. ʿAbd Manāf on his mother's side, and Abū Lahab b. ʿAbd al-Muṭṭalib. These are the people who, Quraysh allege, left the treasure with Duwayk, the *mawlā* of the Banū Mulayḥ, after they had stolen it. When Quraysh accused them of the crime, they informed against Duwayk and his hand was cut off. It is said that they left the stolen treasure with him. They also relate that when Quraysh were certain that al-Ḥārith b. ʿĀmir b. Nawfal b. ʿAbd Manāf had it, they took him to a female Arab soothsayer, who, using her occult skill, pronounced in rhyming prose that he should not enter Mecca for ten years because of his violation of the sanctity of the Kaʿbah. They allege that they expelled him from Mecca and that he remained on its outskirts for ten years.

A ship belonging to a Greek merchant had been driven ashore by rough seas at Jeddah and had been broken to pieces. They took its timbers and prepared them for use in roofing over the Kaʿbah. There was a Copt in Mecca who was a carpenter, and thus they had both the materials for restoring it and a craftsman ready and at hand. There was a snake which used to come out of the well in the Kaʿbah into which votive objects were thrown, and which would lie on top of the Kaʿbah wall every day. People were afraid of it because whenever anyone went near it it would draw itself up, make a rustling noise, and open its mouth. One day, as it was
[1136] lying on top of the Kaʿbah as usual, God sent against it a bird which seized it and carried it off. On seeing this, the Quraysh said, "We may hope that God is pleased with what we intend to do. We have a companion who is a craftsman and we have timber, while God

75. Above, p.1088.
76. Ibn Hishām, *Sīrah*, 122–26. Ibn Hishām omits the passage about Duwayk apart from the first sentence.

has dealt with the snake for us."

This was fifteen years after the Sacrilegious War, when the Messenger of God was thirty-five years old. When they took the decision to demolish and rebuild the Kaʿbah, Abū Wahb b. ʿAmr b. ʿĀʾidh b. ʿImrān b. Makhzūm rose and took a stone from it which leapt from his hand and returned to its place. Then he said, "Men of Quraysh, do not spend on its rebuilding any ill-gotten gains, nor money earned by prostitution, usury, or by wronging any man." Some people wrongly ascribe this saying to al-Walīd b. al-Mughīrah.

Ibn Ḥumayd—Salamah—Muḥammad b. Isḥāq—ʿAbdallāh b. Abī Najīḥ al-Makkī—ʿAbdallāh b. Ṣafwān b. Umayyah b. Khalaf: He saw a son of Jaʿdah b. Hubayrah b. Abī Wahb b. ʿAmr b. ʿĀʾidh b. ʿImrān b. Makhzūm circumambulating the Kaʿbah and asked about him. They said, "This is a son of Jaʿdah b. Hubayrah." Then ʿAbdallāh b. Ṣafwān said, "This man's grandfather—meaning Abū Wahb—is he who, when Quraysh agreed to demolish the Kaʿbah, lifted a stone from it which leapt from his hand and returned to its place. Then he said, 'Men of Quraysh, do not spend on its rebuilding any ill-gotten gains, nor money earned from prostitution, usury, or by wronging any man.' " Abū Wahb was a maternal uncle of the Messenger of God, and was a noble.

Ibn Ḥumayd—Salamah—Muḥammad b. Isḥāq: Quraysh di- [1137]
vided the work on the Kaʿbah between them. The side containing the door went to the Banū ʿAbd Manāf and Zuhrah; the section between the Black Stone and the southern corner went to the Makhzūm, Taym, and the clans of Quraysh who were attached to them; the back of the Kaʿbah went to the Banū Jumaḥ and Banū Sahm; and the side facing the Ḥijr and the Ḥaṭīm went to the Banū ʿAbd al-Dār b. Quṣayy, the Banū Asad b. ʿAbd al-ʿUzzā b. Quṣayy, and the Banū ʿAdī b. Kaʿb. Then, however, they were afraid to demolish it, so al-Walīd b. Mughīrah said, "I will make a start on the demolition for you." He took up his pickaxe and stood by the Kaʿbah, saying, "O God, let the Kaʿbah not fear. O God, we intend nothing but good." Then he demolished part of it near the two corners.[77] They waited to see what would happen to him that

77. Since al-Walīd b. Mughīrah belonged to Makhzūm, these were presumably the two corners of the side assigned to them, that is, what lay between the eastern corner (with the Black Stone) and the southern corner.

night, and they said, "Let us watch; if something happens to him we shall not demolish any more of it and shall restore it as it was, and if nothing happens to him we shall know that God is pleased with what we have done, and we shall demolish it." The next morning al-Walīd went early to his work and continued to demolish, and the others then did so also. At last they came to the foundations, reaching green stones like teeth, interlocked with one another.

[1138] Ibn Ḥumayd—Salamah—Muḥammad b. Isḥāq—certain narrators of traditions *(Ḥadīths):* A man of Quraysh who was among these demolishing it thrust a crowbar between two stones to prise one of them up. When the stone moved, the whole of Mecca shook, and then (they knew that) they had reached the foundations.

The clans then gathered stones to rebuild the Kaʿbah. Each clan gathered them separately and built separately, and when the building reached the place where the Black Stone was to be put they began to dispute about it, since every clan wished to lift the Stone to its place to the exclusion of the other clans. They started to split up into factions, to form alliances, and to make agreements among themselves in preparation for battle. The Banū ʿAbd al-Dār brought a bowl full of blood and made a compact with the Banū ʿAdī b. Kaʿb to support one another to the death. They thrust their hands into this bowl of blood, and were called "the bloodlickers" *(laʿaqat al-dam)* on account of this. The Quraysh remained in this state for four or five days, and then they gathered in the mosque to consult together and to reach an equitable agreement.

Some narrators assert that Abū Umayyah b. al-Mughīrah, who at that time was the oldest member of Quraysh, said, "Men of Quraysh, make the first man who comes in at the door of this mosque the arbiter of your differences so that he may judge on the matter." The first man to come in was the Messenger of God, and when they saw him they said, "This is the trustworthy one *(al-amīn)* with whom we are satisfied. This is Muḥammad." He
[1139] came up to them, and they told him about the matter, and he said, "Bring me a cloak." They brought him one, and he took the Black Stone and placed it on it with his own hands. Then he said, "Let each clan take one side of the cloak, and then lift it up all together." They did so, and when they had brought it to its place he

put it in position with his own hands. Then they built on top of it. Before the revelation first came to him, Quraysh used to call the Messenger of God "the trustworthy one."

The Beginning of the Prophetic Mission

Abū Ja'far (al-Ṭabari): Quraysh's rebuilding of the Ka'bah was fifteen years after the Sacrilegious War. There were twenty years between the Year of the Elephant and the Year of the Sacrilegious War. The early authorities differ as to the age of the Messenger of God when he became a prophet. Some say that it was five years after the Quraysh rebuilt the Ka'bah, when his fortieth birthday had passed.[78]

Those who say this:

Muḥammad b. Khalaf al-'Asqalānī—Ādam—Ḥammad b. Salamah—Abū Jamrah al-Ḍuba'ī—Ibn 'Abbās: The Messenger of God commenced his mission at the age of forty.

'Amr b. 'Alī and Ibn al-Muthannā—Yaḥyā b. Muḥammad b. Qays—Rabī'ah b. Abī 'Abd al-Raḥmān—Anas b. Mālik: The Messenger of God commenced his mission at the end of his fortieth year.

Al-'Abbās b. al-Walīd—his father—al-Awzā'ī—Rabī'ah b. Abī 'Abd al-Raḥmān—Anas b. Mālik: The Messenger of God commenced his mission at the beginning of his fortieth year.

[1140] Ibn 'Abd al-Raḥīm al-Barqī—'Amr b. Abī Salamah—al-Awzā'ī—Rabī'ah b. Abī 'Abd al-Raḥmān—Anas b. Mālik: The Messenger of God commenced his mission at the beginning of his fortieth year.

Abū Shuraḥbīl al-Ḥimṣī—Abū al-Yamān—Ismā'īl b. 'Ayyāsh—Yaḥyā b. Sa'īd—Rabī'ah b. Abī 'Abd al-Raḥmān—Anas b. Mālik:

78. This places the beginning of his prophethood about the year A.D. 610.

The Messenger of God received the revelation when he was aged forty.

Ibn al-Muthannā—al-Ḥajjāj b. al-Minhāl—Ḥammād—ʿAmr b. Dīnār—ʿUrwah b. al-Zubayr: The Messenger of God commenced his mission when he was aged forty.

Ibn al-Muthannā—al-Ḥajjāj—Ḥammād—ʿAmr—Yaḥyā b. Jaʿdah: The Messenger of God said to Fāṭimah, "(Gabriel) has reviewed the Qur'ān with me once a year, but this year he has reviewed it with me twice, and I fancy that my time has come. You are the nearest to me of my kin. Whenever a prophet has been sent, his mission has lasted for a period of half his predecessor's lifetime. Jesus was sent for a period of forty years, and I was sent for twenty."[79]

ʿUbayd b. Muḥammad al-Warrāq—Rawḥ b. ʿUbādah—Hishām—ʿIkrimah—Ibn ʿAbbās: The Messenger of God commenced his mission at the age of forty, and remained in Mecca for thirteen years.[80]

Abū Kurayb—Abū Usāmah and Muḥammad b. Maymūn al-Zaʿfarānī—Hishām b. Ḥassān—ʿIkrimah—Ibn ʿAbbās: The [1141]
Messenger of God commenced his mission and received the revelation when he was aged forty, and remained in Mecca for thirteen years.

Others say that he became a prophet when he was aged forty-three.[81]

Those who say this:

Aḥmad b. Thābit al-Rāzī—Aḥmad—Yaḥyā b. Saʿīd—Hishām—ʿIkrimah—Ibn ʿAbbās: The Prophet received the revelation when he was aged forty-three.

Ibn Ḥumayd—Jarīr—Yaḥyā b. Saʿīd—Saʿīd b. al-Musayyab: The Messenger of God received the revelation when he was aged forty-three.

Ibn al-Muthannā—ʿAbd al-Wahhāb—Yaḥyā b. Saʿīd—Saʿīd, that is, Ibn al-Musayyab: The Messenger of God received the revelation when he was aged forty-three.

---

79. This fits in better with the view that he became a prophet when he was forty-three.

80. Thirteen years would be from A.D. 610 to 622 inclusive.

81. This makes his prophethood begin about the year a.d. 613.

The Day and the Month on Which the Messenger of God Became a Prophet, and the Accounts Concerning This

Abū Jaʿfar (al-Ṭabarī): The sound account is the one related by Ibn al-Muthannā—Muḥammad b. Jaʿfar—Shuʿbah—Ghaylān b. Jarīr—ʿAbdallāh b. Maʿbad al-Zimmānī—Abū Qatādah al-Anṣārī: The Messenger of God was questioned about his Monday fast. He replied, "This is the day on which I was born and the day on which I commenced by mission." Another version has it: "on which I received the revelation."

Aḥmad b. Manṣūr—al-Ḥasan b. Mūsā al-Ashyab—Abū Hilāl—Ghaylān b. Jarīr al-Maʿwalī—ʿAbdallāh b. Maʿbad al-Zimmānī—
[1142] Abū Qatādah— ʿUmar: He said to the Prophet, "O Prophet of God, (what is the reason for) your Monday fast?" He replied, "This is the day on which I was born and the day on which the prophethood descended upon me."

Ibrāhīm b. Saʿīd—Mūsā b. Dā'ūd—Ibn Lahīʿah—Khālid b. Abī ʿImrān—Ḥanash al-Ṣanʿānī—Ibn ʿAbbas: The Prophet was born on a Monday and became a prophet on a Monday.

First Revelation of the Qur'ān

Abū Jaʿfar (al-Ṭabarī): There is no dispute among the scholars on the above point. There is however a dispute as to which Monday this was. Some say that the Qur'ān was revealed to the Messenger of God on the eighteenth of Ramaḍān.

Those who say this:

Ibn Ḥumayd—Salamah—Muḥammad b. Isḥāq—al-Ḥasan b. Dīnār—Ayyūb—Abū Qilābah ʿAbd Allāh b. Zayd al-Jarmī: According to the information which had reached him, the Qur'ān was revealed to the Messenger of God on the eighteenth of Ramaḍān.

Others say that it was revealed on the twenty-fourth of Ramaḍān.

Those who say this:

Ibn Ḥumayd—Salamah—Muḥammad b. Isḥāq—one who is above suspicion—Saʿīd b. Abī ʿArūbah—Qatādah b. Diʿāmah al-

Sadūsī—Abū al-Jald: The *furqān*[82] was revealed on the twenty-fourth of Ramaḍān.

Others say that it was revealed on the seventeenth of Ramaḍān. They quote as evidence for this the words of God:[83] "And that [1143]
which we revealed to Our slave on the day of the *furqān*, on the day when the two armies met.[84] This refers to the meeting (in battle) of the Messenger of God with the polytheists at Badr, which took place on the morning of the seventeenth of Ramaḍān.

Signs of the Approach of Prophethood

Abū Ja'far (al-Ṭabarī): Before Gabriel appeared to him to confer on him his mission as Messenger of God, it is said that he used to see signs and evidences indicating that God wished to ennoble him and to single him out for his favor. One of these is the account which I have previously given[85] of the two angels who came to him, opened up his breast, and removed the hatred and the impurity which were in it. This was when he was with his foster-mother, Ḥalīmah. Another is that it is said that whenever he passed along a road and passed by a tree or a stone, it would greet him.

Al-Ḥārith b. Muḥammad—Muḥammad b. Sa'd—Muḥammad b. 'Umar—'Alī b. Muḥammad b. 'Ubaydallāh b. 'Abdallāh b. 'Umar b. al-Khaṭṭāb—Manṣūr b. 'Abd al-Raḥmān—his mother Barrah bt. Abī Tajrāh: When God willed that Muḥammad should be ennobled and should enter upon prophethood, it came about that whenever he went out to attend his business[86] he would go a great distance, out of sight of houses, and into the ravines and wādī-beds; and then every stone and tree he passed would say, "Peace be upon

82. Here means the Qur'ān, but the word has several other meanings; see *EI* ^{2}, s.v. Furḳān. This paragraph from Ibn Isḥāq is omitted by Ibn Hishām.

83. 8:41.

84. This verse refers to the battle of Badr, and *furqān* might then be understood as the Muslims' "deliverance" from the pagan Meccans; but that also seems to be connected somehow with a revelation of Muḥammad.

85. Though Ṭabarī says "I have previously given," he appears to be referring to what comes subsequently on pp. 1154f.

86. This seems to be the plain meaning of *al-ḥājah*; but "went out about his business" is also possible. The paragraph corresponds to Ibn Sa'd, *Ṭabaqāt*, I:102.17-23.

you, Messenger of God." He would turn to the right and the left and turn round, but could not see anyone.

Predictions of the Appearance of the Prophet

Abū Ja'far (al-Ṭabarī): The various religious communities used to speak of his forthcoming mission, and the scholars of every community used to tell their people of it.

[1144] Al-Ḥārith—Muḥammad b. Sa'd—Muḥammad b. 'Umar—'Alī b. 'Īsā al-Ḥakamī—his father—'Āmir b. Rabī'ah: I heard Zayd b. 'Amr b. Nufayl[87] saying, "I expect a prophet from the descendants of Ishmael, in particular from the descendants of 'Abd al-Muṭṭalib. I do not think that I shall live to see him, but I believe in him, proclaim the truth of his message, and testify that he is a prophet. If you live long enough to see him, give him my greetings. I shall inform you of his description, so that he will not be hidden from you." I said, "Tell me, then," and he said, "He is a man who is neither short nor tall, whose hair is neither abundant nor sparse, whose eyes are always red, and who has the seal of prophethood between his shoulders. His name is Aḥmad,[88] and this town is his birthplace and the place in which he will commence his mission. Then his people will drive him out and hate the message which he brings, and he will emigrate to Yathrib and triumph. Beware lest you fail to recognize him. I have travelled around every land in search of the faith of Abraham. Every person whom I ask, whether Jew, Christian, or Magian, says, 'This faith lies where you have come from,' and they describe him as I have described him to you. They say that no prophet remains but he."[89] 'Āmir said, "When I

87. One of the four men mentioned by Ibn Isḥāq (143-49) as a *ḥanīf* or searcher for a pure monotheism; see Watt, *Muhammad at Mecca*, 162-64. Ibn Sa'd, *Ṭabaqāt*, I:105.23-106.8.

88. Aḥmad is commonly regarded as a variant form of Muḥammad, following the standard interpretation of Qur'ān 61:6, where Jesus says to the Israelites that he brings "good tidings of a messenger who comes after me, whose name is Aḥmad." (Aḥmad is, of course from the same root as Muḥammad, namely ḥ-m-d.) There are strong grounds, however, for thinking that for the first century or so of Islam the word *aḥmadu* was understood as an adjective meaning "more praiseworthy" and not as a proper name; see Watt, "His Name is Aḥmad," *Muslim World*, xliii (1953):110–17.

89. This refers to the standard Muslim interpretation of the phrase "seal of the prophets" applied to Muḥammad in Qur'ān 33:40, namely, that he is the last

became a Muslim, I told the Messenger of God what Zayd b. ʿAmr had said, and I gave him his greetings. He returned his greetings and said, 'May God have mercy on his soul. I saw him in Paradise dressed in flowing robes.' "

Ibn Ḥumayd—Salamah—Ibn Isḥāq—one who is above suspicion —ʿAbdallāh b. Kaʿb the *mawlā* of ʿUthmān: ʿUmar b. al-Khaṭṭāb was sitting with others in the Messenger of God's mosque one day when a beduin came up and entered the mosque looking for ʿUmar (b. al-Khaṭṭāb). When ʿUmar looked at him he said, "This man is still a polytheist, although at one point he abandoned polytheism. He was a soothsayer in the Jāhiliyyah." The man greeted him and then sat down. ʿUmar said to him, "Have you become a Muslim?" [1145]
"Yes," he replied. "Were you a soothsayer in the Jāhiliyyah?" asked ʿUmar. "Praise be to God," the man answered. "You have received me with words which I do not suppose that you have uttered to one of your subjects since you became Caliph." "God forgive me!" said ʿUmar.[90] "During the Jāhiliyyah we used to do worse things than you. We used to worship idols and embrace graven images until God honored us with Islam." "Yes, by God, O Commander of the Faithful," answered the man. "I used to be a soothsayer in the Jāhiliyyah." "Tell me," said ʿUmar, "what is the most amazing saying which your familiar spirit brought you?" "He came to me a month or a year before Islam," said the man, "and said to me:

Have you considered the Jinn[91] and their hopelessness
and their despair of their religion,
and their clinging to young female camels and their saddle cloths?"

---

prophet after whom there will be no other.

90. The point of this story appears to be that the Caliph ʿUmar made a hasty judgement about this man's continuing polytheism, and then had to withdraw it. This account from Ibn Isḥaq is not in the standard text.

91. The jinn (plural; singular *jinnī,* formerly transliterated as "genie") are a third class of intelligent beings along with angels and humans. They are imperceptible to the senses, but may make appearances under different forms. They are capable of having a religion and believing in God; and the Qur'ān (72:1–19; 46:29–32) speaks of Muḥammad preaching to them and of some being converted. In the present passage their "despair of their religion" may be intended as a sort of premonition of the coming of Islam; the reason for the reference to camels is unknown. The jinn play a large part in folklore. See *EI* ^{2}, s.v. Djinn, first part.

Then ʿUmar said to the gathering, "By God, I was by one of the idols of the Jāhiliyyah with a number of men of Quraysh. An Arab had sacrificed a calf to it, and we were waiting for it to be divided up in order to receive a share, when I heard coming from the belly of the calf a voice which was more penetrating than any voice I have ever heard—this was a month or a year before Islam—saying:

O people of Dharīḥ
A matter which has ended in success
A man shouting
Saying, "There is no deity but God."

Ibn Ḥumayd—ʿAlī b. Mujāhid—Ibn Isḥāq—al-Zuhrī—ʿAbdallāh b. Kaʿb the *mawlā* of ʿUthmān b. ʿAffān: a similar account.

Al-Ḥārith—Muḥammad b. Saʿd—Muḥammad b. ʿUmar—Muḥammad b. ʿAbdallāh—al-Zuhrī—Muḥammad b. Jubayr b.
[1146] Muṭʿim—his father: We were sitting by an idol at Buwānah a month before the Messenger of God commenced his mission, having slaughtered camels. Suddenly we heard a voice calling from the belly of one:[92]

Listen to the wonder;
There will be no more eavesdropping to overhear inspiration;
We throw down shooting stars
For a prophet in Mecca;
His name is Aḥmad,[93]
His place of emigration is Yathrib.

We held back and marvelled; then the Messenger of God appeared (that is, he began his mission).

Proofs of Prophethood

Aḥmad b. Sinān al-Qaṭṭān al-Wāsiṭī—Abū Muʿāwiyah—Aʿmash—Abū Ẓibyān—Ibn ʿAbbās: A man of the Banū ʿĀmir came to the Prophet and said, "Show me the seal which is between your shoulders, and if you lie under any enchantment I will cure you, for I am the best enchanter of the Arabs," "Do you wish me to show you a sign?" asked the Prophet. "Yes," said the man, "summon

92. Reading *juzur* instead of *jazūr* with Ibn Saʿd, *Ṭabaqāt*, I:105.12-17.
93. See n. 88.

that cluster of dates." So the Prophet looked at a cluster of dates hanging from a date palm and summoned it, and began to snap his fingers until it stood before him. Then the man said, "Tell it to go back," and it went back. The ʿĀmirī said, "O Banū ʿĀmir, I have never seen a greater magician than I have seen today."

Abū Jaʿfar (al-Ṭabarī): The stories of the proof of his prophethood are too numerous to be counted. We shall devote a book to this subject, if God wills.

The Manner in Which the Qur'ān Was First Revealed

We now return to an account of the condition of the Prophet of God at the time when God began to ennoble him by sending Gabriel to him bearing the revelation.

Abū Jaʿfar (al-Ṭabarī): We have mentioned previously some of the stories related to the first occasion on which Gabriel brought our Prophet Muḥammad the revelation from God and how old the Prophet was at that time. We shall now describe the manner in which Gabriel began to come to him and to appear to him [1147]
bringing the revelation of his Lord.

Aḥmad b. ʿUthmān, known as Abū al-Jawzā—Wahb b. Jarīr—his father—al-Nuʿmān b. Rāshid—al-Zuhrī—ʿUrwah—ʿĀ'ishah: The first form in which the revelation came to the Messenger of God was true vision; this used to come to him like the break of dawn.[94] After that, he grew to love solitude and used to remain in a cave on Ḥirā' engaged in acts of devotion[95] for a number of days before returning to his family. Then he would return to his family and supply himself with provisions for a similar number of days. This continued until the Truth came to him unexpectedly,[96] and said. 'Muḥammad, you are the Messenger of God.' " (Describing what

94. This probably refers to the two visions described in the Qur'ān (53:1–18). These are now interpreted by Muslims as visions of Gabriel, but the use of the word *'abd* (slave) in verse 10 implies that Muḥammad originally took it to be a vision of God, and this is allowed by some of the older commentators. See Ibn Hishām, *Sīrah,* 151.

95. There has been much discussion over the precise meaning of the word *yataḥannathu* (verbal noun, *taḥannuth),* although it is clearly some form of devotional practice; further references in Watt, *Muhammad at Mecca,* 44.

96. In this usage, the Truth *(al-ḥaqq)* is God, and the apparent declaration of Muḥammad's messengership by God supports the view that he originally took the visions to be of God.

happened next,) the Messenger of God said, "I had been standing, but fell to my knees; and crawled away, my shoulders trembling. I went to Khadījah and said, 'Wrap me up! Wrap me up!'[97] When the terror had left me, he came to me and said, 'Muḥammad, you are the Messenger of God.' "

He (Muḥammad) said: I had been thinking of hurling myself down from a mountain crag, but he appeared to me, as I was thinking about this, and said, "Muḥammad, I am Gabriel and you are the Messenger of God." Then he said, "Recite!" I said, "What shall I recite?"[98] He took me and pressed me three times tightly until I was nearly stifled and was utterly exhausted; then he said:[99] "Recite in the name of your Lord who created," and I recited it. Then I went to Khadījah and said, "I have been in fear for my life." When I told her what had happened, she said, "Rejoice, for God will never put you to shame, for you treat your kinsfolk well, tell the truth, deliver what is entrusted to you, endure fatigue, offer hospitality to the guest, and aid people in misfortune."

Then she took me to Waraqah b. Nawfal b. Asad[100] and said to
[1148] him "Listen to your brother's son." He questioned me and I told him what had happened. He said, "This is the Nāmūs[101] which was sent down to Moses, son of ʿImrān. Would that I were a young

---

97. The word *zammilūnī* is masculine plural, and so not addressed to Khadījah alone. The same root is found in Qur'ān 73:1, "O enwrapped one" (*muzzammil*). Somewhat similar is the word in 74:1 *muddaththir* (wrapped in a *dithār* or cloak), and this was held by some scholars to the first sūrah to be revealed. Covering with a cloak is said to have been regarded as a form of protection from the danger involved in the near approach of the divine.

98. The words *mā aqra'u* can mean both "what shall I recite?" and "I do not (cannot) recite," and it is sometimes difficult to decide which meaning is to be preferred. The translations given are thus in a sense conjectural. Muslim scholars debated the question, and some modified the phrase to *mādhā aqra'u*, which can only have the first meaning, others to *mā anā bi-qārin*, which can only have the second. Since *qara'a* can also mean "read," Muḥammad's inability to read was part of later apologetic.

99. 96:1.

100. Waraqah was Khadījah's cousin, their fathers being brothers. He was counted as a *ḥanīf* (see n. 87), and is sometimes said to have become a Christian (Ibn Hishām, *Sīrah*, 143;1151 below); he had certainly studied the Bible. There are other versions of this story in which he does not actually meet Muḥammad. The words "brother's son" may indicate that, as husband of Khadījah, Muḥammad was reckoned as son of her father.

101. The word *nāmūs*, which seems to represent the Greek *nomos* (law), is not found in the Qur'ān. It presumably refers to the five books of Moses (in Arabic usually Tawrāt); but see n. 114 below.

man now, and would that I could be alive when your people drive you out!" I said, "Will they drive me out?" "Yes," he said. "No man has ever brought the message which you have brought without being met with enmity. If I live to see that day, I shall come firmly to your aid."

The first parts of the Qur'ān to be revealed to me after *Iqra'* were:

> Nūn. By the pen, and that which they write. You are not, through your Lord's favor to you, a madman. Yours will be a reward unfailing, and you are of a great nature. You shall see and they shall see.[102]

and:

> O you enveloped in your cloak, arise and warn![103]

and:

> By the forenoon, and by the night when it is still.[104]

Yūnus b. ʿAbd al-Aʿlā—Ibn Wahb—Yūnus—Ibn Shihāb—ʿUrwah—ʿĀ'ishah: A similar account, but omitting the last part from the words "The first parts of the Qur'ān. . . . "

Muḥammad b. ʿAbd al-Malik b. Abī al-Shawārib—ʿAbd al-Wāḥid b. Ziyād—Sulaymān al-Shaybānī—ʿAbd Allāh b. Shaddād: Gabriel came to Muḥammad and said, "O Muḥammad, recite!" He said, "I cannot recite." Gabriel was violent towards him[105] and then said again, "O Muḥammad, recite!" He said, "I cannot recite," and Gabriel again was violent towards him . A third time he said, "O Muḥammad, recite!" He said, "What shall I recite?"[106] and he said:

> Recite in the name of your Lord who creates! He creates man from a clot of blood. Recite: And your Lord is the Most

102. 68:1-5. This is unlikely to be early, since it implies that Muḥammad has been charged with being *majnūn*, mad or possessed by jinn.

103. 74:1-2.

104. 93:1-2. This sūrah contains encouragement to Muḥammad, apparently after a period of depression, possibly the time when Gabriel did not come to him.

105. The word *ghammahu* (he afflicted or grieved him) replaces *ghattanī* of the previous account (he pressed tightly until I was nearly stifled).

106. Muḥammad uses the same words on all three occasions, but the meaning seems to have changed with the third; see n. 98.

> Bountiful, He who teaches by the pen, teaches man what he knew not.[107]

Then he went to Khadījah and said, "Khadījah, I think that I have gone mad." "No, by God," she said. "Your Lord would never do that to you. You have never committed a wicked act." Khadījah
[1149] went to Waraqah b. Nawfal and told him what had happened. He said, "If what you say is true, your husband is a prophet. He will meet adversity from his people. If I live long enough, I shall believe in him."

After this, Gabriel did not come to him for a while, and Khadījah said to him, "I think that your Lord must have come to hate you." Then God revealed to him:

> By the forenoon, and by the night when it is still, your Lord has not forsaken you, nor does he hate you.[108]

Ibn Ḥumayd—Salamah—Muḥammad b. Isḥāq[109]—Wahb b. Kaysān the *mawlā* of the family of al-Zubayr: I heard ʿAbdallāh b. al-Zubayr saying to ʿUbayd b. ʿUmayr b. Qatādah al-Laythi, "Relate to us, ʿUbayd, what the beginning of the Messenger of God's prophetic mission was like when Gabriel came to him." I was present as ʿUbayd related the following account to ʿAbdallāh b. al-Zubayr and those with him. He said, "The Messenger of God used to spend one month in every year in religious retreat on Ḥirā." This was part of the practice of *taḥannuth* in which Quraysh used to engage during the Jāhiliyyah. *Taḥannuth* means self-justification.[110] (Mentioning this practice) Abū Ṭālib said, "By those ascending Ḥirā' and those descending."

The Messenger of God used to spend this month in every year in religious retreat, feeding the poor who came to him. When he had completed his month of retreat the first thing which he would do on leaving, even before going home, was to circumambulate the Kaʿbah seven times, or however many times God willed; then he would go home.

When the month came in which God willed to ennoble him, in

---

107. 96:1-5.
108. 93:1-3.
109. Ibn Hishām, *Sīrah*, 151-54; this omits some sentences kept by Ṭabarī.
110. For *taḥannuth* see n. 95; the word translated "self-justification" is *tabarrur*, which has a wide range of meanings.

the year in which God made him his Messenger, this being the month of Ramaḍān, the Messenger of God went out as usual to Ḥirā' accompanied by his family. When the night came on which [1150]
God ennobled him by making him his Messenger and thereby showed mercy to his servants, Gabriel brought him the command of God. The Messenger of God said, "Gabriel came to me as I was sleeping with a brocade cloth in which was writing. He said, "Recite!" and I said, "I cannot recite."[111] He pressed me tight and almost stifled me, until I thought that I should die. Then he let me go, and said, "Recite!" I said, "What shall I recite?" only saying that in order to free myself from him, fearing that he might repeat what he had done to me. He said:

> Recite in the name of your Lord who creates! He creates man from a clot of blood. Recite: And your Lord is the Most Bountiful, He who teaches by the pen, teaches man what he knew not.

I recited it, and then he desisted and departed. I woke up, and it was as though these words had been written on my heart. There was no one of God's creation more hateful to me than a poet or a madman; I could not bear to look at either of them. I said to myself, "Your humble servant (meaning himself) is either a poet or a madman, but Quraysh shall never say this of me.[112] I shall take myself to a mountain crag, hurl myself down from it, kill myself, and find relief in that way."

I went out intending to do that, but when I was halfway up the mountain I heard a voice from heaven saying, "O Muḥammad, you are the Messenger of God, and I am Gabriel." I raised my head to heaven, and there was Gabriel in the form of a man with his feet set on the horizon, saying, "O Muḥammad, you are the Messenger of God and I am Gabriel." I stood looking at him and this distracted me from what I had intended, and I could go neither forward nor back. I turned my face away from him to all points of

---

111. The phrase *mā aqra'u* seems here to have been given the meaning "I cannot read," since writing is mentioned. The verb *qara'a* can mean "read" as well as "recite."

112. It seems unlikely that it occurred spontaneously to Muḥammad that he was a poet or madman. This is almost certainly a criticism made of him by opponents after he began his public preaching. Later scholars have doubtless introduced the point here in order to explain how Muḥammad came to contemplate suicide.

the horizon, but wherever I looked I saw him in exactly the same form. I remained standing there, neither going forward nor turning back, until Khadījah sent her messengers to look for me. They went as far as Mecca and came back to her, while I was standing in the same place. At last Gabriel left me and I went back to
[1151] my family. When I came to Khadījah, I sat down with my thigh next to hers, and she said to me, "Abū al-Qāsim,[113] where have you been? I sent messengers to look for you all the way to Mecca and back." I said to her, "I am either a poet or a madman," but she answered, "May God save you from that, Abū al-Qāsim! God would not do that to you, considering what I know of your truthfulness, your great trustworthiness, your good character, and your good treatment of your kinsfolk. It is not that, cousin. Perhaps you did see something." "Yes," I said, and then told her what I had seen. "Rejoice, cousin, and stand firm," she said. "By Him is whose hand is Khadījah's soul, I hope that you may be the prophet of this community." Then she rose up, gathered her garments around her, and went to Waraqah b. Nawfal b. Asad, who was her paternal cousin. He had become a Christian, read the Scriptures, and learned from the people of the Torah and the Gospel. She told him what the Messenger of God had told her that he had seen and heard. Waraqah said, "Holy, Holy! By Him in whose hand is the soul of Waraqah, if what you say is true, Khadījah, there has come to him the greatest Nāmūs—meaning by Nāmūs, Gabriel—he who came to Moses[114] (That means that) Muḥammad is the prophet of this community. Tell him to stand firm."

Khadījah went back to the Messenger of God and told him what Waraqah had said, and this relieved his anxiety somewhat. When he had completed his retreat he went back to Mecca and, as was his usual practice, went first to the Kaʿbah and circumambulated it. Waraqah b. Nawfal met him as he was doing this and said, "Son of my brother, tell me what you saw or heard." The Messenger of
[1152] God did so, and Waraqah said to him, "By Him in whose hand is my soul, you are the prophet of this community, and there has come to you the greatest Nāmūs, he who came to Moses. They

113. This is Muḥammad's patronymic or *kunyah* (see n. 22) and a familiar way to address him.

114. This interpretation of Nāmūs differs from that adopted in the translation on p. 1148, which is justified by the use of the verb "sent down" there.

will call you a liar, molest you, drive you out, and fight you. If I live to see that, I will come to God's assistance in a way which he knows." Then he brought his head close and kissed the top of his head. The Messenger of God went home with his resolve strengthened by what Waraqah had said and with some of his anxiety relieved.

Ibn Ḥumayd—Salamah—Muḥammad b. Isḥāq—Ismā'īl b. Abī Ḥakīm the *mawlā* of the family of al-Zubayr: He was told that Khadījah said to the Messenger of God, to keep him steadfast in the prophethood with which God had ennobled him, "Cousin, can you tell me when this companion of yours who visits you comes?" He replied, "Yes," and she said, "Tell me then, when he comes." Gabriel came to him as before, and the Messenger of God said to Khadījah, "Khadījah, here is Gabriel who has come to me." She said, "Yes? Come and sit by my left thigh, cousin." He came and sat by her, and she said, "Can you see him?" He replied, "Yes," and she said, "Move around and sit by my right thigh." He did so, and she said, "Can you see him?" He replied, "Yes," and she said, "Move around and sit in my lap." He did so, and she said, "Can you see him?" He replied, "Yes." Then she was grieved, and flung off her veil while the Messenger of God was sitting in her lap. Then she said, "Can you see him?" and he replied, "No." At that she said, "Cousin, be steadfast and rejoice. By God, this being is an angel and no devil."[115]

Ibn Humayd—Salamah—Muhammad b. Ishāq: I related this tradition (*ḥadīth*) to 'Abdallāh b. al-Ḥasan, and he said, "I heard my mother Fāṭimah bt. al-Ḥusayn relating this *Ḥadīth* on the authority of Khadījah, except that I heard her saying that Khadījah put the Messenger of God inside her shift next to her body, and that thereupon Gabriel departed. Then she said, 'This being is an angel and no devil.' " [1153]

Ibn al-Muthannā—'Uthmān b. 'Umar b. Fāris—'Alī b. al-Mubārak—Yaḥyā, that is, Ibn Abī Kathir: I asked Abū Salamah which part of the Qur'ān had been revealed first, and he replied:

"O you enveloped in your cloak, arise and warn!"[116]

115. The thought is that an angel respects a woman's modesty, whereas a devil or demon would not.

116. 74:1.

I said, "They say that it was

Recite in the name of your Lord",[117]

but Abū Salamah replied, "I asked Jābir b. ʿAbdallāh which part of the Qurʾān had been revealed first, and he said, "O you enveloped in your cloak." I said, "What about 'Recite in the name of your Lord?' " but he answered, "What I am telling you is what the Prophet told me. He said, "I was in retreat on Ḥirāʾ, and when I had completed my retreat I came down the mountain and went into the bottom of the wādī. Then I heard a voice calling me; I looked right and left, behind me and in front of me, but could not see anything. Then I looked up, and there he was sitting on a throne between heaven and earth, and I was afraid of him (*fa-khashītu minhu*). Ibn al-Muthannā: These were ʿUthmān b. ʿUmar's words, but the correct version is "I was terror-stricken by him." (*fa-juʾiththu minhu*) Then I went to Khadījah and said, "Envelop me!" So they enveloped me in a cloak and poured water over me, and then "O you enveloped in your cloak, arise and warn!" was revealed to me.

Abū Kurayb—Wakīʿ—ʿAlī b. al-Mubārak—Yaḥyā b. Abī Kathīr: I asked Abū Salamah which part of the Qurʾān had been revealed first, and he said, "It was 'O you enveloped in your cloak.' " I said, "They say that it was 'Recite in the name of your Lord who created,' " but he said, "I asked Jābir b. ʿAbdallāh, and he said 'I am only telling you what the Messenger of God told me. He said, "I was in retreat on Ḥirāʾ, and when I had completed my retreat I
[1154] came down the mountain and heard a voice. I looked left and right and saw nothing, and behind me and saw nothing. Then I raised my head and saw something, and went to Khadījah and said, 'Envelop me, and pour water on me.' So they enveloped me in a cloak and poured water on me, and then 'O you enveloped in your cloak' was revealed to me."

Hishām b. Muḥammad: Gabriel came to the Messenger of God for the first time on Saturday night and Sunday night.[118] On Monday he brought him the commission as Messenger of God, and taught him the ritual ablution, the prayer ritual, and the passage

117. 96:1.
118. The Arab day begins at sunset, so that by Western reckoning this would be the nights of Friday and Saturday.

"Recite in the name of your Lord who created." On the Monday on which he received the revelation, the Messenger of God was forty years old.

Aḥmad b. Muḥammad b. Ḥabīb al-Ṭūsī—Abū Dāūd al-Ṭayālisī—Ja'far b. 'Abdallāh b. 'Uthmān al-Qurashī—'Umar b. 'Urwah b. al-Zubayr—'Urwah b. al-Zubayr—Abū Dharr al-Ghifārī: I said, "O Messenger of God, how did you first know with absolute certainty that you were a prophet?" "Abū Dharr," he replied, "two angels came to me while I was somewhere in the Valley of Mecca. One of them came down to earth, while the other remained between heaven and earth. One of them said to the other, 'Is this he?' and the other replied, 'It is he.' 'Weigh him against a man,' he said, so I was weighed against a man and outweighed him. 'Weigh him against ten,' he said, so he weighed me against ten and I outweighed them. Then he said, 'Weigh him against a hundred,' so he weighed me against a hundred and I outweighed them. Then he said, 'Weigh him against a thousand.' So he weighed me against a thousand and I outweighed them. People began to be scattered over me from the pan of the balance, and one angel said to the other, 'If you were to weigh him against the whole of his community he would outweigh them.'

"Then one said to the other, 'Open his breast.' He opened my breast, and then he said, 'Take out his heart' or 'open his heart.' He [1155]
opened my heart, and took out from it the pollution of Satan and the clot of blood, and threw them away. Then one said to the other, 'Wash his breast as you would a receptacle—or, wash his heart as you would a covering.' Then he summoned the *sakīnah*,[119] which looked like the face of a white cat, and it was placed in my heart. Then one of them said to the other, 'Sew up his breast.' So they sewed up my breast and placed the seal between my shoulders. No sooner had they done this than they turned away from me. While this was happening I was watching it as though I were a bystander."[120]

---

119. The word *sakīnah* occurs six times in the Qur'ān. In five instances it is usually taken to mean a "peace of reassurance" sent down by God upon Muḥammad or the believers; but in the other instance (2:48) it is a material object contained in the sacred ark of the Israelites. Because of the uncertainty about its meaning, the word lent itself to various interpretations, of which there is an example here. It corresponds to the Hebrew *shekhīnah*; see *EI* [1] s.v. *Sakīna*.

120. Ibn Isḥāq (Ibn Hishām *Sīrah*, 105–6) describes events similar to the above,

Muḥammad b. ʿAbd al-Aʿlā—Ibn Thawr—Maʿmar—al-Zuhrī: The inspiration ceased to come to the Messenger of God for a while, and he was deeply grieved. He began to go to the tops of mountain crags, in order to fling himself from them; but every time he reached the summit of a mountain, Gabriel appeared to him and said to him, "You are the Prophet of God." Thereupon his anxiety would subside and he would come back to himself.

The Prophet used to relate this story as follows: "I was walking one day when I saw the angel who used to come to me at Ḥirā' on a throne between heaven and earth. I was terror-stricken by him, and I went back to Khadījah and said, "Wrap me up!" So we wrapped him up (*zammalnāhu*), that is, enveloped him in a cloak (*daththarnāhu*), and God revealed:

> O you enveloped in your cloak, arise and warn! Your Lord magnify, your raiment purify.[121]

Al-Zuhrī: The first thing to be revealed to him was "Recite in the name of your Lord who creates ... " as far as the words "what he knew not."

Yūnus b. ʿAbd al-Aʿlā—Ibn Wahb—Yūnus—Ibn Shihāb—Abū Salamah b. ʿAbd al-Raḥmān—Jābir b. ʿAbdallāh al-Anṣārī: The Messenger of God said, relating the story of the interruption or gap
[1156] in the revelation, "As I was walking, I heard a voice from heaven. I looked up, and suddenly saw the angel who came to me at Ḥirā' seated on a throne between heaven and earth. I was terror-stricken and went (to Khadījah) and said "Wrap me up! Wrap me up" They enveloped me in my cloak, and God revealed, "O you enveloped in your cloak, arise and warn ... " as far as "and pollution shun."

After that, the revelation came in regular succession.

Khadījah the First to Believe in the Messenger of God

Abū Jaʿfar (al-Ṭabarī): God commanded his Prophet to rise up and to warn his people that God would punish them for their ingratitude to their Lord and for their worship of false gods and idols to the exclusion of Him who created them and gave them their daily bread. He was also to tell them of his Lord's bounty to himself,

---

but during Muḥammad's childhood; see also 1157 below.

121. 74:1-4; there is an awkward change of person in the previous sentence.

with the words: "Of the bounty of your Lord let your discourse be." According to Ibn Isḥāq, this refers to his prophethood.[122]

Ibn Ḥumayd—Salamah—Ibn Isḥāq: The words "Of the bounty of your Lord let your discourse be" mean "Of God's bounty and generosity in bestowing Prophethood upon you, Let your discourse be," that is, "proclaim it and summon people to it." Thereupon the Messenger of God began to proclaim God's bounty to himself and to (God's) servants in conferring prophethood upon him. He did this in private to those of his family who trusted in him. It is related that of God's creatures the first to hold him truthful, to believe in him, and to follow him was his wife Khadījah.

Al-Ḥārith—Ibn Sa'd—al-Wāqidī: Our fellow scholars are agreed that the first of the people of the Qiblah to respond to the Messenger of God was Khadījah bt. Khuwaylid.

The First Rituals of Islam Are Prescribed

Abū Ja'far (al-Ṭabarī): The first of the duties of Islam to be prescribed for Muḥammad by God, after that of confessing God's oneness, disavowing graven images and idols, and repudiating false gods, is said to have been that of ritual prayer or worship (*ṣalāt*).[123]

Ibn Ḥumayd—Salamah—Muḥammad b. Isḥāq—certain scholars:[124] When ritual prayer was prescribed for the Messenger of God,
Gabriel came to him while he was in the upper part of Mecca, [1157]
and dug his heel into the side of the wādī, whereupon a spring gushed out. While the Messenger of God watched him, Gabriel then performed the ritual ablution in order to show him how to purify himself for prayer. Then the Messenger of God performed the ritual ablution as he had seen Gabriel do. Next, Gabriel rose up and led him in prayer, and the Prophet followed his actions. Then Gabriel departed, and the Messenger of God went to Khadījah and performed the ablution for her in order to show her how to purify

122. Ibn Hishām, *Sīrah,* 158; the verse is 93:11.

123. The word *ṣalāt* is commonly translated "prayer," although "worship" would be more appropriate, since there is virtually no petition or intercession. The *ṣalāt* consists of a series of acts accompanied by expressions of praise or adoration. The climax is touching the ground with the forehead in acknowledgement of God's majesty. Each Muslim is now required to accomplish the *ṣalāt* five times a day, though originally the number of times was probably not fixed.

124. Ibn Hishām, *Sīrah,* 158.

herself for prayer, as Gabriel had shown him. She performed the ablution as he had done, and then he led her in prayer as Gabriel had led him, and she followed his actions.

The Prophet Ascends to the Seventh Heaven [125]

Ibn Ḥumayd—Hārūn b. al-Mughīrah and Ḥakkām b. Salm—ʿAnbasah—Abū Hāshim al-Wāṣiṭī—Maymūn b. Siyāh—Anas b. Mālik: At the time when the Prophet became a prophet, he used to sleep around the Kaʿbah as did the Quraysh. On one occasion two angels, Gabriel and Michael, came to him and said, "Which of the Quraysh were we ordered to come to?" Then they said, "We were ordered to come to their chief," and went away. After this they came from the Qiblah and there were three of them. They came upon him as he slept, turned him on his back, and opened his breast. Then they brought water from Zamzam and washed away the doubt, or polytheism, or pre-Islamic beliefs, or error, which was in his breast. Then they brought a golden basin full of faith and wisdom, and his breast and belly were filled with faith and wisdom.

Then he was taken up to the earthly heaven. Gabriel asked for
[1158] admittance, and they said, "Who is it?" "Gabriel," he said. "Who is with you?" they said. "Muḥammad," he answered. "Has his mission commenced?" they asked. "Yes," he said. "Welcome," they said, and called down God's blessings on him. When he went in, he saw before him a huge and handsome man. "Who is this, Gabriel?" he asked. "This is your father, Adam," he replied. Then they took him to the second heaven. Gabriel asked for admission, and they said the same as before. Indeed, the same questions were asked and the same answers given in all the heavens. When Muḥammad went in to the second heaven he saw before him two men. "Who are these, Gabriel?" he asked. "John and Jesus, the two maternal cousins," he replied. Then he was taken to the third heaven, and when he went in he saw before him a man. "Who is this, Gabriel?" he asked. He replied, "Your brother Joseph who was given preeminence in beauty over other men as is the full moon over the stars at night." Then he was taken to

125. Ibid. 263–71, with slightly different material.

the fourth heaven, and he saw before him a man and said, "Who is this, Gabriel?" "This is Idrīs," he said,[126] and recited:

> And we raised him to high station.

Then he was taken to the fifth heaven, and he saw before him a man and said, "Who is this, Gabriel?" "This is Aaron," he said. Then he was taken to the sixth heaven, and he saw before him a man and said, "Who is this, Gabriel?" "This is Moses," he said. Then he was taken to the seventh heaven, and he saw before him a man and said, "Who is this, Gabriel?" "This is your father Abraham," he said.

Then he took him to Paradise, and there before him was a river whiter than milk and sweeter than honey, with pearly domes on either side of it. "What is this, Gabriel?" he asked. Gabriel replied, "This is al-Kawthar, which your Lord has given to you, and these are your dwellings." Then Gabriel took a handful of its earth and lo! it was fragrant musk. Then he went out to the Sidrat al-Muntahā,[127] which was a lote tree bearing fruits the largest of which were like earthenware jars and the smallest like eggs. Then his Lord drew nigh,

"Till he was distant two bows' length or nearer." Because of [1159]
the nearness of its Lord the lote tree became covered by the like of such jewels as pearls, rubies, chrysolites, and colored pearls. God made revelation to his servant, caused him to understand and know, and prescribed for him fifty prayers (daily).

Then he went back past Moses, who said to him, "What did he impose your community?" "Fifty prayers," he said. "Go back to your Lord," said Moses, "and ask him to lighten the burden for your community, for your community is the weakest in strength and the shortest-lived." Then he told Muḥammad what he himself had suffered at the hands of the Children of Israel. The Messenger of God went back, and God reduced the number by ten.

---

126. See n. 55. The verse is 19:57.

127. The "lote tree of the utmost boundary" is spoken of in the description of Muḥammad's second vision in Sūrah 53:14. The following phrase about being "distant two bows' length or nearer" is from verse 9 describing the first vision. Though many Muslim scholars associate the second vision with Muḥammad's "night journey" or ascent to heaven, this is improbable since the main verse referring to the "night journey" (17:1) was revealed about the middle of the Meccan period, whereas the passage 53:13–18 almost certainly refers to a very early experience.

Then he passed Moses again, who said, "Go back to your Lord and ask him to lighten the burden further." This continued until he had gone back five times. Once more Moses said, "Go back to your Lord and ask him to lighten the burden," but the Messenger of God said, "I am not going back, although I do not wish to disobey you," for it had been put into his heart that he should not go back. God said, "My speech is not to be changed, and my decision and precept is not to be reversed, but he (Muḥammad) lightened the burden of prayer on my community to a tenth of what it was at first."[128]

Anas: I never encountered any scent, not even the scent of a bride, more fragrant than the skin of the Messenger of God. I pressed my skin to his and smelt it.

The First Male to Believe in the Messenger of God

ʿAlī b. Abī Ṭālib

Abū Jaʿfar (al-Ṭabarī): There is a difference of opinion among the early scholars as to who after his wife Khadījah bt. Khuwaylid first followed the Messenger of God, believed in him, held true the message which he brought from God, and prayed with him. Some say that the first male to believe in the Messenger of God, pray with him, and hold the truth of the message which he brought from God was ʿAlī b. Abī Ṭālib.

Among those who take this view, whose reports we have heard, are the following:

[1160] Ibn Humayd—Ibrāhīm b. al-Mukhtār—Shuʿbah—Abū Balj—ʿAmr b. Maymūn—Ibn ʿAbbās: The first to perform the prayer was ʿAlī.

Zakariyyā b. Yaḥyā al-Ḍarīr—ʿAbd al-Ḥamīd b. Baḥr—Sharīk b. ʿAbdallah b. Muḥammad b. ʿAqīl—Jābir: The Prophet was commissioned as prophet on Monday, and ʿAlī performed the prayer on Tuesday.

Ibn al-Muthannā—Muḥammad b. Jaʿfar—Shuʿbah—ʿAmr b. Murrah—Abū Ḥamzah—Zayd b. Arqam: The first to accept Is-

128. Literally, this runs: "he lightened the prayer for my community to a tenth." The translation adopted assumes that these words are a continuation of the speech of God, and seems to make best sense of "my"; but there are other possibilities.

lam with the Messenger of God was ʿAlī b. Abī Ṭālib. I mentioned this to al-Nakhaʿī, and he denied it, saying, "Abū Bakr was the first to accept Islam."

Abū Kurayb—Wakīʿ—Shuʿbah—ʿAmr b. Murrah—Abū Ḥamzah the *mawlā* of the Anṣār—Zayd b. Arqam: The first to accept Islam with the Messenger of God was ʿAlī b. Abī Ṭālib.

Abu Kurayb—ʿUbayd b. Saʿīd—Shuʿbah—ʿAmr b. Murrah—Abū Ḥamzah, a man of the Anṣār—Zayd b. Arqam: The first to perform the prayer with the Messenger of God was ʿAlī.

Aḥmad b. al-Ḥasan al-Tirmidhī—ʿUbaydallāh b. Mūsā—al-ʿAlā'—al-Minhāl b. ʿAmr—ʿAbbād b. ʿAbdallāh: I heard ʿAlī saying, "I am the servant of God and the brother of his Messenger, and I am the most righteous one (*al-ṣiddīq al-akbar*).[129] No one other than I can say this but a liar and an inventor of falsehoods. I performed the prayer with the Messenger of God seven years before other men.

Muḥammad b. ʿUbayd al-Muḥāribī—Saʿīd b. Khuthaym—Asad b. ʿAbdah al-Baljī—Yaḥyā b. ʿAfīf—ʿAfīf: During the Jāhiliyyah I came to Mecca and stayed with al-ʿAbbās b. ʿAbd al-Muṭṭalib. [1161]
When the sun came up and rose into the sky, while I was looking at the Kaʿbah a young man came up and gazed at the sky. Then he turned to face the Kaʿbah and stood facing it. Soon afterwards a youth came and stood on his right, and soon after that a woman came and stood behind them. The young man bowed, and the youth and woman bowed; then the young man stood erect, followed by the youth and the woman, and then the young man prostrated himself, and they did so with him. I said, "ʿAbbās, this is a weighty matter." "It is a weighty matter indeed," he said. "Do you know who this is?" "No", I said. "This is Muḥammad b. ʿAbdallāh b. ʿAbd al-Muṭṭalib, my brother's son," he said. "Do you know who this is with him?" "No," I said. "This is ʿAlī b. Abī Ṭālib b. ʿAbd al-Muṭṭalib, my brother's son," he said. "Do you know who this woman is who is behind them?" "No," I said. "This is Khadījah bt. Khuwaylid, my nephew's wife," he said "My nephew has told me that his Lord,[130] the Lord of Heaven, has commanded them to do what you see them doing. God's oath, I do not

---

129. This is an implicit claim that ʿAlī is superior to Abū Bakr, since "the righteous one" (*al-ṣiddīq*) is a kind of by-name regularly given to Abū Bakr by Sunnites.

130. Following the variant *rabbahu* instead of the *rabbaka* of the printed text.

know anyone on the face of the earth but these three who follow this religion."

Abū Kurayb—Yūnus b. Bukayr—Muḥammad b. Isḥāq—Yaḥyā b. Abī al-Ash'ath al-Kindī, a Kūfan scholar—Ismā'īl b. Iyās b. 'Afīf—his father—his grandfather:[131] I was a merchant, and I came during the pilgrimage and stayed with al-'Abbās. While we were
[1162] with him, a man came out to pray and stood facing the Ka'bah. Then a woman came out and stood praying with him, followed by a youth who stood praying with him. I said, "'Abbās, what is this religion? I do not know what this religion is." He answered, "This is Muḥammad b. 'Abdallāh, who claims that God has sent him as His Messenger with this (religion), and that the treasures of Chusroes and Caesar will be given to him by conquest. This woman is his wife Khadījah bt. Khuwaylid, who has believed in him, and this youth is his cousin 'Alī b. Abī Tālib, who has believed in him."

'Afīf: Would that I had believed in him that day, so that I had been the third.

Ibn Ḥumayd—Salamah b. al-Faḍl and 'Alī b. Mujāhid: (then) Salamah—Muḥammad b. Isḥāq—Yaḥyā b. Abī al-Ash'ath (Abū Ja'far (al-Ṭabarī): elsewhere in my book the name is given as Yaḥyā b. al-Ash'ath)—Ismā'īl b. Iyās b. 'Afīf al-Kindī ('Afīf was the maternal halfbrother of al-Ash'ath b. Qays al-Kindī, and the son of his paternal uncle)—his father—his grandfather, 'Afīf: Al-'Abbās b. 'Abd al-Muṭṭalib was a friend of mine. He used to go to the Yemen to buy perfume and sell it during the pilgrimage season. While I was staying with al-'Abbas b. 'Abd al-Muṭṭalib at Minā there came to him a man in the prime of life who performed the ritual ablution thoroughly and then stood praying. Then a woman came out, performed the ablution, and stood praying. Then a youth just past the age of puberty came out, performed the ablution, and stood by his side praying. I said, "Whatever is this, 'Abbās" He replied, "This is my brother's son Muḥammad b. 'Abdallāh b. 'Abd al-Muṭṭalib, who claims that God has sent him as a messenger; this is my brother's son 'Alī b. Abī Ṭālib who has followed him in his
[1163] religion, and this is Muḥammad's wife Khadījah bt. Khuwaylid who has followed him in his religion." After 'Afīf had become a

131. This and the following paragraph are omitted by Ibn Hishām. See Guillaume, p.113.

Muslim and Islam had become firmly rooted in his heart, he used to say, "Would that I had been a fourth."

Ibn Humayd—ʿĪsā b. Sawādah b. al-Jaʿd—Muḥammad b. al-Munkadir, Rabīʿah b. Abī ʿAbd al-Rahmān, Abū Ḥāzim al-Madanī and al-Kalbī: ʿAlī was the first to accept Islam. According to al-Kalbī, he accepted Islam at the age of nine.

Ibn Ḥumayd—Salamah—Ibn Isḥāq:[132] The first male to believe in the Messenger of God, to pray with him, and to accept the truth of the message he brought from God was ʿAlī b. Abī Ṭālib, who at that time was ten years old.

One of the favors which God bestowed on ʿAlī b. Abī Ṭālib was that the Messenger of God was his guardian before Islam.

Ibn Ḥumayd—Salamah—Muḥammad b. Isḥāq—ʿAbdallāh b. Abī Najīḥ—Mujāhid b. Jabr Abū al-Ḥajjāj: A mark of God's favor to ʿAlī b. Abī Ṭālib and his beneficence and benevolence towards him was the following. When Quraysh were afflicted by a severe drought, the Messenger of God, seeing that Abū Ṭālib had many dependents, said to his uncle al-ʿAbbās, who was one of the richest of the Banū Hāshim, "ʿAbbās, your brother Abū Ṭālib has many dependents, and you see how people are suffering from this drought. Come with me and let us lighten the burden of his dependents. I will take one of his sons and you take one, and we will look after them for him." Al-ʿAbbās agreed, and they went to Abū Ṭālib and said, "We wish to lighten the burden of your dependents until the hardship from which the people are suffering lifts." [1164]

Abū Ṭālib said to them, "As long as you leave me ʿAqīl, do as you wish." The Messenger of God took ʿAlī and made him a member of his household, and al-ʿAbbās did likewise with Jaʿfar. ʿAlī b. Abī Ṭālib continued to live with the Messenger of God until the latter became a prophet, and then followed him, believed in him, and accepted the truth of his message. Jaʿfar remained with al-ʿAbbās until he (Jaʿfar) professed Islam and became financially independent of him.

Ibn Ḥumayd—Salamah—Muḥammad b. Isḥāq: Some scholars mention that when the time for prayer came, the Messenger of God would go out to the ravines of Mecca, accompanied by ʿAlī b. Abī Ṭālib, in order to conceal himself from his uncle Abū Ṭālib,

132. Ibn Hishām, *Sīrah,* 158-60.

his other uncles, and the rest of his clan. They would pray together there, and then as evening fell, would return. They continued in this fashion as long as God willed that they should. One day, however, Abū Ṭālib came across them as they were praying and said to the Messenger of God, "Nephew, what is this religion which I see you following?" He replied, "Uncle, this is the religion of God, of His angels, of His messengers and of our forefather Abraham," or words to that effect; "God has sent me as Messenger to His servants with this religion, and you, my uncle, are the most deserving person to whom I could give sincere advice and whom I could summon to right guidance, and you are the most deserving person to answer my call and assist me in this matter," or words to this effect. Abū Ṭālib replied, "Nephew, I cannot leave my religion and the religion of my forefathers and their practices, but, by God, as long as I live nothing unpleasant shall befall you."

Ibn Ḥumayd—Salamah—Muhammad b. Isḥāq: They allege that he said to ʿAlī b. Abī Ṭālib, "My son, what is this religion which
[1165] I see you practicing?" He replied, "Father, I believe in God and His Messenger. I accept the truth of the message which he has brought, and I pray to God with him." They also allege that Abū Ṭālib said "He calls you to nothing but good, so adhere to him."

Al-Ḥārith—Ibn Saʿd—Muḥammad b. ʿUmar—Ibrāhīm b. Nāfiʿ—Ibn Abī Najīḥ—Mujāhid: ʿAli became a Muslim when he was ten years old.

Al-Ḥārith—Ibn Saʿd—al-Wāqidi: Our fellow scholars are agreed that ʿAlī accepted Islam a year after the Messenger of God began his prophetic mission, and that he remained in Mecca for twelve years.

Abū Bakr

Others say that Abū Bakr was the first male to accept Islam.

Those who say this:

Sahl b. Mūsā al-Rāzī—ʿAbd al-Raḥmān b. Maghrā,—Mujālid—al-Shaʿbī: I said to Ibn ʿAbbās, "Who was the first to accept Islam?" He answered, "Have you not heard the lines of Ḥassān b. Thābit,[133]

If you call to mind trustworthy men to grieve for them,
mention your brother Abū Bakr and his deeds.

---

133. *Dīwān*, ed. Arafat, I:125.

The best of men, the most pious and the most just
after the Prophet, and the most faithful in fulfilling
what he undertook.
The second, the follower, may his tomb be praised,
and the first of men to believe in the prophets.

Sa'īd b. 'Anbasah al-Rāzī—al-Haytham b. 'Adī—Mujālid—al-Sha'bī—Ibn 'Abbās: A similar account. [1166]

Ibn Ḥumayd—Yaḥyā b. Wāḍiḥ—al-Haytham b. 'Adī—Mujālid—al-Sha'bī—Ibn 'Abbās: A similar account.

Baḥr b. Naṣr al-Khawlānī—'Abdallāh b. Wahb—Mu'awiyah b. Ṣāliḥ—Abū Yaḥyā and Ḍamrah b. Ḥabīb and Abū Ṭalhah—Abū Umānah al-Bāhilī—'Amr b. 'Abasah: I came to the Messenger of God when he was staying at 'Ukāẓ[134] and said, "O Messenger of God, who has followed you in this religion?" He replied, "Two men have followed me in it, a free man and a slave; Abū Bakr and Bilāl." Then I accepted Islam and reckoned myself at that time to be one quarter of those who believe in Islam.

Ibn 'Abd al-Raḥīm al-Barqī—'Amr b. Abī Salamah—Ṣadaqah—Naṣr b. 'Alqamah—his brother—Ibn 'Ā'idh—Jubayr b. Nufayr: Both Abū Dharr and Ibn 'Abasah used to say, "I reckoned myself to be a quarter of those who believed in Islam, for no one had accepted Islam before me but the Prophet, Abū Bakr and Bilāl." Neither knew when the other accepted Islam.

Ibn Ḥumayd—Jarīr—Mughīrah—Ibrāhīm: The first to accept Islam was Abū Bakr.

Abū Kurayb—Wakī'—Shu'bah—'Amr b. Murrah—Ibrāhīm al-Nakha'ī: Abū Bakr was the first to accept Islam.

Others say that a number of people accepted Islam before Abū Bakr.

Those who say this: Ibn Ḥumayd—Kinānah b. Jabalah— [1167]
Ibrāhīm b. Ṭahmān—al-Ḥajjāj b. al-Ḥajjāj—Qatādah—Sālim b. Abī al-Ja'd—Muḥammad b. Sa'd: I said to my father, "Was Abū Bakr the first of them to accept Islam?" He answered, "No, more than fifty people accepted Islam before him, but he was the best Muslim among us."

---

134. Site of an annual fair, lying between Nakhlah and al-Ṭā'if.

Zayd b. Ḥārithah

Others say that the first man to believe and follow the Prophet was Zayd b. Ḥārithah, his *mawlā*.

Those who say this:

Al-Ḥārith—Muḥammad b. Sa'd—al-Wāqidī—Ibn Abī Dhi'b: I asked al-Zuhrī who was the first person to accept Islam. He replied, "The first woman was Khadījah and the first man was Zayd b. Ḥārithah."

Al-Ḥārith—Muḥammad b. Sa'd—Muḥammad b. 'Umar—Mus'ab b. Thābit—Abū al-Aswad—Sulaymān b. Yasār: The first to accept Islam was Zayd b. Ḥārithah.

Al-Ḥārith—Muḥammad b. Sa'd—Muḥammad (that is Ibn 'Umar)—Rabī'ah b. 'Uthmān—'Imrān b. Abī Anas: A similar report.

'Abd al-Raḥmān b. 'Abdallāh b. 'Abd al-Ḥakam—'Abd al-Malik b. Maslamah—Ibn Lahī'ah—Abū al-Aswad—'Urwah: The first to accept Islam was Zayd b. Ḥārithah.

Ibn Isḥāq's account[135]

Ibn Isḥāq's account, as transmitted by Ibn Ḥumayd—Salamah, is as follows: Then Zayd b. Ḥārithah, the *mawlā* of the Messenger of God, accepted Islam. He was the first male to accept Islam and
[1168] to pray after 'Alī b. Abī Ṭālib. Then Abū Bakr b. Abī Quḥāfah al-Ṣiddīq accepted Islam. When he did so, he proclaimed this openly and summoned others to God and to his Messenger. He was well-liked among his tribe, popular and easy to get on with. He was also the most expert of Quraysh on the genealogy of the tribe and the best informed of them about their good and bad qualities. He was a merchant, upright and well-known, and, for various purposes, the men of his tribe used to come to him and associate with him because of his knowledge, his commercial skill, and the excellence

135. The passage from al-Wāqidī has not been located. That from Ibn Isḥāq is Ibn Hishām, *Sīrah*, 160. Zayd b. Ḥārithah had been captured in war as a boy and sold as a slave to Khadījah. When Muḥammad freed him, he would become his "client" (*mawlā*). Usually, however, he is called Muḥammad's "adoptive son," and is even said to have been named Zayd b. Muḥammad. This "adoption" was presumably not like that practiced in the West, but some kind of social usage about which we are not fully informed, perhaps due to the fact that Zayd chose to remain with Muḥammad and Khadījah. This question became important when Muḥammad married Zaynab bt. Jaḥsh after Zayd had divorced her; see Watt, *Muhammad at Medina*, 282, 329–31.

of his company. He began to summon to Islam trustworthy members of his tribe who came and joined in his social gatherings. I have heard that ʿUthmān b. ʿAffān, ʿAbd al-Raḥmān b. ʿAwf, Saʿd b. Abī Waqqāṣ and Ṭalḥah b. ʿUbaydallāh accepted Islam at his hands. When they responded to his summons, he took them to the Messenger of God, where they accepted Islam and joined in the prayer. These eight men were the first group to accept Islam, to pray, to accept the truth of his message, and to believe in the revelation which he brought from God. After that, people entered Islam in unbroken succession, both men and women, until Islam became a general topic of conversation in Mecca and everyone talked of it.

Al-Wāqidī's account

Al-Wāqidī's account, as transmitted by al-Ḥārith—Ibn Saʿd, is as follows: Our fellow scholars are agreed that the first of the people of the Qiblah to respond to the Messenger of God's call was Khadījah bt. Khuwaylid. After this, there is a difference of opinion among us as to which of three men, Abū Bakr, ʿAlī, and Zayd b. Ḥārithah, was the first to accept Islam. Khālid b. Saʿīd b. al-ʿĀs accepted Islam with them and made a fifth. According to some Abū Dharr accepted Islam fourth or fifth, while ʿAmr b. ʿAbasah al-Sulamī accepted Islam fourth or fifth according to others. There is a difference of opinion among us as to which of these men accepted Islam first and there are many accounts concern- [1169]
ing this. There are disagreements about the first three and about those whose names we have given after them.

Al-Ḥārith—Ibn Saʿd—Muḥammad b. ʿUmar—Musʿab b. Thābit—Abū al-Aswad Muḥammad b. ʿAbd al-Raḥmān b. Nawfal: Al-Zubayr became a Muslim after Abū Bakr and he was the fourth or fifth.

Ibn Isḥāq: Khālid b. Saʿīd b. al-ʿĀs and his wife Humaynah bt. Khalaf b. Asʿad b. ʿĀmir b. Bayāḍah of Khuzāʿah became Muslims after a large number of people other than those whom I have mentioned by name as being early converts to Islam.[136]

---

136. Ibn Hishām, *Sīrah,* 164. It is not clear why Ṭabarī has selected these two names from a list of early Muslims given by Ibn Isḥāq.

Events of the Life of the Messenger of God

(Continued)

The Messenger of God Begins to Preach Openly

Three years after the commencement of his mission,[137] God commanded His Prophet to proclaim the divine message which he had received, to declare it publicly to the people, and to summon them to it. God said to him:

> So proclaim that which you are commanded, and withdraw from the polytheists.[138]

In the previous three years of his mission, until he was commanded to summon people openly to God, he had kept his preaching secret and hidden. Then God revealed:

> And warn your tribe of near kindred, and lower your wing (in kindness) to those believers who follow you. And if they (your kinsfolk) disobey you, say: "I am innocent of what they do."[139]

When the Messenger of God's Companions, prayed they went to the ravines and concealed themselves from their fellow tribesmen. Once while Sa'd b. Abī Waqqāṣ and a number of the Messenger of God's Companions were in one of the ravines of Mecca, a group of polytheists suddenly appeared before them as they were praying, expressed their disapproval and reproached the believers for what they were doing. Finally, they came to blows, and Sa'd b.

---

137. Ibid., 166.
138. 15:94
139. 26:214-16.

Abī Waqqāṣ struck one of the polytheists with a camel's jawbone [1170]
and split his head open. This was the first blood shed in the time of Islam.

Abū Kurayb and Abū al-Sā'ib—Abū Muʿāwiyah—al-Aʿmash—ʿAmr b. Murrah—Saʿīd b. Jubayr—Ibn ʿAbbās: One day the Messenger of God mounted al-Ṣafā and called out, "Beware this morning!" Quraysh gathered around him and said, "What is the matter?" Then he said, "If I were to tell you that the enemy would come upon you this morning or this evening, would you believe me?" "Certainly," they replied. He said, "I am a warner to you in the face of a terrible doom." Then Abū Lahab said, "May you perish! Did you call us together for this?" Then God revealed: "The power of Abū Lahab will perish and he will perish" ... reciting to the end of the sūrah.[140]

Abū Kurayb—Abū Usāmah—al-Aʿmash—ʿAmr b. Murrah—Saʿīd b. Jubayr—Ibn ʿAbbās: When God revealed the verse, "and warn your tribe of near kindred," the Messenger of God went out, mounted al-Ṣafā, and called out, "Beware this morning!" Some said, "Who is that calling out?" and others said, "It is Muḥammad." Then he said, "Banū so-and-so, Banū ʿAbd al-Muṭṭalib, Banū ʿAbd Manāf!" They gathered round him, and he said, "If I were to tell you that horsemen were coming out at the foot of that mountain, would you believe me?" They replied, "We have never known you to tell a lie." Then he said, "I am 'a warner to you in the face of a terrible doom.'" Abū Lahab said, "May you perish! Did you only bring us together for this?" Then the following sūrah was revealed: "The power of Abū Lahab will perish, and he will perish ... " reciting to the end of the sūrah.

Ibn Ḥumayd—Salamah—Muḥammad b. Isḥāq—ʿAbd al- [1171]
Ghaffār b. al-Qāsim—al-Minhāl b. ʿAmr—ʿAbdallāh b. al-Ḥārith b. Nawfal b. al-Ḥārith b. ʿAbd al-Muttalib—ʿAbdallāh b. ʿAbbās—ʿAlī b. Abī Ṭālib:[141] When the verse "and warn your tribe of near kindred" was revealed to the Messenger of God, he called me and said to me, "ʿAlī, God has commanded me to warn my tribe of near

140. Abū Lahab was the uncle of Muḥammad who succeeded Abū Ṭālib as chief of the clan of Hāshim, and then refused to continue to let Muḥammad have the protection of the clan. It was probably at that time that Sūrah lll was revealed and not on the occasion described here. The verses quoted are 34:46 and 111:1-5.

141. This section is omitted by Ibn Hishām.

kindred. I was troubled by this, for I knew that when I broached the matter to them they would respond in a way which I would not like. I kept silent until Gabriel came to me and said, "Muḥammad, if you do not do what you are commanded, your Lord will punish you. So prepare a measure of wheat for us, add a leg of mutton to it, fill a large bowl of milk for us, and then assemble the Banū 'Abd al-Muṭṭalib for me so that I may speak to them and tell them what I have been commanded to tell them."

I did what he had told me to do and then called them to him. At that time they numbered forty men, more or less, including his uncles Abū Ṭālib, Ḥamzah, al-'Abbās, and Abū Lahab. When they had gathered together, he called on me to bring the food which I had prepared. I brought it, and when I put it down the Messenger of God took a piece of meat, broke it with his teeth, and threw it towards the dish. Then he said, "Take, in the name of God." They ate until they could eat no more, and yet the food was as it had been, except for where their hands had been. I swear by God, in
[1172] whose hand 'Alī's soul rests, that a single man could have eaten the amount of food which I put before all of them. Then he said, "Give them something to drink," so I brought them that bowl and they drank from it until they had drunk their fill, and I swear by God that one man could have drunk that amount.[142]

When the Messenger of God wanted to speak to them, Abū Lahab forestalled him and said, "Your host has long since bewitched you." Then they dispersed without the Messenger of God speaking to them. On the following day he said to me, 'Alī, this man forestalled me by saying what you heard him saying, so that the people dispersed before I could speak to them. Prepare the same food for us as you did yesterday, and assemble them here."

I did this, assembled them, and brought the food to them when he called me. He did as he had done the previous day, and they ate until they could eat no more. Then he said, "Bring the bowl," and they drank until they could drink no more. Then he spoke to them, saying, "Banū 'Abd al-Muṭṭalib, I know of no young man among the Arabs who has brought his people something better than what I have brought to you. I bring you the best of this world

142. This is an example of the miracles invented for Muḥammad by later Muslim scholars in order to refute the Christian argument that he could not be a prophet because he had performed no miracles.

and the next, for God has commanded me to summon you to him. Which of you will aid me in this matter, so that he will be my brother, my agent *(waṣī)* and my successor *(khalīfah)* among you?"

They all held back, and although I was the youngest and the most bleary-eyed,[143] pot-bellied, and spindly-legged of them, I said, "I will be your helper, Prophet of God." He put his hand on the back of my neck and said, "This is my brother, my agent, and my successor among you, so listen to him and obey him." They rose up laughing and saying to Abū Ṭālib, "He has commanded you to [1173] listen to your son and to obey him!"

Zakariyyā' b. Yaḥyā al-Ḍarīr—'Affān b. Muslim—Abū 'Awānah—'Uthmān b. al-Mughīrah—Abū Ṣādiq—Rabī'ah b. Nājid: A man said to 'Alī, "Commander of the Faithful, how did you become the heir of your cousin to the exclusion of your paternal uncle?"[144] 'Alī said, "Ahem" three times until everybody craned their necks and pricked up their ears, and then said, "The Messenger of God assembled (or: invited) the whole of the Banū 'Abd al-Muṭṭalib, including his own closest relatives, to eat a year-old lamb and to drink some milk.[145] He also prepared a quantity of wheat[146] for them, and they ate until they were full, while the food remained as it was, as though it had not been touched. Then he called for a drinking cup and they drank until they could drink no more, while the drink remained as though it had not been touched and they had not drunk.

"Then he said, 'Banū 'Abd al-Muṭṭalib, I have been sent to all men in general and to you in particular. Now that you have seen what you have seen, which of you will swear an oath of allegiance to me to become my brother, my companion and my inheritor?' Not one of them rose up, so I stood before him, although I was the youngest there. He said. 'Sit down.' He repeated the words he had spoken three times, while I would rise up and would say to me, 'Sit down.' On the third occasion, he struck his hand on mine. In

143. The word *armaṣ* is literally "with eyes encrusted with matter."
144. This presumably refers to al-'Abbās, the ancestor of the 'Abbāsid dynasty.
145. Literally, "to drink a *farq*" which was a liquid measure used especially in al-Madīnah.
146. Literally "a *mudd* of wheat," but it is impossible to say even approximately how much this was.

this way I became the heir of my cousin to the exclusion of my uncle."

Ibn Ḥumayd—Salamah—Muḥammad b. Isḥāq—ʿAmr b. ʿUb-
[1174] ayd—al-Ḥasan b. Abī al-Ḥasan: When the verse "and warn your tribe of near kindred" was revealed to the Messenger of God, he rose up in the Valley and said, "Banū ʿAbd al-Muṭṭalib, Banū ʿAbd Manāf, Banū Quṣayy!" Then he named the various groups of Quraysh, clan by clan, until he had come to the last of them, and said, "I summon you to God and warn you of his punishment."

Al-Ḥārith—Ibn Saʿd—Muḥammad b. ʿUmar—Jāriyah b. Abī ʿImrān—ʿAbd al-Raḥmān b. al-Qāsim—his father:[147] The Messenger of God was commanded to proclaim the divine message which he had received, to declare it publicly to the people, and to summon them to God.

147. Ibn Saʿd, *Ṭabaqāt*, I:132.22-5.

Other Events up to the Hijrah

Quraysh Begin to Oppose the Messenger of God

Ibn Ḥumayd—Salamah—Ibn Isḥāq:[148] The Messenger of God proclaimed God's message openly and declared Islam publicly to his fellow tribesmen. When he did so, they did not withdraw from him or reject him in any way, as far as I have heard, until he spoke of their gods and denounced them. When he did this, they took exception to it and united in opposition and hostility to him, except for those of them whom God had protected from error by means of Islam. The latter were few in number and practiced their faith in secret. His uncle Abū Ṭālib was friendly to him, however, and protected him and shielded him from harm. The Messenger of God continued to do God's work and to proclaim his message, undeterred by anything. When Quraysh saw that he would not give them any satisfaction, they objected to his departing from their ways and denouncing their gods, and, seeing that Abū Ṭālib protected him, shielded him from harm, and would not hand him over to them, a number of the nobles of Quraysh, [1175]
consisting of such men as ʿUtbah b. Rabīʿah, Shaybah b. Rabīʿah, Abū al-Bakhtarī b. Hishām, al-Aswad b. al-Muṭṭalib, al-Walīd b. al-Mughīrah, Abū Jahl b. Hishām, al-ʿĀṣ b. Wā'il, and Nubayh and Munabbih, the sons of al-Ḥajjāj,[149] went to Abū Ṭālib and said, "Abū Ṭālib, your nephew has reviled our gods, denounced our re-

148. Ibn Hishām, *Sīrah*, 166–8; Ibn Hishām omits the previous section from Ibn Isḥāq.

149. These were leading men from the clans of ʿAbd Shams (2), Asad (2), Makhzūm (2), and Sahm (3). In the politics of pre-Islamic Mecca, these clans tended to be opposed to Hāshim and its associated clans.

ligion, derided our traditional values and told us that our forefathers were misguided. Either curb his attacks on us or give us a free hand to deal with him, for you are just as opposed to him as we are, and we will deal with him for you." Abū Ṭālib gave them a mild answer and declined courteously, and they left him. The Messenger of God continued as before, proclaiming the faith of God and summoning people to it.

After this, Muḥammad was estranged from the Quraysh, and they withdrew from him and harbored a secret hatred for him. They talked about him frequently amongst themselves and urged one another against him. Eventually they went to Abū Ṭālib once again. "Abū Ṭālib," they said, "we hold you in respect among us on account of your age, your nobility, and your standing. We asked you to forbid your nephew to attack us, but you did not do so. By God, we can no longer endure this vilification of our forefathers, this derision of our traditional values and this abuse of our gods. Either you restrain him or we shall fight both of you over this until one side or the other is destroyed," or words to that effect. Then they left. This breach and enmity with his tribe weighed heavily on Abū Ṭālib, but he could not reconcile himself to surrendering the Messenger of God to them or deserting him.

Muḥammad b. al-Ḥusayn—Aḥmad b. al-Mufaḍḍal—Asbāṭ—al-Suddī: A number of men of the Quraysh gathered together, includ-
[1176] ing Abū Jahl b. Hishām, al-ʿĀṣ b. Wāʾil, al-Aswad b. al-Muṭṭalib and al-Aswad b. ʿAbd Yaghūth, together with a number of other shaykhs of the Quraysh, and said to one another, "Let us go to Abū Ṭālib and speak to him about Muḥammad, so that he will give us justice against him and order him to desist from reviling our gods; and we will leave him to the god whom he worships, for we fear that this old man may die and we may do something which the Arabs will reproach us for and say, 'They let him alone until his uncle died, and then they laid hands on him.'"

They sent one of their number, whose name was al-Muṭṭalib,[150] to Abū Ṭālib to ask permission for them to enter. He said, "Here are the shaykhs and nobles of your tribe asking permission to visit you." He told him to ask them to come in, and when they had

150. This is not, of course, al-Muṭṭalib, the brother of Hāshim, who had been dead for a long time. It may have been al-Muṭṭalib b. Ḥantab from the clan of Makhzūm.

done so they said, "Abū Ṭālib, you are our elder and our chief, so give us justice against your nephew and order him to desist from reviling our gods, and we will leave him to his god."

Abū Ṭālib sent for the Messenger of God, and when he came in he said, "Nephew, here are the shaykhs and nobles of your tribe. They have asked for justice against you, that you should desist from reviling their gods and they will leave you to your god." "Uncle," he said, "shall I not summon them to something which is better for them than their gods?" "What do you summon them to?" he asked. He replied, "I summon them to utter a saying through which the Arabs will submit to them and they will rule over the non-Arabs." Abū Jahl said from among the gathering, "What is it, by your father? We will give you it and ten like it." He answered, "That you should say; "There is no deity but God." They took fright at that and said, "Ask for anything rather than that!" But he said, "If you were to bring me the sun and put it into [1177]
my hand, I would not ask you for anything other than this."

They rose up to leave in anger and said, "By God, we shall revile you and your god who commands you to do this!" "The chiefs among them hurried about, exhorting; Go and be staunch to your gods! This is a thing designed ... " to the words "naught but an invention."[151]

Muḥammad turned toward his uncle, who said to him, "Nephew, why did you go too far with them?" He turned again toward his uncle and called upon him, saying, "Utter a saying by means of which I shall testify for you on the day of resurrection. Say, 'There is no deity but God.'" He replied, "Were it not that the Arabs would consider this shameful for you (all), and say that I was afraid of death, I would grant you this; but I must remain in the religion of my ancestors." Then came the revelation of the verse:

> You guide not whom you love, but God guides whom he will.[152]

Abū Kurayb and Ibn Wakī'—Abū Usāmah—al-A'mash—'Abbād—Sa'īd b. Jubayr—Ibn 'Abbās: When Abū Ṭālib fell ill, a number of Quraysh visited him, among them Abū Jahl, who said,

---

151. 38:6-7.
152. 28:56.

"Your nephew is reviling our gods and doing and saying all sorts of things. Why do you not send for him and forbid him to do this?" He sent for him, and the Prophet came and entered the room. There was just room for one man to sit between Abū Ṭalib and his visitors, and Abū Jahl, being afraid that Abū Ṭālib would be more sympathetic to him if he sat beside him, leapt up and sat in that place himself, so that the Messenger of God could not find anywhere near his uncle to sit down and had to sit by the door. Abū Ṭālib said to him, "Nephew, how is it that your tribe are complaining of you and claiming that you are reviling their gods and saying this, that, and the other?" They showered accusations
[1178] upon him, and then the Messenger of God spoke and said, "Uncle, I want them to utter one saying. If they say it, the Arabs will submit to them and the non-Arabs will pay the *jizyah* [153] to them." They were perturbed at this utterance and said, "One saying? Yes, by your father, and ten! What is it?" Abū Ṭālib said, "What saying is it, nephew" He replied, "There is no deity but God." They rose up in alarm, shaking the dust off their garments and saying, "Does he make the gods one god? This is indeed an astounding thing." Then came the revelation beginning with the words just spoken by these men and ending "they have not yet tasted my doom."[154] These are the exact words of Abū Kurayb's account.

Returning to Ibn Isḥāq's narrative.[155]

Ibn Ḥumayd—Salamah—Muḥammad b. Isḥāq—Ya'qūb b. 'Utbah b. al-Mughīrah b. al-Akhnas: He was told that when the Quraysh said this to Abū Ṭālib, he sent for the Messenger of God and said to him, "Nephew, your tribe have come to me and said such-and-such. Spare me and yourself, and do not put a greater burden on me than I can bear." The Messenger of God thought that his uncle had changed about him and was going to abandon him and hand him over, and that his determination to aid him and stand by him had weakened, so he said, "Uncle, if they were to place the sun in my right hand and the moon in my left, on condition that I should abandon (carrying on) my preaching before God gave it the victory or I died in the attempt, I should not abandon

153. The *jizyah* was the poll tax paid by members of "protected minorities" (*dhimmīs*) under the Caliphate.

154: 38:5-8.

155. Ibn Hishām, *Sīrah*, 168–70; Ṭabarī omits a poem ascribed to Abū Ṭālib.

it." Then the Messenger of God burst into tears and wept, and rose up. When he turned away, Abū Ṭālib called him back and said, "Come here, nephew." The Messenger of God came up to him, and he said, "Go, nephew, and say what you like. By God, I [1179] will never hand you over for any reason."

When the Quraysh discovered that Abū Ṭālib had refused to abandon the Messenger of God and to hand him over, and was determined to break with them on this issue and become their enemy, they brought ʿUmārah b. al-Walīd b. al-Mughīrah to him and said, I have been told, "Abū Ṭālib, this is ʿUmārah b. al-Walīd, the bravest, most poetically gifted and most handsome young man in Quraysh. Take him, and his intelligence and his support are yours. Take him as a son, and he is yours; and hand over your nephew who has opposed your religion and the religion of your forefathers, who has sowed discord among your tribe and who has derided their traditional values, and we shall kill him. A man for a man."

Abū Ṭālib said, "This is an evil bargain which you are offering me. Will you give me your son so that I can feed him for you, while I give you my son so that you can kill him? By God, this shall never be." Al-Muṭʿim b. ʿAdī b. Nawfal b. ʿAbd Manāf said, "By God, Abū Ṭālib, your tribe have treated you fairly, and have tried hard to avoid putting you in an unpleasant situation. I do not think that you wish to accept any proposal from them." Abū Ṭālib replied to al-Muṭʿim, "By God, they have not treated me fairly. You have decided to abandon me and to support the rest of the tribe against me. Do what you think fit." These, or something like them, were his words.

After this, the situation deteriorated, hostility became more bitter, and people withdrew from one another and showed open hatred to one another. Then the Quraysh incited one another against those in their various clans who had become Companions of the Messenger of God and had accepted Islam with him. Every clan fell upon those of its members who were Muslims, tormenting them and trying to force them to leave their religion. God pro- [1180] tected his Messenger from them by means of his uncle Abū Ṭālib who saw what the Quraysh were doing among the Banū Hāshim and the Banū al-Muṭṭalib and called on them to follow him in protecting and defending the Messenger of God. They gathered round him, stood by him, and responded to his call to defend the Messenger of God, with the exception of Abū Lahab. Abū Ṭālib was overjoyed when he saw how serious they were in supporting him and how solicitous they were for him, and he began to praise them and to extol the Messenger of God's merits and his standing among them in order to reinforce their decision.

The Emigration to Abyssinia

ʿAlī b. Naṣr b. ʿAlī al-Jahḍamī and ʿAbd al-Wārith b. ʿAbd al-Ṣamad b. ʿAbd al-Wārith—ʿAbd al-Ṣamad b. ʿAbd al-Wārith—Abān al-ʿAṭṭār—Hishām b. ʿUrwah—ʿUrwah: He wrote to ʿAbd al-Malik as follows, referring to the Messenger of God: When he summoned his people to the guidance and light which had been revealed to him and for which God had sent him, they did not withdraw from him at the beginning of his preaching, and were on the point of listening to him. When, however, he spoke of their idols, some wealthy men of Quraysh who had come from al-Ṭā'if took exception to this and reacted strongly against him, not liking what he said. They instigated those over whom they had influence against him, and the mass of the people turned away from him and abandoned him, except for those of them whom God pro-
[1181] tected, and these were few in number. Matters remained thus as long as God willed, and then their chiefs conspired together to seduce from God's religion those of their sons, brothers, and fellow clansmen who had followed him. It was a trial which severely shook the people of Islam who had followed the Messenger of God. Some were seduced, but God protected from error those whom He wished to protect. When the Muslims were treated in this way, the Messenger of God commanded them to emigrate to Abyssinia. In Abyssinia there was a righteous king called the Negus in whose land no one was oppressed and who was praised for his righteousness. Abyssinia was a land with which Quraysh traded and in which they found an ample living, security, and a good market. When the Messenger of God commanded them to do this, the main body of them went to Abyssinia because of the coercion they were being subjected to in Mecca. His fear was that they would be seduced from their religion. He himself remained, and did not leave Mecca. Several years passed in this way, during

which Quraysh pressed hard upon those of them who had become Muslims. After this, Islam spread in Mecca and a number of their nobles entered Islam.[156]

Abū Ja'far (al-Ṭabarī): There is a difference of opinion as to the number of those who emigrated to Abyssinia in this, the first emigration. Some say that there were eleven men and four women.[157]

Those who say this:

Al-Ḥārith—Ibn Sa'd—Muḥammad b. 'Umar—Yūnus b. Muḥammad al-Ẓafarī—his father—a man of his tribe; also 'Ubaydallāh b. 'Abbās al-Hudhalī—al-Ḥārith b. al-Fuḍayl: Those who emigrated in the first emigration did so by stealth and in secret, and numbered eleven men and four women. They went to al-Shu'aybah, some riding and some walking. As they arrived, God caused two [1182] merchant ships to halt there for the Muslims, and in these they were carried to Abyssinia for half a dīnār. This took place in the month of Rajab in the fifth year from the time of the Messenger of God's commissioning as a prophet. Quraysh set out in pursuit of them and reached the sea at the place where the Muslims had embarked, but did not capture any of them. The emigrants said, "We came to Abyssinia and were hospitably lodged by the best of hosts. We had security to practice our religion, and we worshipped God without being persecuted and without hearing unpleasant words."

Al-Ḥārith—Muḥammad b. Sa'd–Muḥammad b. 'Umar–Yūnus b. Muḥammad—his father; also 'Abd al-Ḥamīd—Muḥammad b. Yaḥyā b. Ḥibbān: The names of this group, men and women, were: 'Uthmān b. 'Affān and his wife Ruqayyah, the daughter of the Messenger of God; Abū Ḥudhayfah b. 'Utbah b. Rabī'ah and his wife Sahlah bt. Suhayl b. 'Amr; al-Zubayr b. al-'Awwām b. Khuwaylid b. Asad; Muṣ'ab b. 'Umayr b. Hāshim b. 'Abd Manāf b. 'Abd al-Dār; 'Abd al-Raḥmān b. 'Awf b. 'Abd 'Awf b. al-Ḥārith b. Zuhrah; Abū Salamah b. 'Abd al-Asad b. Hilāl b. 'Abdallāh b. 'Umar b. Makhzūm and his wife Umm Salamah bt. Abī Umayyah b. al-Mughīrah b. 'Abdallāh b. 'Umar b. Makhzūm; 'Uthmān b. [1183] Maẓ'ūn al-Jumaḥī; 'Āmir b. Rabī'ah al-'Anzī (from the tribe of 'Anz b. Wā'il, not from that of 'Anazah), the confederate of the

156. Reading *dakhala fīhi* for *fīhā* of the printed text. This is part of the letter to the Caliph 'Abd al-Malik.

157. For the emigrations to Abyssinia, see Introduction, p.46. The two following passages from al-Wāqidī are found in Ibn Sa'd, *Ṭabaqāt*, I:136. 9-137.2.

Banū ʿAdī b. Kaʿb, and his wife Laylā bt. Abī Ḥathmah; Abū Sabrah b. Abī Ruhm b. ʿAbd al-ʿUzzā al-ʿĀmirī; Ḥāṭib b. ʿAmr b. ʿAbd Shams; Suhayl b. Bayḍā', from the Banū al-Ḥārith b. Fihr; and ʿAbdallāh b. Masʿūd, the confederate of the Banū Zuhrah.

Abū Jaʿfar (al-Ṭabarī): Others say that those Muslims who went to Abyssinia and emigrated there, apart from their children who went with them when they were young or were born there, were eighty-two men, if ʿAmmār b. Yāsir, who is doubtful, is included among them.

Those who say this:

Ibn Ḥumayd—Salamah—Muḥammad b. Isḥāq:[158] The Messenger of God saw the sufferings which were inflicted on his Companions and saw that, although he himself was spared such treatment by virtue of his standing with God and his uncle Abū Ṭālib, he could not defend his Companions against the sufferings they were experiencing. He therefore said to them, "Why do you not go to Abyssinia? There is a king there under whom no one is oppressed, and it is a land of truth. Stay there until God creates a relief from the situation in which you find yourselves." Thereupon the Messenger of God's Muslim Companions went to Abyssinia, fearing they might be seduced and fleeing to God with their religion. This was the first emigration in Islam.

[1184] The first Muslims to emigrate were as follows: from the Banū Umayyah b. ʿAbd Shams b. ʿAbd Manāf, ʿUthman b. ʿAffān b. Abī al-ʿĀṣ b. Umayyah, accompanied by his wife Ruqayyah, the daughter of the Messenger of God. From the Banū ʿAbd Shams, Abū Ḥudhayfah b. ʿUtbah b. Rabīʿah b. ʿAbd Shams b. ʿAbd Manāf, accompanied by his wife Sahlah bt. Suhayl b. ʿAmr, one of the Banū ʿĀmir b. Lu'ayy. From the Banū Asad b. ʿAbd al-ʿUzzā b. Quṣayy, al-Zubayr b. al-ʿAwwām. After this, Ibn Isḥāq gives the same list of people as al-Wāqidī, except that he says: From the Banū ʿĀmir b. Lu'ayy b. Ghālib b. Fihr, Abū Sabrah b. Abī Ruhm b. ʿAbd al-ʿUzzā b. Abī Qays b. ʿAbd Wudd b. Naṣr b. Mālik b. Ḥisl b. ʿĀmir b. Lu'ayy; but some people say that this was not so and that it was Abū Ḥāṭib b. ʿAmr b. ʿAbd Shams b. ʿAbd Wudd b. Naṣr b. Mālik b. Ḥisl b. ʿĀmir b. Lu'ayy. He is said to have been the first of all to go to Abyssinia. Ibn Isḥāq makes their number ten, say-

158. Ibn Hishām, *Sīrah*, 208–9; Ṭabarī omits Ibn Isḥaq's second longer list, 209–16.

ing: These ten, according to what I have been told, were the first Muslims to emigrate to Abyssinia.

Then Ja'far b. Abī Ṭālib emigrated, and after that there was a steady flow of Muslims. They assembled in Abyssinia and remained there, some coming with their families and some singly, without their families. Ibn Isḥāq then reckons that there were eighty-two men in all, including the ten I have mentioned by name, some who had their families and children with them, some who had children born in Abyssinia, and some who had no family with them.

Quraysh Show Increased Hostility to the Messenger of God

Abū Ja'far (al-Ṭabarī): When those of the Messenger of God's Companions who emigrated to Abyssina had departed, the Messenger of God remained in Mecca preaching in secret and openly, protected by God through his uncle Abū Ṭālib and by those of his clan who answered his call for support. When Quraysh saw that they had no means of attacking him physically, they accused him of sorcery, soothsaying, and madness, and of being a poet. They began to keep away from him those whom they feared might listen to him and follow him. The most serious step which they are reported to have taken at that time was the following. [1185]

Ibn Ḥumayd—Salamah—Muḥammad b. Isḥāq—Yaḥyā b. 'Urwah b. al-Zubayr—his father 'Urwah—'Abdallāh b. 'Amr b. al-'Āṣ:[159] I said to him, "What was the worst attack you saw by Quraysh upon the Messenger of God when they openly showed their enmity to him?" He replied, "I was with them when their nobles assembled one day in the Ḥijr and discussed the Messenger of God. They said, 'We have never seen the like of what we have endured from this man. He has derided our traditional values, abused our forefathers, reviled our religion, caused division among us, and insulted our gods. We have endured a great deal from him,' or words to that effect. While they were saying this, the Messenger of God suddenly appeared and walked up and kissed the Black Stone. Then he passed by them while performing the circumambulation,

159. Ibid., 183f.

and as he did so they made some slanderous remarks about him. I could see from the Messenger of God's face that he had heard them, but he went on. When he passed the second time they made similar remarks, and I could see from his face that he had heard them, but again he went on. Then he passed them the third time, and they made similar remarks; but this time he stopped and said, 'Hear, men of Quraysh. By Him in whose hand Muḥammad's soul
[1186] rests, I have brought you slaughter.' They were gripped by what he had said, and it was as though every man of them had a bird perched on his head;[160] even those of them who had been urging the severest measures against him previously spoke in a conciliatory way to him, using the politest expressions they could think of, and said, 'Depart in true guidance, Abū al-Qāsim; by God, you were never ignorant.'

"The Prophet left, and the next day they gathered in the Ḥijr, and I (ʿAbdallāh b. ʿAmr b. al-ʿĀṣ) was again present. They said to one another, 'You were talking about the unpleasantness which you have endured and the things which Muḥammad has done to you, but when he openly said something disagreeable you shrank from him.' While they were saying this, the Messenger of God suddenly appeared, and they leapt upon him as one man and surrounded him, saying, 'Is it you who says this and that?' repeating what they had heard of his denunciation of their gods and their religion. The prophet said, 'Yes, I am the one who says that.' "

"Then I saw one of them grabbing his cloak, but Abū Bakr stood in front of him weeping and saying, 'Woe upon you all! Would you kill a man because he says, My Lord is God?'[161] Then they left him, and that is the worst thing I ever saw Quraysh do to him."

Yunūs b. ʿAbd al-Aʿlā—Bishr b. Bakr—al-Awzāʿī—Yaḥyā b. Abī Kathīr—Abū Salamah b. ʿAbd al-Raḥmān: I said to ʿAbdallāh b. ʿAmr, "Tell the worst thing which you saw the polytheists do to the Messenger of God." He said, "ʿUqbah b. Abī Muʿayṭ came up while the Messenger of God was by the Kaʿbah, twisted his robe round his neck, and throttled him violently. Abū Bakr stood behind him, put his hand on his shoulder, and pushed him away

160. In his translation, Guillaume interprets this as "not one of them but stood silent and still."

161. Abū Bakr quotes a verse from the Qur'ān (40:28) referring to a threat to kill Moses.

from the Messenger of God. Then he said, 'People, would you kill a man because he says, My Lord is God? ... ' to the words 'God guides not one who is prodigal, a liar?' " [1187]

Ḥamzah Accepts Islam

Ibn Isḥāq—a man from Aslam, who had a good memory:[162] Abū Jahl b. Hishām passed by the Messenger of God as he was sitting by al-Ṣafā and abused him, reviled him, and spoke to him offensively, denouncing his religion and trying to humiliate him. The Messenger of God did not say anything, but a woman client (*mawlāh*) of ʿAbdallāh b. Judʿān al-Taymī, who was in her house above al-Ṣafā, overheard this. Then Abū Jahl left him, went to the assembly of the Quraysh at the Kaʿbah, and sat down with them. Soon afterwards, Ḥamzah b. ʿAbd al-Muṭṭalib came up with his bow slung over his shoulder, on his way back from the hunt. He was a great huntsman and used to go out for game with his bow and arrows. When he came back from the hunt he would not go back to his family until he had circumambulated the Kaʿbah, after which, if he passed by an assembly of the Quraysh, he would always stop, greet them, and talk with them. He was the strongest man of Quraysh, and the most unyielding. By the time he went past the woman, the Messenger of God had risen and gone home, and she said to him, "Abū ʿUmārah, if only you had seen what your nephew Muḥammad had to endure just now, before you came, from Abū al-Ḥakam b. Hishām.[163] He found him sitting here and reviled him, abused him and spoke to him offensively, and then left him, while Muḥammad said nothing in return."

Ḥamzah was carried away by a fury, as it was God's will to honor him in this way, and went off quickly, not stopping to speak to anyone as he used to do when intending to circumambulate the Kaʿbah, ready to attack Abū Jahl when he saw him. When he entered the mosque, he saw him sitting among the people and went up to him. When he was standing next to him he raised his bow

162. Ibn Hishām, *Sīrah*, 184f.

163. Out of politeness, this woman addresses Ḥamzah by his *kunyah* (see n. 22) and refers to Abū Jahl by his, that is, Abū al-Ḥakam. Since Jahl is not a boy's name, Abū Jahl is not a proper *kunyah* but rather a kind of nickname, possibly meaning "father of violence (or bravado)." His primary name was ʿAmr. Similarly the name of Muḥammad's uncle Abū Lahab means something like "father of brightness."

and gave him a blow with it which split his head open in an ugly way, and said, "Do you revile him when I am a member of his religion and say what he says? Return that blow against me if you can!"

[1188] The men of Banū Makhzūm (the clan of Abū Jahl), rose up to come to Abū Jahl's assistance against Ḥamzah, but Abū Jahl said, "Leave Abū ʿUmārah, for, by God, I insulted his nephew gravely."

Ḥamzah persevered in his Islam. Quraysh recognized that by Ḥamzah's acceptance of Islam the Messenger of God had been strengthened and that Ḥamzah would protect him; after this, they curbed some of their attacks on him.

ʿAbdallāh b. Masʿūd Recites the Qur'ān Aloud to Quraysh

Ibn Ḥumayd—Salamah—Muḥammad b. Isḥāq—Yaḥyā b. ʿUrwah b. al-Zubayr—his father:[164] The first to recite the Qur'ān aloud in Mecca after the Messenger of God was ʿAbdallāh b. Masʿūd. One day the companions of the Messenger of God were assembled together and said, "By God, Quraysh have never heard this Qur'ān recited aloud to them. Who will let them hear it?" ʿAbdallāh b. Masʿūd said, "I will." They said, "We fear what they will do to you. What we want is a man who has a clan who will protect him against them if they seek to harm him." He replied, "Let me do it. God will protect me."

The next day, Ibn Masʿūd went to the Maqām[165] in the late morning when the Quraysh were gathered in their groups. When he was standing at the maqām, he said, "In the name of God, the Compassionate, the Merciful," raising his voice as he did so, "The Compassionate has made known the Qur'ān. He has created man." He turned toward them as he recited, and they took notice of him and began to say, "What is this son of a slave's mother saying?" Then they said, "He is reciting some of what Muḥammad has brought," and rose up and began to hit him in the face. He continued to recite as much as God willed that he should, and then went back to his companions with the marks of their blows

164. Ibn Hishām, *Sīrah,* 202f.

165. Presumably the spot near the Kaʿbah known as "the standing place of Abraham" (*maqām Ibrāhīm*). The verses recited are 55:1-3.

on his face. They said, "This is what we feared would happen to you," but he replied, "The enemies of God were never more despicable in my sight than they are now. If you wish, I will do the [1189] same thing to them tomorrow." They replied, "No, you have done enough. You have made them hear what they do not wish to hear."

Quraysh Boycott the Banū Hāshim and the Banū al-Muṭṭalib[166]

Abū Ja'far (al-Ṭabarī): When those who had emigrated to Abyssinia had settled down in the land of the Negus and were living in security, Quraysh conferred together about taking some action against those Muslims who had taken refuge there. They then sent 'Amr b. al-'Āṣ and 'Abdallāh b. Abi Rabī'ah b. al-Mughīrah al-Makhzūmī to the Negus with many gifts for him and for his generals, telling them to ask the Negus to hand back those Muslims whom he had accepted into his country. 'Amr and 'Abdallāh travelled to him on this mission and carried out the task which their people had entrusted to them, but did not achieve the results from the Negus which their tribe had hoped for, and went home in disgrace.

'Umar b. al-Khaṭṭāb, who was a staunch, sturdy, and mighty warrior, had accepted Islam, as had Ḥamzah b. 'Abd al-Muṭṭalib before him, and the Messenger of God's Companions began to feel stronger. Islam had begun to spread among the clans, and the Negus had given protection to those Muslims who had taken refuge in his country. When all of these things happened, the Quraysh gathered together to confer and decided to draw up a document in which they undertook not to marry women from the Banū Hāshim and the Banū al-Muṭṭalib, or to give them women in marriage, or to sell anything to them or buy anything from them. They drew up a written contract to that effect and solemnly pledged themselves to observe it. Then they hung up the document in the interior of the Ka'bah to make it even more binding upon themselves. When Quraysh did this, the Banū Hāshim and the Banū al-Muṭṭalib joined with Abū Ṭālib, went with him to his valley [1190] and gathered round him there; but Abū Lahab 'Abd al-'Uzzā b.

166. There is similar material in Ibn Hishām, *Sīrah*, 230-32.

ʿAbd al-Muṭṭalib left the Banū Hāshim and went to the Quraysh, supporting them against Abū Ṭālib. This state of affairs continued for two or three years, until the two clans were exhausted, since nothing reached any of them except what was sent secretly by those of the Quraysh who wished to maintain relations with them.

It is related that Abū Jahl met Ḥakīm b. Ḥizām b. Khuwaylid b. Asad with a slave carrying some wheat which he intended to take to his aunt Khadījah bt. Khuwaylid, who was with the Messenger of God in the valley. He hung on to him and said, "Are you taking food to the Banū Hāshim? By God, you and your food will not move until I disgrace you in Mecca!" Abū al-Bakhtarī b. Hishām b. al-Ḥārith b. Asad came up and said, "What is going on between you two?" Abū Jahl said, "He is taking food to the Banū Hāshim," but Abū al-Bakhtarī replied, "It is food belonging to his aunt which he has stored and which she has now sent for. Would you prevent him from taking her own food to her? Let the man pass." Abū Jahl refused, and in the end they came to blows. Abū al-Bakhtarī took hold of a camel's jawbone, struck him with it, split his head open, and trampled upon him violently. Ḥamzah b. ʿAbd al-Muṭṭalib was near by observing this. They did not want the Messenger of God and his Companions to hear of this and rejoice at their discomfiture. During all of this period of years the Messenger of God was calling upon his people in secret and openly, by night and by day, while the revelation from God was coming to him continuously, commanding and forbidding, threatening those who showed open hostility to him, and vindicating the Messenger
[1191] of God against those who opposed him.

Quraysh Attempt to Induce the Messenger of God to Cease His Attacks on Their Gods

It is said that the nobles of his tribe gathered together to speak to him one day.

Muḥammad b. Mūsā al-Ḥarashī—Abū Khalaf ʿAbdallāh b. ʿĪsā—Dāūd—ʿIkrimah—Ibn ʿAbbās: Quraysh promised the Messenger of God that they would give him so much wealth that he would become the richest man in Mecca, would give him as many wives as he wanted in marriage, and would submit to his commands.

They said, "This is what we will give you, Muḥammad, so desist from reviling our gods and do not speak evilly of them. If you will not do so, we offer you one means which will be to your advantage and to ours." "What is it?" he asked. They said, "You will worship our gods, al-Lāt and al-ʿUzzā, for a year, and we shall worship your god for a year." "Let me see what revelation comes to me from my Lord," he replied. Then, the following inspiration came from the Preserved Tablet:

> Say: O disbelievers! I worship not that which you worship; nor do you worship that which I worship. And I shall not worship that which you worship, nor will you worship that which I worship. To you your religion, and to me my religion.

God also revealed:

> Say: Do you bid me serve other than God? O fools! ... (reciting to the words) ... Nay, but God must you serve, and be among the thankful![167]

Yaʿqūb b. Ibrāhīm—Muḥammad b. Isḥāq—Saʿīd b. Mīna the *mawlā* of Abū al-Bakhtarī:[168] Al-Walīd b. al-Mughīrah, al-ʿĀṣ b. Wā'il, al-Aswad b. al-Muṭṭalib, and Umayyah b. Khalaf met the Messenger of God and said, "Muḥammad, come and let us worship that which you worship and you worship that which we worship, and we shall make you a partner in all of our undertakings. If what you have brought is better than what we already have, we will be partners with you in it and take our share of it, and if what we have is better than what you have, you shall be partner with us in what we have, and you shall take your share of it." Then God revealed: "Say: O disbelievers ... (reciting) to the end of the [1192]
sūrah.[169]

Satan Casts a False Revelation on the Messenger of God's Tongue

The Messenger of God was eager for the welfare of his people and

167. The verses revealed are 109:1-6 and 39:64-66.
168. Ibn Hishām seems to have omitted this section, although Guillaume has not noticed the fact.
169. 109.

wished to effect a reconciliation with them in whatever ways he could. It is said that he wanted to find a way to do this, and what happened was as follows.[170]

Ibn Ḥumayd—Salamah—Muḥammad b. Isḥāq—Yazīd b. Ziyād al-Madanī—Muḥammad b. Ka'b al-Quraẓī: When the Messenger of God saw how his tribe turned their backs on him and was grieved to see them shunning the message he had brought to them from God, he longed in his soul that something would come to him from God which would reconcile him with his tribe. With his love for his tribe and his eagerness for their welfare it would have delighted him if some of the difficulties which they made for him could have been smoothed out, and he debated with himself and fervently desired such an outcome. Then God revealed:[171]

> By the Star when it sets, your comrade does not err, nor is he deceived; nor does he speak out of (his own) desire . . .

and when he came to the words:

> Have you thought upon al-Lāt and al-'Uzzā and Manāt, the third, the other?

Satan cast on his tongue, because of his inner debates and what he desired to bring to his people, the words:

> These are the high-flying cranes; verily their intercession is accepted with approval.[172]

When Quraysh heard this, they rejoiced and were happy and delighted at the way in which he spoke of their gods, and they listened to him, while the Muslims, having complete trust in their Prophet in respect of the messages which he brought from God, did not suspect him of error, illusion, or mistake. When he came to the prostration, having completed the sūrah, he prostrated himself and the Muslims did likewise, following their Prophet, trusting in the message which he had brought and following his example. Those polytheists of the Quraysh and others who were in the

---

170. This section is also omitted by Ibn Hishām, perhaps because he felt it was discreditable to the Prophet.

171. Sūrah 53; the verses quoted are 1-3 and 19-20.

172. An alternative reading to *turtaḍā* is *turtajā*, meaning, "is to be desired or hoped for."

mosque[173] likewise prostrated themselves because of the reference to their gods which they had heard, so that there was no one in the mosque, believer or unbeliever, who did not prostrate himself. The one exception was al-Walīd b. al-Mughīrah, who was a very old man and could not prostrate himself; but he took a handful of soil from the valley in his hand and bowed over that. Then they all dispersed from the mosque. The Quraysh left delighted by the mention of their gods which they had heard, saying, "Muḥammad has mentioned our gods in the most favorable way possible, stating in his recitation that they are the high-flying cranes and that their intercession is received with approval." [1193]

The news of this prostration reached those of the Messenger of God's Companions who were in Abyssinia and people said, "The Quraysh have accepted Islam." Some rose up to return, while others remained behind. Then Gabriel came to the Messenger of God and said, "Muḥammad, what have you done? You have recited to the people that which I did not bring to you from God, and you have said that which was not said to you." Then the Messenger of God was much grieved and feared God greatly, but God sent down a revelation to him, for He was merciful to him, consoling him and making the matter light for him, informing him that there had never been a prophet or a messenger before him who desired as he desired and wished as he wished but that Satan had cast words into his recitation, as he had cast words on Muḥammad's tongue. Then God cancelled what Satan had thus cast, and established his verses by telling him that he was like other prophets and messengers, and revealed:

> Never did we send a messenger or a prophet before you but that when he recited (the Message) Satan cast words into his recitation *(umniyyah)*.God abrogates what Satan casts. Then God established his verses. God is knower, wise.[174]

---

173. The sacred area around the Ka'bah was not, of course, an Islamic mosque at this period, though the word *masjid,* "place of prostration, mosque," seems to have been applied to it.

174. 22-52. The translation deviates here from that of Pickthall in order to make it correspond with what is required by Ṭabarī's account. The meanings for *tamannā* and *umniyyah,* "recite" and "recitation," are well attested (see *Lisān* s.v. *M-N-Y).* An alternative rendering for this verse would be: "Never did we send a messenger or a prophet before you but that when he formed a wish Satan threw (some vanity) into his desire . . . ."

Thus God removed the sorrow from his Messenger, reassured him about that which he had feared and cancelled the words
[1194] which Satan had cast on his tongue, that their gods were the high-flying cranes whose intercession was accepted with approval. He now revealed, following the mention of "al-Lāt, al-ʿUzza and Manāt, the third, the other," the words:

> Are yours the males and his the females? That indeed were an unfair division! They are but names which you have named, you and your fathers ...

to the words:

> to whom he wills and accepts.[175]

This means, how can the intercession of their gods avail with God?

When Muḥammad brought a revelation from God cancelling what Satan had cast on the tongue of His Prophet, the Quraysh said, "Muḥammad has repented of what he said concerning the position of your gods with God, and has altered it and brought something else." Those two phrases which Satan had cast on the tongue of the Messenger of God were in the mouth of every polytheists, and they became even more ill-disposed and more violent in their persecution of those of them who had accepted Islam and followed the Messenger of God.

Those of the Companions of the Messenger of God who had left Abyssinia upon hearing that Quraysh had accepted Islam by prostrating themselves with the Messenger of God now approached. When they were near Mecca, they heard that the report that the people of Mecca had accepted Islam was false. Not one of them entered Mecca without obtaining protection or entering secretly. Among those who came to Mecca and remained there until they emigrated to al-Madīnah and were present with the Prophet at Badr, were, from the Banū ʿAbd Shams b. ʿAbd Manāf b. Quṣayy, ʿUthmān b. ʿAffān b. Abī al-ʿĀs b. Umayyah, accompanied by his wife Ruqayyah the daughter of the Messenger of God; Abū Hudhayfah b. ʿUtbah b. Rabīʿah b. ʿAbd Shams, accompanied by his
[1195] wife Sahlah bt. Suhayl; together with a number of others number-

175. 53:21-23,26, Ṭabarī explains *ḍīzā*, "unfair," as meaning *ʿawjā*, "crooked."

ing thirty-three men.

Al-Qāsim b. al-Ḥasan—al-Ḥusayn b. Dāūd—Ḥajjā—Abū Ma'shar—Muḥammad b. Ka'b al-Quraẓī and Muḥammad b. Qays: The Messenger of God was sitting in a large gathering of Quraysh, wishing that day that no revelation would come to him from God which would cause them to turn away from him. Then God revealed:

> By the Star when it sets, your comrade does not err, nor is he deceived . . .

and the Messenger of God recited it until he came to:

> Have you thought upon al-Lāt and al-'Uzzā and Manāt, the third, the other?

when Satan cast on his tongue two phrases:

> These are the high flying cranes; verily their intercession is to be desired.[176]

He uttered them and went on to complete the sūrah. When he prostrated himself at the end of the sūrah, the whole company prostrated themselves with him. Al-Walīd b. al-Mughīrah raised some dust to his forehead and bowed over that, since he was a very old man and could not prostrate himself. They were satisfied with what Muḥammad had uttered and said, "We recognize that it is God who gives life and death, who creates and who provides sustenance, but if these gods of ours intercede for us with him, and if you give them a share, we are with you."

That evening Gabriel came to him and reviewed the sūrah with him, and when he reached the two phrases which Satan had cast upon his tongue he said, "I did not bring you these two." Then the Messenger of God said, "I have fabricated things against God and have imputed to Him words which He has not spoken." Then God revealed to him:

> And they indeed strove hard to beguile you away from what we have revealed to you, that you should invent other than it against us . . .

176. Sūrah 53. This version of the false verses has *la-turjā*, "to be desired or hoped for."

to the words:

> and then you would have found no helper against us.[177]

He remained grief-stricken and anxious until the revelation of the verse:

[1196] Never did we send a messenger or a prophet before you . . . to the words . . . God is knower, wise.[178]

When those who had emigrated to Abyssinia heard that all the people of Mecca had accepted Islam, they returned to their clans, saying, "They are more dear to us"; but they found that the people had reversed their decision when God cancelled what Satan had cast upon the Messenger of God's tongue.

The Boycott Is Repealed

Ibn Ḥumayd—Salamah—Ibn Isḥāq.[179] Then a number of the Quraysh took steps to repeal the agreement which the Quraysh had drawn up amongst themselves directed against the Banū Hāshim and the Banū al-Muṭṭalib. The most creditable part in this was played by Hishām b. ʿAmr b. al-Ḥārith al-ʿĀmirī of ʿĀmir b. Luʾayy. He was the son of the maternal half-brother of Naḍlah b. Hāshim b. ʿAbd Manāf, and he went to Zuhayr b. Abī Umayyah b. al-Mughīrah b. ʿAbdallāh b. ʿUmar b. Makhzūm, whose mother was ʿĀtikah bt. ʿAbd al-Muṭṭalib, and said, "Zuhayr, are you content to eat food, wear clothes, and marry women while your maternal uncles are in the condition in which you know them to be, unable to buy or sell, and unable to give or take in marriage? I swear by God that if they were the maternal cousins of Abū al-Ḥakam b. Hishām[180] and you were to call on him to do what he has called on you to do, he would never agree to do it." "For goodness' sake, Hishām," he replied, "What can I do? I am only one man. By God, if I had another man with me I would take steps to repeal it and would continue until I had had it repealed." "You have found

177. 17:73,75.
178. 22:52.
179. Ibn Hishām, *Sīrah*, 247-49.
180. This is the man usually called Abū Jahl, who was one of the most vehement opponents of Muḥammad.

a man," he said. "Who?" he asked. "Myself," he replied. Then Zuhayr said, "Find me a third man."

[1197] So he went to al-Muṭʿim b. ʿAdī b. Nawfal b. ʿAbd Manāf and said to him, "Muṭʿim, are you content that two clans of the Banū ʿAbd Manāf are perishing while you look on,[181] agreeing with Quraysh on the matter? By God, if you allow them to do this, you will find that they will soon do the same to you." He replied, "For goodness' sake, what can I do? I am only one man." "You have found a second," he said. "Who?" he asked. "Myself," he replied. Then he said, "Find me a third." "I have already done so," he replied. "Who?" he asked. "Zuhayr b. Abī Umayyah," he said. Then he said, "Find me a fourth."

So he went to Abū al-Bakhtarī b. Hishām and said the same to him as he had said to al-Muṭʿim b. ʿAdī. He answered, "Is there anyone who will help in this?" "Yes," he said. "Who?" he asked. He said, "Zuhayr b. Abī Umayyah and al-Muṭʿim b. ʿAdī, and I am with you." "Find me a fifth," he said.

Then he went to Zamʿah b. al-Aswad b. al-Muṭṭalib b. Asad, spoke to him, and reminded him of how closely they were related to him and of his duty to them. He said, "Is there anyone who will help in this matter in which you are calling upon me to take part?" "Yes," he replied, and named them.

They promised to meet him at Khaṭm al-Ḥajūn, which is in the high ground above Mecca. When they gathered there, they agreed upon their course of action, and pledged themselves to deal with the document and to have it repealed. Zuhayr said, "I will be the first to begin and will be the first to speak." The next morning they went to their groups, and Zuhayr appeared in a gown, circumambulated the Kaʿbah seven times, and then went up to the people and said, "People of Mecca, shall we eat food, drink drink, and wear clothes while the Banū Hāshim are perishing, neither buying nor selling? By God, I shall not sit down until this unjust [1198] document which severs relationships is torn up." Abū Jahl, who was at one side of the mosque, said, "You lie, by God. It shall not be torn up." Zamʿah b. al-Aswad said, "By God, you are a greater liar. We did not approve of its being written when it was written."

181. ʿAbd Manāf had four sons, ancestors of four clans. The two who are perishing are Hāshim and al-Muṭṭalib. Muṭʿim belongs to a third, Nawfal, and the fourth is ʿAbd Shams.

Then Abū al-Bakhtarī said, "Zamʿah has spoken the truth. We do not approve of what was written in it, and we do not acknowledge it." Then al-Muṭʿim b. ʿAdī said, "You have both spoken the truth, and anyone who says otherwise is lying. We are full of guilt for it before God and for what is written in it." Hishām b. ʿAmr said much the same. Then Abū Jahl said, "This is something which has been decided during the night, and which has been decided elsewhere than in this place." Abū Ṭālib was sitting at one side of the mosque. Al-Muṭʿim b. ʿAdī went up to the document to tear it up, and found that it had been eaten by termites except for the part on which had been written, "In your name, O God." These were the words with which the Quraysh prefaced their documents when they wrote anything.

I have heard that the writer of the document which the Quraysh drew up against the Messenger of God and his relatives from the Banū Hāshim and the Banū al-Muṭṭalib was Manṣūr b. ʿIkrimah b. Hāshim b. ʿAbd Manāf b. ʿAbd al-Dār b. Quṣayy. (For having done so) his hand withered.

The Messenger of God Is Subjected to Further Insults

The rest of the emigrants remained in Abyssinia until the Messenger of God sent ʿAmr b. Umayyah al-Ḍamrī to the Negus for them. He transported them in two ships and brought them to the Messenger of God while he was in Khaybar after al-Ḥudaybiyah. The total number of those who came in the two ships was sixteen men.[182]

The Messenger of God continued to live in Mecca with Quraysh, calling them to God secretly and openly, enduring their molestation of him, their calling him a liar, and their derision of him. Things came to such a pitch that one of them, it is said,
[1199] would throw a sheep's womb upon him as he was praying or would throw it into his cooking pot when it was set up for him. Finally, I have been told, he took a large stone and sheltered behind it when he prayed.

Ibn Ḥumayd—Salamah—Ibn Isḥāq—ʿUmar b. ʿAbdallāh b. ʿUr-

182. This final return was early in the year 7/628. Many others had returned before Muḥammad left Mecca.

wah b. al- Zubayr—'Urwah b. al-Zubayr:[183] The Messenger of God used to bring this out on a stick when it was thrown into his house and stand at his door and say, "Banū 'Abd Manāf, what protection is this?" Then he would throw it into the road.

The Deaths of Abū Ṭālib and Khadījah

After this Abū Ṭālib and Khadījah died in a single year.

Ibn Ḥumayd—Salamah—Ibn Isḥāq:[184] This was three years before his emigration to al-Madīnah. Their death was a great affliction to the Messenger of God. This is because after the death of Abū Ṭālib, Quraysh went to greater lengths in molesting him than they had ever done during his lifetime. One of them even poured dust upon his head.

Ibn Ḥumayd—Salamah—Ibn Isḥāq—Hishām b. 'Urwah—his father: When that foolish person poured dust upon the Messenger of God's head, he went into his house with the dust still on his head. One of his daughters stood next to him washing off the dust and weeping, while the Messenger of God said to her, "Do not weep, daughter, for God will protect your father." The Messenger of God used to say, "Quraysh never did anything unpleasant to me until Abū Ṭālib died."

The Messenger of God Goes to al-Ṭā'if

When Abū Ṭālib died, the Messenger of God went to al-Ṭā'if to seek support and protection against his own people from Thaqīf. It is said that he went to them alone.

Ibn Ḥumayd—Salamah—Ibn Isḥāq—Yazīd b. Ziyād—Muḥam- [1200]
mad b. Ka'b al-Quraẓī:[185] When the Messenger of God reached al-Ṭā'if, he went to a group of men of Thaqīf who were at that time the chiefs and nobles of the tribe. They were three brothers, 'Abd Yālayl b. 'Amr b. 'Umayr, Mas'ud b. 'Amr b. 'Umayr, and Ḥabīb b. 'Amr. b. 'Umayr. One of them had a wife from Quraysh, from

---

183. Ibn Hishām, *Sīrah,* 277.

184. Ibid., 277.

185. Ibid., 279-81. Thaqīf was the dominant tribe in al-Ṭā' if. They had been forced into an alliance with the Meccans, and Muḥammad may have hoped that anti-Meccan feeling would lead men to support him.

the Banū Jumaḥ. He sat down with them and called them to God, and spoke to them of the requests which he had come to them to make, (that is,) that they should come to his aid in defense of Islam and take his side against those of his own tribe who opposed him. One of them said, "If God has sent you, I will tear off the covering of the Kaʿbah;" another said, "Could God find no-one but you to send?" and the third said, "By God, I shall never say a single word to you, for if you are a messenger from God as you say, you are too important for me to reply to you, and if you are lying against God, it is not right for me to speak to you."

The Messenger of God rose up and left them, despairing of getting any good out of Thaqīf. I have been told that he said to them, "If that is your decision, do not tell anyone about it," for he did not want his tribe to hear about this matter and be emboldened against him. However, they did not comply with his request, but incited against him their ignorant rabble and their slaves, who reviled him and shouted at him until a crowd gathered and forced him to take refuge in a garden belonging to ʿUtbah b. Rabīʿah and Shaybah b. Rabīʿah, who were in it at the time.[186] Those of the rabble of Thaqīf who had followed him went back, and he went to the shade of a trellised vine and sat there while the two sons of Rabīʿah watched him, seeing what he had to endure from the rabble of Thaqīf.

[1201] I have been told that the Messenger of God met that woman from the Banū Jumaḥ[187] and said to her, "What have I had to endure from your husband's relatives?" I have been told that when he felt secure the Messenger of God said, "O God, I make complaint to You of the weakness of my power, the fewness of my expedients, and the contempt in which I am held by men. O most merciful of the merciful, You are the Lord of the oppressed, and You are my Lord. To whom will You entrust me? To a stranger who will regard me with displeasure or to an enemy to whom You have given power over me? If You are not angry with me, I do not care, but Your protection is wide enough for me. I take refuge in the light of Your countenance by which the darkness is illumi-

186. These were two Meccans of the clan of ʿAbd Shams. Many wealthy Meccans had property in al-Ṭāʾif because, being higher up in the mountains, it had a much better climate.

187. The wife of one of the leaders of Thaqīf with whom he had been speaking.

nated, and in which this world and the next are rightly ordered, refuge from the descent of Your anger upon me or the falling of Your wrath upon me. You shall have satisfaction from me until You are content. There is no might and no power except in You."

When the two sons of Rabīʿah, ʿUtbah and Shaybah, saw what had happened to him, they were moved by pity for their kinsman[188] and, calling a Christian slave of theirs named ʿAddās, they said to him, "Take a bunch of these grapes, put it in this dish, take it to that man, and tell him to eat of it." ʿAddās did so, went up to him and put it before the Messenger of God. When he stretched out his hand he said, "In the name of God," and then ate. ʿAddās looked him in the face and said, "By God, these words are not used by the people of this country." The Messenger of God said to him, "From what country do you come, ʿAddās, and what is your religion?" He replied, "I am a Christian, from the people of Nineveh." The Messenger of God said, "From the town of the
righteous man Jonah the son of Mattā?"[189] "How do you know [1202]
about Jonah the son of Mattā?" he asked. The Messenger of God replied, "He is my brother. He was a prophet, and I am a prophet." ʿAddās bent down before the Messenger of God, kissing his head, his hands, and his feet. The two sons of Rabīʿah said one to the other, "As far as your slave is concerned, Muḥammad has corrupted your slave for you." When ʿAddās came back to them they said to him, "Woe betide you, ʿAddās, what made you kiss that man's head, hands, and feet?" He replied, "Masters, there is no one better in the world than that man. He has told me something which none but a prophet knows." They said, "Woe betide you, ʿAddās, do not let him turn you away from your religion. Your religion is better than his."

The Messenger of God Returns to Mecca

When the Messenger of God despaired of getting any positive response from Thaqīf, he left al-Ṭā'if to return to Mecca. When he was at Nakhlah, he rose in the middle of the night to pray, and, as God has told, a number of the jinn passed by. Muḥammad b. Isḥāq says that he was told that they were seven jinn from Naṣībīn of

188. As being all descendants of ʿAbd Manāf.
189. In the Bible his father is called Amittai.

the Yemen.[190] They listened to him, and when he had completed his prayer they went back to their people to warn them, having believed and responded to what they had heard. God mentioned their story when he said:

> And when we inclined toward you certain of the jinn, who wished to hear the Qur'ān and, when they were in its presence, said: Give ear! and when it was finished, turned back to their people, warning. They said: O our people! We have heard a scripture which has been revealed after Moses, confirming that which was before it, guiding to the truth and a right road. O our people! respond to God's summoner and believe in him. He will forgive you some of your sins and guard you from a painful doom.[191]

God also said:

> Say: It is revealed to me that a company of the jinn gave ear, and they said: It is a marvellous Qur'ān.

[1203] Muḥammad (Ibn Isḥāq) says that he has heard that the names of the jinn who listened to the revelation were Ḥassā, Massā, Shāṣir, Nāṣir, Aynā al-Ard, Aynayn, and al-Aḥqam.[192]

Then the Messenger of God came back to Mecca, and found that its people were even more determined to oppose him and to abandon his religion, except for a few weak people who believed in him. Some say that when the Messenger of God left al-Ṭā'if for Mecca[193] a certain Meccan passed by, and the Messenger of God

190. This phrase seems incorrect, since the well-known Naṣībīn is on the border between eastern Syria and Turkey. Another version of the story reads "on their way from Naṣībīn to the Yemen" (see Leiden text, footnote).

191. 46:29-31. Ṭabarī gives only the beginning and the end of this passage, but it has been given in full to make the story more intelligible. The following verse is 72:1.

192. These names are not vocalized in the text and the forms given here are hypothetical; the fifth and sixth names are particularly dubious.

193. This story implies (though there is no explicit statement) that following the death of Abū Ṭālib, Muḥammad had been deprived of the protection of his own clan of Hāshim by the new chief Abū Lahab. For this reason he had to obtain the protection of another clan before he could return to Mecca in safety. Al-Akhnas b. Sharīq, though technically a confederate from al-Ṭā'if, appears to have been the leading man of the Meccan clan of Zuhrah. Suhayl b. 'Amr was chief of the clan of 'Āmir. When he speaks of Banū Ka'b he means all the main clans of Quraysh except his own and al-Ḥārith b. Fihr (see table in the Introduction, p.xxx). Al-Muṭ'im

said, "Will you deliver a message which I entrust to you?" He agreed, and he said, "Go to al-Akhnas b. Sharīq and say to him, 'Muḥammad asks you if you will give him protection so that he can deliver the message of his Lord.' The man went to him and delivered the message, and al-Akhnas replied, "The confederate does not give protection against the men of pure blood." He went back to the Prophet and gave him this reply. Muḥammad then asked him if he would go back again, and when he indicated that he would, said, "Go to Suhayl b. ʿAmr and say to him, 'Muḥammad asks you if you will give him protection so that he can deliver the message of his Lord.'" He went to him and delivered the message, and he replied, "The Banū ʿĀmir b. Luʾayy do not give protection against the Banū Kaʿb." The man went back to the Prophet and gave him this reply. Muḥammad asked him if he would go back yet again, and when he indicated that he would, he said, "Go to al-Muṭʿim b. ʿAdī and say to him, 'Muḥammad asks if you will give him protection so that he can deliver the message of his Lord.'" Al-Muṭʿim replied, "Yes, let him enter."

The man went back and told him this, and the next morning al-Muṭʿim b. ʿAdī, his sons, and his brother's sons appeared wearing their weapons and entered the mosque. When Abū Jahl saw him, he said, "Are you offering protection to someone or following a call to arms?" "I am offering protection," he said. Abū Jahl replied, "We shall protect whomever you protect." The Prophet entered Mecca and remained there. One day he went into the sacred mosque while the polytheists were by the Kaʿbah. When Abū
Jahl saw him he said, "This is your prophet, Banū ʿAbd Manāf."[194] [1204]
To this ʿUtbah b. Rabīʿah said, "Is there anything wrong with there being a prophet or a king from among us?" The Prophet was told of this or heard it, and he went to them and said, "As for you, ʿUtbah b. Rabīʿah, by God, you were not angered on behalf of God or

b. ʿAdī was head of the clan of Nawfal, and had been one of those instrumental in ending the boycott. In his translation, Guillaume regards the whole story as derived by Ṭabarī from Ibn Isḥāq, but in this he appears to be mistaken. The introductory words "some say..." (*dhakara baʿḍuhum*) indicate a different unspecified source. It is unlikely, too, that Ibn Hishām would have omitted the story at this point (Ibn Hishām, *Sīrah,* 281), if it had been present in Ibn Isḥāq, since he gives the gist of it in his own additional note at an earlier point (Ibid., 251).

194. The designation Banū ʿAbd Manāf includes the clans of ʿAbd Shams and Nawfal as well as Hāshim and al-Muṭṭalib. Pride in his ancestry makes ʿUtbah b. Rabīʿah (of ʿAbd Shams) defend Banū ʿAbd Manāf against the taunt of Abū Jahl.

his Prophet, but were angered on behalf of your own pride; and as for you, Abū Jahl b. Hishām, by God, not long will pass before you laugh little and weep much; and as for you, council *(mala')* of Quraysh, by God, not long will pass before you will enter unwillingly into that which you dislike."

The Messenger of God Preaches to the Arab Tribes

The Messenger of God used to appear at the times of pilgrimage before the Arab tribes, summoning them to God, informing them that he himself was a prophet sent by God, and asking them to believe his words and defend him so that he might make manifest the message from God he had been sent to convey.

Ibn Ḥumayd—Salamah—Muḥammad b. Isḥāq—Ḥusayn b. 'Abdallāh b. 'Ubaydallāh b. 'Abbās:[195] I heard Rabī'ah b. 'Abbād telling my father: "I was in Minā with my father when I was a young man while the Messenger of God was stopping at the encampments of the Arab tribes and saying, Banū so-and-so, I am God's Messenger to you, commanding you to worship God and not to associate anything with Him, to cast off whatever idols you worship other than Him, to believe in me, and the truth of my message, and to defend me so that I may make manifest the message of God I have been sent to convey".

Behind him was a freshly washed man with a squint, with two locks of hair, wearing an 'Adanī robe. When the Messenger of God had completed his speech and his appeal, the man would say, "Banū so-and-so, this man is calling upon you to cast off al-Lāt and
[1205] al-'Uzzā from your necks, both you and your confederates from the jinn of the Banū Mālik b. Uqaysh, and to accept the heresy and the error which he has brought; so do not obey him and do not listen to him." I said to my father, "Father, who is that man who is following Muḥammad and contradicting what he says?" He answered, "That is his uncle, 'Abd al-'Uzzā Abū Lahab b. 'Abd al-Muṭṭalib."

Ibn Ḥumayd—Salamah—Muḥammad b. Isḥāq—Muḥammad b. Muslim b. Shihāb al-Zuhrī: The Messenger of God went to the Kindah—among whom was one of their chiefs called Mulayh—

195. From here to p. 1224 Ṭabarī follows Ibn Hishām, *Sīrah*, 282–301, with some omissions.

in their encampments, and summoned them to God and offered himself to them, but they refused him.

Ibn Ḥumayd—Salamah—Muḥammad b. Isḥāq—Muḥammad b. ʿAbd al-Raḥmān b. ʿAbdallāh b. Ḥuṣayn: He went to a clan of Kalb called the Banū ʿAbdallāh in their encampments, summoned them to God and offered himself to them, and finally said, "Banū ʿAbdallāh, God has given your ancestor an excellent name." However, they did not accept what he offered them.

Ibn Ḥumayd—Salamah—Muḥammad b. Isḥāq—one of his companions—ʿAbdallāh b. Kaʿb b. Mālik: The Messenger of God went to the Banū Ḥanīfah in their encampments, summoned them to God and offered himself to them, but not one of the Arabs gave him an uglier answer than they.

Ibn Ḥumayd—Salamah—Muḥammad b. Isḥāq and Muḥammad b. Muslim b. Shihāb al-Zuhrī: He went to the Banū ʿĀmir b. Ṣaʿṣaʿah, called them to God and offered himself to them. One
of them called Bayḥarah b. Firās said, "By God, if I could take [1206]
this young man from Quraysh I could conquer all the Arabs with him." Then he said, "Do you think that if we follow you and God gives you victory over your opponents we shall have the command after you?" He replied, "Command belongs to God, who places it where He wills." Bayḥarah said, "Are we to expose our throats to the Arabs in your defense, and when you are victorious the command will go to someone else? We do not need your religion." So they refused him. When the pilgrims dispersed, the Banū ʿĀmir (b. Ṣaʿṣaʿah) went back to one of their shaykhs who was so old that he was unable to participate in the pilgrimage with them. On returning to him they would tell him what had happened during the pilgrimage. In this particular year he asked them on their return what had happened during the pilgrimage, and they said, "A young man from the Quraysh, one of the Banū ʿAbd al-Muṭṭalib, who claimed that he was a prophet, came to us and called upon us to defend him, stand with him, and bring him back with us to our country." The old man put his hand to his head and said, "Banū ʿĀmir, is there any way we can put this right? Can we regain our lost opportunity? By him in whose hand my soul rests, no descendant of Ishmael has ever falsified this. It is indeed the truth! What happened to your ability to judge him?"

The Messenger of God continued in this manner. Whenever

people gathered for the pilgrimage, he would go to them, summon the tribes to God and to Islam, and offer them himself together with the right guidance and mercy which he had brought to them
[1207] from God. Whenever he heard of an arrival who had name and nobility among the Arabs, he would give special attention to him, summon him to God, and offer him his message.

The First Madīnans Said to Have Accepted Islam

Ibn Ḥumayd—ʿĀṣim b. ʿUmar b. Qatādah al-Ẓafarī—some shaykhs of his people: Suwayd b. Ṣāmit the brother of the Banū ʿAmr b. ʿAwf came to Mecca on the pilgrimage or the *ʿumrah.* [196] Among themselves Suwayd's people called him al-Kāmil (the perfect one) on account of his steadfastness, his poetry, his descent, and his nobility. He is the author of the following lines:

Many a man is there whom you call a friend, but if
 you knew
what he says behind your back, his slanders would
 grieve you.
His words are like fat when he is in your presence,
 but when you are absent they are a sword pointed
 at the base of your throat.
His outward appearance delights you, but beneath his skin
 is false slander which cuts through the sinews of your
 back.
His eyes show you what he is concealing
 for there is no concealing hatred and the malignant
 glance.
[1208] Aid me with good deeds, for you have been weakening me
 for too long;
 the best friends are those who aid without weakening.

He also composed many other poems.

---

196. The *ʿumrah* or "lesser pilgrimage" consisted of those rites of the full pilgrimage (*ḥajj*) which took place in Mecca itself, and it could be performed at any time of the year. Banū ʿAmr b. ʿAwf was an important clan of the tribe of al-Aws in al-Madīnah. The phrase "brother of (a clan)" is common in al-Madīnah and seems to be equivalent to "member of" the clan; it is perhaps to be explained by the persistence in al-Madīnah of matrilineal kinship; see Watt, *Muhammad at Medina*, 378–85, etc.

When the Messenger of God heard of his arrival, he was attentive to him and summoned him to God and to Islam. Suwayd said to him, "Perhaps what is with you is like what is with me." The Messenger of God asked, "What is with you?" "The book of Luqmān," he replied, meaning the wisdom of Luqmān.[197] The Messenger of God said, "Expound it to me." He expounded it to him, and he said, "This speech is good, but I have a speech better than this, a Qur'ān which God has revealed to me, guidance and light." Then the Messenger of God recited the Qur'ān to him and summoned him to Islam. He was close to accepting, and said, "This is indeed an excellent saying." He left him and went back to al-Madīnah, and soon afterwards was killed by the Khazraj. His clan used to say that he was a Muslim when he was killed; his death took place before (the battle of) Bu'āth.[198]

Ibn Ḥumayd—Salamah—Muḥammad b. Isḥāq—al-Ḥuṣayn b. 'Abd al-Raḥmān b. 'Amr b. Sa'd b. Mu'ādh, brother of the Banū 'Abd al-Ashhal—Maḥmūd b. Labīd, brother of the Banū 'Abd al-Ashhal: When Abū al-Ḥaysar Anas b. Rāfi' came to Mecca accompanied by some young men of the Banū 'Abd al-Ashhal,[199] including Iyās b. Mu'ādh, seeking an alliance with the Quraysh against their fellow citizens from the Khazraj, the Messenger of God heard of their arrival, came to them and sat down with them. He said to them, "Would you like something better than what you have come for?" "What is that?" they asked. He said, "I am the Messenger of God whom He has sent to His servants that I may call them to God, so that they may worship God and not associate anything with Him. He has revealed the Book to me." Then he told them about Islam and recited the Qur'ān to them. Iyās [1209] b. Mu'ādh, who was a young lad, said, "My people, by God, this is better than what we came for." Abū al-Ḥaysar Anas b. Rāfi' took up a handful of dust from the valley, threw it in the face of Iyās b.

197. Luqmān was a legendary wise man of Arab tradition, also mentioned in the Qur'ān, Sūrah 31.

198. The battle of Bu'āth between two factions of the inhabitants of al-Madīnah, and involving nearly all of them, occurred about the year a.d. 617; see *EI*², s.v. Bu'āth. The story illustrates the rivalry between clans and tribes to claim priority in the acceptance of Islam.

199. Banū 'Abd al-Ashhal was another important clan of the tribe of al-Aws. The story has been handed down in the clan as a claim to have had one of the first Muslims in al-Madīnah.

Mu'ādh, and said, "Enough of that. By my life, we did not come here for this." Iyās remained silent, the Messenger of God rose up to leave them, and they went back to al-Madīnah, where the battle of Bu'āth took place between the Aws and the Khazraj. Iyās b. Mu'ādh died soon afterwards.

Maḥmūd b. Labīd: Those of my clan who were with him when he died told me that they heard him saying continually until he died, "There is no deity but God," "God is very great," "Praise be to God," "Glory be to God." They had no doubt that he died a Muslim, having embraced Islam at that meeting when he heard the Messenger of God saying what he said.

The First Deputation from al-Madīnah

When God wished to make His religion victorious, to render His Prophet mighty, and to fulfil His promise to him, the Messenger of God went out during that pilgrimage in which he met the group of the Anṣār,[200] and appeared before the Arab tribes as he had been doing in every pilgrimage season. While he was at al-'Aqabah, he met a party of the Khazraj to whom God wished good.

Ibn Ḥumayd—Salamah—Muḥammad b. Isḥāq—'Āṣim b. 'Umar b. Qatādah—some shaykhs of his tribe: When the Messenger of God met them he said to them, "Who are you?" They said, "We are a group of the Khazraj." "Mawlās[201] of the Jews?" he asked. "Yes," they said. "Will you not sit down so that I may speak to you?" he asked. "Certainly," they said. So they sat down with him, and he summoned them to God, expounded Islam to them, and recited the Qur'ān to them.

One of the things which God had done for them in order to pre-
[1210] pare them for Islam was that the Jews lived with them in their land. The Jews were people of scripture and knowledge, while the Khazraj were polytheists and idolaters. They had gained the mastery over the Jews in their land, and whenever any dispute arose

200. The Anṣār ("helpers") are the Muslims of al-Madīnah as a whole, but the name, given in honor for their support of Muḥammad, was not conferred until after this date.

201. *Mawālī* is the plural of *mawlā*, which can mean either "client" or "patron"; the latter would be more appropriate here, since most of the Arab clans of al-Madīnah were now politically stronger than the Jewish groups allied with them, as is indicated below.

among them the Jews would say to them, "A prophet will be sent soon. His time is at hand. We shall follow him, and with him as our leader we shall kill you as 'Ād and Iram[202] were killed." When the Messenger of God spoke to this group of people and called them to God, they said to one another, "Take note! This, by God, is the prophet with whom the Jews are menacing you. Do not let them be before you in accepting him." They responded to his call, believed in the truth of his message, and accepted the Islam which he expounded to them, saying, "We have left our people behind us, and no people is as divided by enmity and malice as they are. Perhaps God will reunite them by means of you;[203] we shall go to them, summon them to your proposals, and expound to them this religion which we have accepted from you. If God reunites them in it, there will be no man mightier than you."

Then they left the Messenger of God to go back to their country, believing and accepting the truth of his message. I have been told that they were six men of the Khazraj; from the Banū al-Najjār, who are Taym Allāh, in particular from the Banū Mālik b. al-Najjār b. Tha'labah b. 'Amr b. al-Khazraj b. Ḥārithah b. Tha'labah b. 'Amr b. 'Āmir: As'ad b. Zurārah b. 'Udas b. 'Ubayd b. Tha'labah b. Ghanm b. Mālik b. al-Najjār, who is Abū Umāmah, and 'Awf b. al-Ḥārith b. Rifā'ah b. Sawād b. Mālik b. Ghanm b. Mālik b. al-Najjār, who is Ibn 'Afrā'; from the Banū Zurayq b. 'Āmir b. 'Abd [1211]
Ḥārithah b. Mālik b. Ghaḍb b. Jusham b. al-Khazraj b. Ḥārithah b. Tha'labah b. 'Amr b. 'Amr b. 'Āmir: Rāfi' b. Mālik b. al-'Ajlān b. 'Amr b. 'Āmir b. Zurayq; from the Banū Salimah b. Sa'd b. 'Alī b. Asad b. Sāridah b. Tazīd b. Jusham b. al-Khazraj b. Ḥārithah b. Tha'labah b. 'Amr b. Āmir, in particular from the Banū Sawād: Quṭbah b. 'Āmir b. Ḥadīdah b. 'Amr b. Sawād b. Ghanm b. Ka'b b. Salimah; from the (subclan) Banū Ḥarām b. Ka'b b. Ghanm b. Ka'b b. Salimah: 'Uqbah b. 'Āmir b. Nābī b. Zayd b. Ḥarām; and from the (subclan) Banū 'Ubayd b. 'Adī b. Ghanm b. Ka'b b. Salimah: Jābir b. 'Abdallāh b. Ri'āb b. al-Nu'mān b. Sinān b. 'Ubayd.

When they went back to their people in al-Madīnah, they told them about the Messenger of God and summoned them to Islam,

202. Two Arab tribes mentioned in the Qur'ān, but extinct by this time.

203. The hope of overcoming the divisions in al-Madīnah which had reached a climax in the battle of Bu'āth (n. 176), was an important motive for the acceptance of Islam there.

so that it spread among them, and there was not a single dwelling among the dwellings of the Anṣār in which the Messenger of God was not spoken of.

The First Pledge of al-ʿAqabah

The following year, twelve of the Anṣār came on the pilgrimage and met the Messenger of God at al-ʿAqabah, this being the first al-ʿAqabah, and took an oath of allegiance to him according to the terms of the "pledge of women."[204] This was before the duty of making war was laid upon them.

[1212] They were; from the Banū al-Najjār: Asʿad b. Zurārah b. ʿUdas b. ʿUbayd b. Thaʿlabah b. Ghanm b. Mālik b. al-Najjār, who is Abū Umāmah, ʿAwf and Muʿādh, sons of al-Ḥārith b. Rifāʿah b. Sawād b. Mālik b. Ghanm b. Mālik b. al-Najjār, who are the sons of ʿAfrāʾ; from the Banū Zurayq b. ʿĀmir: Rāfiʿ b. Mālik b. al-ʿAjlān b. ʿAmr b. ʿĀmir b. Zurayq and Dhakwān b. ʿAbd Qays b. Khaldah b. Mukhallad b. ʿĀmir b. Zurayq; from the Banū ʿAwf b. al-Khazraj: from the (subclan) Banū Ghanm b. ʿAwf, who are al-Qawāqil, ʿUbādah b. al-Ṣāmit b. Qays b. Aṣram b. Fihr b. Thaʿlabah b. Ghanm b. ʿAwf b. al-Khazraj and Abū ʿAbd al-Raḥmān, who is Yazīd b. Thaʿlabah b. Khazmah b. Aṣram b. ʿAmr b. ʿAmmārah, one of the Banū Ghudaynah of the tribe of Balī, a confederate of theirs; from the Banū Sālim b. ʿAwf b. ʿAmr b. ʿAwf b. al-Khazraj: ʿAbbās b. ʿUbādah b. Naḍlah b. Mālik b. al-ʿAjlān b. Zayd b. Ghanm b. Sālim b. ʿAwf; from the Banū Salimah, from the (subclan) Banū Ḥarām: ʿUqbah b. ʿĀmir b. Nābī b. Zayd b. Ḥarām b.
[1213] Kaʿb b. Ghanm b. Kaʿb b. Salimah; from the (subclan) Banū Sawād, Quṭbah b. ʿĀmir b. Ḥadīdah b. ʿAmr b. Sawād b. Ghanm b. Kaʿb b. Salimah. From (the tribe of) al-Aws b. Ḥārithah b. Thaʿlabah b. ʿAmr b. ʿĀmir, from the clan of the Banū ʿAbd al-Ashhal, there was present Abū al-Haytham b. al-Tayyihān, whose name is Mālik, a confederate of theirs, and from (the clan of) the Banū ʿAmr b. ʿAwf: ʿUwaym b. Sāʿidah b. Ṣalʿajah, a confederate of theirs.

---

204. This was a pledge to accept and practice the religion of Islam, but without any undertaking to protect Muḥammad. It is called "the pledge of women" because in Sūrah 60:12 Muḥammad is told to require something like this from believing women wanting to become Muslims. A modified version of the Qurʾānic requirements is given below on p.1213.

Ibn Ḥumayd—Salamah—Muḥammad b. Isḥāq—Yazīd b. Abī Ḥabīb—Marthad b. ʿAbdallāh al-Yazanī–Abū ʿAbdallāh ʿAbd al-Raḥmān b. ʿUsaylah al-Ṣunājī—ʿUbādah b. al-Ṣāmit: I was among those who were present at the first al-ʿAqabah. There were twelve of us, and we took an oath of allegiance to him according to the terms of the "pledge of women," this being before the duty of making war was laid upon us. The terms were that we should not associate anything with God, should not steal, should not commit adultery, should not kill our children, should not produce any lie we have devised between our hands and feet, and should not disobey him in what was proper. If we fulfilled this, we should have paradise, and if we committed any of these sins, we should be punished with the prescribed penalties in this world, which would be an expiation for them, while if we concealed them to the Day of Resurrection, then the matter was in God's hands; if He wished, He would punish us, and if He wished He would forgive us.

Ibn Ḥumayd—Salamah—Ibn Isḥāq—Ibn Shihāb—ʿĀʾidh Allāh b. ʿAbdallāh Abū Idrīs al-Khawlānī—ʿUbādah b. al-Ṣāmit—the Prophet: A similar account.

Islam Begins to Spread in al-Madīnah

Ibn Ḥumayd—Salamah—Ibn Isḥāq: When they left the Messenger of God he sent with them Muṣʿab b. ʿUmayr b. Hāshim b. ʿAbd [1214] Manāf b. ʿAbd al-Dār b. Quṣayy, commanding him to teach them to recite the Qurʾān, to teach them Islam, and to instruct them in their religion. In al-Madīnah Muṣʿab was called "al-Muqriʾ" (the Qurʾān reciter) and lodged with Asʿad b. Zurārah b. ʿUdas Abū Umāmah.

Ibn Ḥumayd—Salamah—Muḥammad b. Isḥāq—ʿUbaydallāh b. al-Mughīrah b. Muʿayqīb and ʿAbdallāh b. Abī Bakr b. Muḥammad b. ʿAmr b. Ḥazm: Asʿad b. Zurārah went out with Muṣʿab b. ʿUmayr to take him to the dwellings of the Banū ʿAbd al-Ashhal and the Banū Ẓafar. Saʿd b. Muʿādh b. al-Nuʿmān b. Imruʾ al-Qays was the son of Asʿad b. Zurārah's maternal aunt. Asʿad took Muṣʿab into one of the gardens of the Banū Ẓafar by a well called Biʾr Marq, and the two sat down there, while some of those who had become Muslims gathered around them. Saʿd b. Muʿādh and Usayd b. Ḥuḍayr were at that time the two chiefs of their clan, the

Banū ʿAbd al-Ashhal, and both of them were polytheists according to the religion of their people. When they heard of the arrival of Asʿad and Muṣʿab, Saʿd b. Muʿādh said to Usayd b. Ḥuḍayr, "My excellent friend, go to those two men who have come to our quarter to make fools of our weaker members, drive them off, and forbid them to return to our quarter. If it were not that, as you know, Asʿad b. Zurārah is related to me, I would do it for you, but he is my maternal aunt's son, and I cannot tackle him in any way."

Usayd b. Ḥuḍayr took his javelin and went up to them. When Asʿad b. Zurārah saw him he said to Muṣʿab, "This is the chief of his clan who has come to you, so be true to God in dealing with him." Muṣʿab answered, "If he sits down I will speak to him." Usayd stood by them with a grim expression on his face and said,
[1215] "Why have you come to us to make fools of our weaker members? Depart from us, if you set any value on your lives." Muṣʿab said to him, "Why do you not sit down and listen? If you like anything which we say, you can accept it, and if not, then what you dislike will have been removed from you." Usayd replied, "You have spoken fairly," planted his javelin in the ground and sat down with them. Muṣʿab spoke to him of Islam and recited the Qur'ān to him. It is reported that the two (Muṣʿab and Asʿad) said of this, "By God, we recognized Islam in (Usayd's) face, in its radiance and easiness, before he spoke." Then (Usayd) said, "How fair and beautiful is this. What do you do when you wish to enter this religion?" The two (Asʿad and Muṣʿab) replied, "Wash, purify yourself, pronounce the *shahādah* of Truth and then pray two *rakʿahs*."[205]

Usayd rose up, washed himself, purified himself, pronounced the *shahādah* of truth, and then rose and performed two *rakʿahs*. After this he said, "I have come from a man not one of whose clan, if he were to follow you, would lag behind him. I shall send him to you now. His name is Saʿd b. Muʿādh." He took his javelin and went to Saʿd and his people, who were sitting in their assembly. When Saʿd b. Muʿādh saw him coming he said, "I swear, by God, that Usayd b. Ḥuḍayr is coming back to you with a differ-

205. The *shahādah* is the "witnessing" that "there is no deity but God, Muḥammad is the Messenger of God." A *rak'ah* is a cycle of actions and words constituting part of the prayer or formal worship (*ṣalāt*). Each *ṣalāt* has two, three, or four *rak'ahs*, according to the time of day, as well as an introduction and a conclusion.

ent face from that with which he left you." When Usayd stood by the assembly, Sa'd said to him, "What did you do?" He answered, "I spoke to the two men, and I did not find any harm in them. I forbade them to come here, and they said, 'We will do what you wish.' However I have been told that the Banū Ḥārithah[206] have come out against As'ad b. Zurārah in order to kill him; they want to show that you cannot protect your kin, for they know that he is your maternal aunt's son."

Sa'd rose in anger and in haste, being alarmed by what Usayd had told him about the Banū Ḥārithah. He took the javelin from Usayd's hand, saying, "By God, I think that you are useless," and went up to As'ad and Muṣ'ab. When he saw that they were at ease, he realized that Usayd had only wanted him to listen to them. He [1216]
stood by them with a grim expression on his face, and then said to As'ad b. Zurārah, "Abū Umāmah, if we were not related, you would not seek to do this to me, coming to us in our dwellings with a message which we do not want." As'ad had said to Muṣ'ab, "By God, Muṣ'ab, there has come to you the acknowledged chief of his clan, no two of whom will oppose you if he follows you." Accordingly, Muṣ'ab said to Sa'd, "Will you not sit and listen? If you are pleased with anything or desire it, you can accept it, and if you do not like it we shall take away from you that which you dislike." Sa'd replied, "You have spoken justly," stuck the javelin into the ground and sat down. Then Muṣ'ab expounded Islam to him and recited the Qur'ān to him. The two (Muṣ'ab and As'ad) said of this, "We recognized Islam in (Sa'd's) face, in its radiance and easiness, before he spoke of it." Then Sa'd said, "What do you do when you accept Islam and enter into this religion?" They said to him, "Wash, purify yourself, pronounce the *shahādah* of truth and pray two *rak'ahs.*"

He rose up, washed himself, purified himself, pronounced the *shahādah* of truth and prayed two *rak'ahs.* Then he took his javelin and headed for his people's assembly accompanied by Usayd b. Ḥuḍayr. When his people saw him coming, they said to one another, "We swear, by God, that Sa'd is coming back to you with a different face from that with which he left you." When Sa'd stood by them he said, "Banū 'Abd al-Ashhal, what do you recog-

206. A clan whose ancestor Ḥārithah was reckoned to be a brother of 'Abd al-Ashhal.

nize my position to be amongst you?" They replied, "You are our chief, the best of us in judgement and the most blessed of us in spirit." Then he said, "It is forbidden to me to speak to any man or woman of you until you believe in God and in His Messenger."

By that evening there was not a man or woman in the dwellings of the Banū ʿAbd al-Ashhal who had not accepted Islam. Asʿad and Muṣʿab went back to Asʿad b. Zurārah's house, and Muṣʿab remained with him calling people to Islam until there was not a dwelling place among the dwellings of the Anṣār in which
[1217] there were not Muslim men and women, except for those in the dwellings of the Banū Umayyah b. Zayd, Khaṭmah, Wā'il, and Wāqif; these were the group Aws Allāh, of (the tribe of al-Aws b. Ḥārithah.[207] The reason for this was that Abū Qays b. al-Aslat, whose name was Ṣayfī, was among them. He was their poet and their leader, whom they used to heed and obey. He caused them to hold back from Islam, and continued in this course until the Messenger of God had emigrated to al-Madinah and the battles of the first Badr, Uḥud, and the Trench had taken place.

The Second Pledge of al-ʿAqabah

After this Muṣʿab b. ʿUmayr went back to Mecca. Some of the Muslim Anṣār went on the pilgrimage together with polytheist pilgrims from their people, and when they came to Mecca they agreed to meet the Messenger of God at al-ʿAqabah in the middle of the days of *al-tashrīq.*[208] Thus God wished to honor them, to aid his Prophet, to make Islam and its followers mighty, and to humble polytheism and its followers.

Ibn Ḥumayd—Salamah—Muḥammad b. Isḥāq—Maʿbad b. Kaʿb b. Mālik b. Abī Kaʿb b. al-Qayn, brother of the Banū Salimah—his brother ʿAbdallāh b. Kaʿb, who was one of the most learned men of

207. The four small clans Umayyah b. Zayd, Khaṭmah, Wā'il, and Wāqif were collectively known as Aws Allāh, originally Aws Manāt. They were a small section of the tribe of al-Aws, but of little political importance and perhaps to some extent dependent on Jewish clans. This last point may explain why they did not at first become Muslims.

208. The three days of *tashrīq* are the eleventh to the thirteenth of the month of Dhū al-Ḥijjah, following on the day of sacrifice on the tenth. The pilgrims have to spend these days at Minā and are not to fast. The original meaning of *tashrīq* is uncertain.

the Anṣār—his father Kaʿb b. Mālik, who was one of those present at al-ʿAqabah and swore the oath of allegiance to the Messenger of God ther:e We set out among the pilgrims of our tribe, having prayed and become instructed in our religion. With us was al-Barāʾ b. Maʿrūr, our chief and our oldest member. When we set off on our journey and left al-Madīnah al-Barāʾ said to us, "By God, I have made a decision, and I do not know whether you will agree with me in it or not." We said, "What is that?" and he said, "I have decided that I shall not turn my back on this building (meaning [1218]
the Kaʿbah) and that I shall pray toward it." We said, "By God, we have not heard that our Prophet prays in any other direction than toward Syria, and we do not wish to differ from him.[209] He answered, "I shall pray toward the Kaʿbah." "We shall not do so," we said.

When the time for prayer came, we prayed toward Syria and he prayed toward the Kaʿbah. This continued until we came to Mecca. We reproached him for what he was doing, but he insisted upon continuing the practice. When we came to Mecca he said to me, "Nephew, let us go to the Messenger of God so that I can ask him about what I have done during my journey, for I became concerned about it when I saw how you opposed me over it." We went to ask for the Messenger of God, as we did not know him and had not seen him before. We met a man from Mecca and asked him about the Messenger of God. "Do you know him?" he asked. "No," we said. "Do you know al-ʿAbbās b. ʿAbd al-Muṭṭalib, his uncle?" he asked. We said that we did, as we knew al-ʿAbbās, who came frequently to us on business. He said, "When you go into the mosque, he is the man sitting with al-ʿAbbās b. ʿAbd al-Muṭṭalib."

We went into the mosque, and there was al-ʿAbbās sitting down, with the Messenger of God sitting with him. We greeted him, and then sat down with him. The Messenger of God said to al-ʿAbbās, "Do you know these two men, Abū al-Faḍl?" "Yes," he said. "This is al-Barāʾ b. Maʿrūr, the chief of his people (that is, the clan of Salimah) and this is Kaʿb b. Mālik." By God, I shall never forget how the Messenger of God asked, "The poet?" to which al-ʿAbbās replied, "Yes."

---

209. Facing towards Syria means, of course, facing towards Jerusalem as the Jews did. The final change of *qiblah* (direction faced in prayer), from Jerusalem to Mecca occurred about February A.D. 624.

Al-Barā' b. Ma'rūr said to him, "O Prophet of God, I set out on my journey, having been guided by God to Islam, and I decided that I would not turn my back on this building, and so I prayed
[1219] toward it. My companions opposed me in this, and I became concerned about it. What is your opinion, O Messenger of God?" The Messenger of God replied, "You would indeed have had a *qiblah*, had you kept to it patiently."[210] Then al-Barā' returned to the Messenger of God's *qiblah* and prayed with us toward Syria. His family assert that he prayed toward the Ka'bah until he died, but it is not as they say. We know more about the matter than they do.

Then we went on the pilgrimage, and agreed to meet the Messenger of God at al-'Aqabah in the middle of the days of *al-tashrīq*. When we had finished (the rites of) the pilgrimage, the night came upon which we had promised to meet the Messenger of God. We had with us 'Abdallāh b. 'Amr b. Ḥarām Abū Jābir. We had concealed our purpose from the polytheists among our people who were with us, but we told him about this meeting and spoke to him as follows: "Abū Jābir, you are one of our chiefs and one of our nobles, and we do not wish you to remain in your present state, which is that you will be fuel for the flames of Hell on the morrow." Then we summoned him to Islam, and informed him of the Messenger of God's arrangement to meet us at al-'Aqabah. He accepted Islam and was present at al-'Aqabah with us, and became a *naqīb*.[211]

We spent that night encamped with our people, but when a third of the night had gone by we left our encampment to meet the Messenger of God. We slipped away secretly, moving as silently as sand grouse, and met in the ravine by al-'Aqabah. We were seventy men and two women, Nusaybah bt. Ka'b Umm 'Umārah, a woman of the Banū Māzin b. al-Najjār, and Asmā' bt. 'Amr b. 'Adī, a woman of the Banū Salimah, who was Umm Manī'. We gathered in the ravine to wait for the Messenger of God. He came to us ac-
[1220] companied by his paternal uncle al-'Abbās b. 'Abd al-Muṭṭalib, who at that time still adhered to the religion of his people, but wished to be present when his nephew was negotiating and to

210. The meaning of this reply is ambiguous.

211. Muḥammad asked that each clan which had accepted Islam should appoint a "representative" (*naqīb*), presumably to form a council of some sort, but there is no record of them ever functioning as such (see below p.1221).

see that there was a firm agreement. When he had sat down, al-ʿAbbās b. ʿAbd al-Muṭṭalib was the first to speak, and said, "People of the Khazraj (the Arabs used to call the Anṣar, the Khazraj and the Aws together, by the name of the Khazraj), you know what Muḥammad's position is among us. We have protected him against those of our people who have the same religious views as ourselves. He is held in honor by his own people and is safe in his country. He is determined to leave them and to join you, so if you think that you can fulfil the promises which you made in inviting him to come to you and can defend him against his enemies, then assume the responsibilities which you have taken upon yourselves. But if you think that you will abandon him and hand him over after he has come to you, then leave him alone now, for he is honored by his people and is safe in his country."

We said to him, "We have heard what you have said. Speak, Messenger of God, and choose what you want for yourself and your Lord." The Messenger of God spoke, recited the Qur'ān, summoned us to God, and made us desirous of Islam. Then he said, "I will enter a contract of allegiance with you, provided that you protect me as you would your wives and children."

Then al-Barā' b. Maʿrūr took his hand and said, "By Him who sent you with the truth, we shall defend you as we would our womenfolk. Administer the oath of allegiance to us, O Messenger of God, for we are men of war and men of coats of mail; we have inherited this from generation to generation."

He was interrupted as he was speaking to the Messenger of God by Abū al-Haytham b. al-Tayyihān, the confederate of the Banū ʿAbd al-Ashhal, who said, "O Messenger of God, there are ties between us and other people which we shall have to sever (meaning the Jews). If we do this and God gives you victory, will you perhaps return to your own people and leave us?" The Messenger of God smiled and then said, "Rather, blood is blood, and blood shed [1221]
without retaliation is blood shed without retaliation. You are of me and I am of you. I shall fight whomever you fight and make peace with whomever you make peace with." Then he said, "Appoint twelve representatives *(naqīb)* from among you for me, who will see to their people's affairs." They appointed twelve representatives, nine from the Khazraj and three from the Aws.

Ibn Ḥumayd—Salamah—Muḥammad b. Isḥāq—ʿAbdallāh b.

Abī Bakr b. Muḥammad b. 'Amr b. Ḥazm: the Messenger of God said to the representatives, "You are to see to your people's affairs; you are a surety for them, as the disciples were for Jesus, son of Mary, and I am for my people." They agreed to this.

Ibn Ḥumayd—Salamah—Muḥammad b. Isḥāq—'Āṣim b. 'Umar b. Qatādah: When they gathered to take the oath of allegiance to the Messenger of God, al-'Abbās b. 'Ubādah b. Naḍlah al-Anṣāri, the brother of the Banū Sālim b. 'Awf, said, "People of the Khazraj, do you know what you are pledging yourselves to in swearing allegiance to this man?" "Yes," they said. He continued, "In swearing allegiance to him you are pledging yourselves to wage war against all mankind. If you think that when your wealth is exhausted by misfortune and your nobles are depleted by death you will give him up, then stop now, for, by God, it is disgrace in this world and the next if you later give him up. But if you think that you will be faithful to the promises which you made in inviting him, even if your wealth is exhausted and your nobles killed, then take him, for, by God, he is the best thing for you in this world and the next." They answered, "We shall take him even if it brings the loss of our wealth and the killing of our nobles. What shall we gain for this, O Messenger of God, if we are faithful?" He answered, "Par-
[1222] adise." "Stretch out your hand," they said. He stretched out his hand, and they swore alleginace to him. According to 'Āṣim b. 'Umar b. Qatādah, al-'Abbās (b. 'Ubādah) only said this in order to make the contract more binding upon them, while according to 'Abdallāh b. Abī Bakr he only said it in order to delay them that night in the hope that 'Abdallāh b. Ubayy b. Salūl[212] would come, which would give more weight to the people's decision; but God knows best which version is true. The Banū al-Najjār claim that Abū Umāmah As'ad b. Zurārah was the first to clasp hands, while the Banū 'Abd al-Ashhal say that on the contrary it was Abū al-Haytham b. al-Tayyihān.

Ibn Ḥumayd—Salamah—Muḥammad (b. Isḥāq)—Ma'bad b. Ka'b b. Mālik; and also Sa'īd b. Yaḥyā b. Sa'īd—his father—Muḥammad b. Isḥāq—Ma'bad b. Ka'b—his father Ka'b b. Mālik:

212. This is the man who a year or two later became the leader of the Hypocrites (*munāfiqūn*), that is, those men of al-Madīnah who had accepted Islam but were not happy to have Muḥammad as their leader. It is said that before Muḥammad's arrival 'Abdallāh b. Ubayy had hoped to become ruler of al-Madīnah.

The first to clasp the hand of the Messenger of God was al-Barā' b. Ma'rūr, and after this they clasped his hand one after another. When we had all sworn the oath of allegiance to the Messenger of God Satan shouted from the top of al-'Aqabah in the most piercing voice I have ever heard, "people of the stations[213] of Minā, do you want a blameworthy person and the apostates with him[214] who have gathered together to wage war on you?" The Messenger of [1223]
God said, "What does the Enemy of God say? This is the (devil) Azabb of al-'Aqabah, the son of the devil Azyab.[215] Listen, Enemy of God. By God, I shall deal with you!"

The Messenger of God told them to disperse to their encampments, and al-'Abbās b. 'Ubādah b. Naḍlah said to him, "By Him who sent you with the truth, if you wish we shall fall upon the people of Minā with our swords tomorrow." The Messenger of God replied, "We have not been commanded to do this; go back to your encampments."

We went back to our beds and slept upon them until the morning, when the chief men of Quraysh came to us in our encampments and said to us, "Men of the Khazraj, we have heard that you have come to this companion of ours to take him from our midst and to swear an oath of allegiance to him to wage war against us. By God, there is not tribe of the Arabs between whom and ourselves we should be more unwilling for war to break out than you." Those of the polytheists of our people who were there immediately swore to them by God that nothing of the sort had taken place and that they knew nothing about it. They were telling the truth, for they did not know.

We looked at one another, and the men of Quraysh rose up, among them al-Ḥārith b. Hishām b. al-Mughīrah al-Makhzūmī, who was wearing a pair of new sandals. I (Ka'b b. Mālik) spoke a few words as though I wished to associate all of our people with what our polytheists had said; "Abū Jābir,[216] can you not get sandals like those of this young man of Quraysh (that is al-

213. The place where the stomachs (*jabājib*) of the sacrificial victims were scattered.

214. "Blameworthy" (*mudhammam*) is an insulting way of referring to Muḥammad, whose name can mean "praiseworthy." The *ṣubāt* (plural of *ṣābi'*) are people who have changed their religion.

215. Nothing further is known about this matter.

216. This is 'Abdallāh b. 'Amr of the subclan Ḥarām of the clan of Salimah.

Ḥārith), seeing that you are one of our chiefs?" Al-Ḥārith heard these words, took the sandals off his feet, and threw them at me,
[1224] saying, "By God, put them on your feet!" Abū Jābir said, "Gently! By God, you have annoyed the young man! Give him back his sandals." I replied, "By God, I will not! It is a good omen. If the omen proves true I shall plunder him." This is Kaʿb b. Mālik's account of al-ʿAqabah and what he witnessed there.

Abū Jaʿfar (al-Ṭabarī): Other authorities than Ibn Isḥāq say that those of the Anṣār who came to swear allegiance to the Prophet came in (the month of) Dhū al-Ḥijjah. After this the Messenger of God remained in Mecca for the rest of that Dhū al-Ḥijjah and for the months of Muḥarram and Ṣafar, and emigrated to al-Madīnah in the month of Rabīʿ I (July-September 622) arriving there on Monday, the twelfth of that month (24 September).

ʿAlī b. Naṣr b. ʿAlī and ʿAbd al-Wārith b. ʿAbd al-Ṣamad b. ʿAbd al-Wārith—ʿAbd al-Ṣamad b. ʿAbd al-Wārith—his father—Abān al-ʿAttār—Hishām b. ʿUrwah—ʿUrwah: When those who had emigrated to Abyssinia before the Messenger of God's emigration to al-Madinah came back from there, the number of Muslims began to increase and multiply. Many of the Anṣār in al-Madinah accepted Islam, which spread widely there, and the people of al-Madinah began to come to the Messenger of God in Mecca. When the Quraysh saw this, they urged one another to torment the Muslims and treat them harshly. They seized them and were eager to torment them, and the Muslims suffered great hardship. This was the second trial; there were two trials, one which forced out those of them who emigrated to Abyssinia, when the Messenger of God commanded them to do so and gave them permission to go there, and one they came back and saw the people of al-Madinah coming to them.

The seventy representatives,[217] chiefs of those who had accepted
[1225] Islam, came to the Messenger of God from al-Madīnah met him during the pilgrimage, and swore an oath of allegiance to him at al-ʿAqabah. They gave him their pledge in the following words: "We are of you and you are of us; whoever comes to us of your Companions, or you yourself if you come to us, we shall defend you as we

217. The word *naqīb* is used here in a general sense. They did in a sense represent their clans, but not all of them were the "representatives" asked for by Muḥammad.

would defend ourselves." After this Quraysh began to treat them harshly, and the Messenger of God commanded his Companions to go to al-Madīnah This was the second trial, during which the Messenger of God told his Companions to emigrate and himself emigrated. It was concerning this that God revealed:

> And fight them until persecution is no more, and religion is all for God.[218]

Ibn Ḥumayd—Salamah—Muḥammad b. Isḥāq—ʿAbdallāh b. Abī Bakr b. Muḥammad b. ʿAmr b. Ḥazm:[219] They (the Quraysh) came to ʿAbdallāh b. Ubayy b. Salūl and said much the same as Kaʿb b. Mālik reports them as saying. He replied, "This is a weighty matter; my people are not men to make a decision without consulting me in such a matter, and I have no knowledge that it has taken place." They then left him.

When the people dispersed from Minā, Quraysh investigated the report thoroughly, and found that there had indeed been an agreement. They went out in pursuit of the (men of al-Madīnah), and overtook Saʿd b. ʿUbādah at al-Ḥājir together with Al-Mundhir b. ʿAmr the brother of the Banū Sāʿidah b. Kaʿb b. al-Khazraj; both of these were representatives. Al-Mundhir evaded capture, but they took Saʿd, tied his hands to his neck with the thong of his camel's saddle girth and went back to Mecca with him, beating him and dragging him by his hair, for he had very luxuriant hair.

Saʿd said of this, "By God, I was in their hands when a group of the Quraysh came up to me, among them a white, clean, tall, pleasant-looking man. I said to myself, 'If there is any good among them, it will be in this man.' When he came near me, he raised his hand and gave me a severe blow. I said to myself, 'By God, there is no good in them after this.' I was in their hands and they were dragging me along, when one of the men with them was moved by pity for me and said, 'For heaven's sake! Don't you have any bond of protection or any compact with any of the Quraysh?' 'Certainly,' I said, 'I used to protect Jubayr b. Muṭʿim b. ʿAdī b. Nawfal b. ʿAbd Manāf's commercial agents and defend them against anyone who

---

218. This verse (8:39) was probably not revealed until after the battle of Badr. The almost identical verse 2:193 seems not to have been revealed until shortly before the conquest of Mecca.

219. Ibn Hishām, *Sīrah*, 301f.

wished to wrong them in my country, and I did the same for al-Ḥārith b. Umayyah b. ʿAbd Shams b. ʿAbd Manāf.' 'Well then,' he said, 'call out these two men's names and say what links there are between you and them.'

"I did so, and he went to them and found them in the mosque by the Kaʿbah. He told them that a man of the Khazraj was being beaten in the valley and that he was calling upon them and saying that there were bonds of protection between himself and them. They asked who it was, and he said that it was Saʿd b. ʿUbādah. They said, 'He speaks the truth, by God. He used to protect our agents and defend them against oppression in his country.' They
[1227] came and released me from my captors' hands, and I departed. The person who punched me was Suhayl b. ʿAmr, the brother of the Banū ʿĀmir b. Lu'ayy."

Abū Jaʿfar (al-Ṭabarī): When they came to al-Madīnah they proclaimed Islam there. There were among their people some of their shaykhs who remained in their polytheistic religion, among whom was ʿAmr b. al-Jamūḥ b. Zayd b. Ḥarām b. Kaʿb b. Ghanm b. Salimah, whose son Muʿādh b. ʿAmr had been present at al-ʿAqabah and had sworn an oath of allegiance to the Messenger of God along with others of their young men. Those members of the Aws and the Khazraj who took the oath of allegiance at the second al-ʿAqabah took the pledge of war, when, in contrast to the terms of the first al-ʿAqabah, God permitted fighting. The first was the pledge of women, as I have mentioned above on the authority of ʿUbādah b. al-Ṣāmit. The second pledge of al-ʿAqabah was to wage war against all men,[220] as I have mentioned above on the authority of ʿUrwah b. al-Zubayr.

Ibn Ḥumayd—Salamah—Muḥammad b. Isḥāq—ʿUbādah b. al-Walīd b. ʿUbādah b. al-Ṣāmit—his father al-Walīd—ʿUbādah b. al-Ṣāmit, who was one of the representatives:[221] We took the oath of allegiance to the Messenger of God according to the terms of the pledge of war. ʿUbādah was one of the twelve who took the pledge at at first al-ʿAqabah.

---

220. That is, on anyone who injured or killed Muḥammad.
221. Ibn Hishām, *Sīrah,* 304.

The Messenger of God Commands the Muslims to Emigrate to al-Madīnah[222]

Abū Ja'far (al-Ṭabarī): After God had given his Messenger permission to fight by revealing the verse:[223] "And fight them until persecution is no more, and religion is all for God," and the Anṣār had pledged themselves to support him according to the terms which I have described, the Messenger of God commanded those of his Companions from among the Muslims who were with him at Mecca to emigrate, go to al-Madīnah, and join their brethren, the Anṣār. He told them, "God has made for you brethren and an abode in which you will be safe." They went in groups. The Messenger of God remained in Mecca waiting for his Lord to [1228]
give him permission to leave Mecca and go to al-Madīnah. The first of the Messenger of God's Companions to emigrate to al-Madīnah was from the Quraysh, from the Banū Makhzūm. He was Abū Salamah b. 'Abd al-Asad b. Hilāl b. 'Abdallāh b. 'Umar b. Makhzūm, who emigrated to al-Madīnah a year before the people of al-'Aqabah took the oath of allegiance to the Messenger of God. He had come to the Messenger of God in Mecca from Abyssinia, and when Quraysh persecuted him and he heard that some of the Anṣār had accepted Islam, he went to al-Madīnah as an Emigrant. The first of the emigrants to go to al-Madīnah after Abū Salamah was 'Āmir b. Rabī'ah the confederate of the Banū 'Adī b. Ka'b, accompanied by his wife Laylā bt. Abī Ḥathmah b. Ghānim b. 'Abdallāh b. 'Awf b. 'Abīd b. 'Awīj b. 'Adī b. Ka'b, and after him 'Abdallāh b. Jaḥsh b. Ri'āb and Abū Aḥmad b. Jaḥsh, who was blind and used to go about Mecca, both the upper and the lower parts, without a guide. After this, the Companions of the Messenger of God went to al-Madīnah in successive groups, but the Messenger of God remained in Mecca after his Companions had emigrated, waiting to be given permission to emigrate.[224] None of the Emigrants remained behind with him in Mecca except those who had been seized and imprisoned (by their families) or who had been

222. This follows Ibn Hishām, *Sīrah,* 314, 316 closely, though Ṭabarī does not mention the fact.

223. 8:39.

224. From this point to p.1234, Ṭabarī follows Ibn Hishām, *Sīrah,* 323-26, apart from a paragraph on p.1232.

seduced (from Islam).The only exceptions were ʿAlī b. Abī Ṭālib and Abū Bakr b. Abī Quḥāfah. Abū Bakr would often ask the Messenger of God for permission to emigrate, but the Messenger of God would say to him, "Do not do so; perhaps God will provide a companion for you." Abū Bakr hoped that the Messenger of God would be that companion.

The Quraysh Plot to Kill the Messenger of God

[1229] When Quraysh saw that the Messenger of God had acquired a following and Companions from a tribe other than themselves in a region other than theirs, and when they saw his Emigrant Companions going to join them, they realized that these had found a home and were safe from their attacks. The Quraysh were now anxious about the Messenger of God going to the people of al-Madīnah as they knew that he had decided to join the Madīnans in order to make war on the Quraysh. They therefore met together about this matter in the House of Assembly, formerly the house of Quṣayy b. Kilāb, where Quraysh had always made their decisions, and there they deliberated what to do about the Messenger of God, since they had come to be afraid of him.

Ibn Ḥumayd—Salamah—Muḥammad b. Isḥāq—ʿAbdallāh b. Abī Najīḥ—Mujāhid b. Jabr Abū al-Ḥajjāj—Ibn ʿAbbās; also al-Kalbī—Abū Ṣāliḥ—Ibn ʿAbbās and al-Ḥasan b. ʿUmārah—al-Ḥakam b. ʿUtaybah—Miqsam—Ibn ʿAbbās: They gathered together for this purpose and at the fixed time went into the House of Assembly to deliberate there about the Messenger of God. On the morning of the day fixed (the day called al-Zaḥmah) they went there, and the Devil met them in the form of a venerable old man wearing a coarse garment and stood at the door of the house. When they saw him standing at the door they said, "Who is this old man?" He said, "I am an old man from Najd who has heard what you have arranged to meet for and has come to be with you to
[1230] hear what you say; perhaps you will not lack judgement and good advice from him." They replied, "Certainly, come in," so he went in with them. All the nobles of Quraysh, of every clan, had gathered there; from the Banū ʿAbd Shams, Shaybah and ʿUtbah the sons of Rabīʿah and Abū Sufyān b. Ḥarb; from the Banū Nawfal b. ʿAbd Manāf, Ṭuʿaymah b. ʿAdī, Jubayr b. Muṭʿim and al-Ḥārith b.

'Amir b. Nawfal; from the Banū 'Abd al-Dār b. Quṣayy, al-Naḍr b. al-Ḥārith b. Kaladah; from the Banū Asad b. 'Abd al-'Uzzā, Abū al-Bakhtarī b. Hishām, Zam'ah b. al-Aswad b. al-Muṭṭalib and Ḥakim b. Ḥizām; from the Banū Makhzūm, Abū Jahl b. Hishām; from the Banū Sahm, Nubayh and Munabbih the sons of al-Ḥajjāj; and from the Banū Jumaḥ, Umayyah b. Khalaf. In addition there were others, some from the Quraysh and others who were not counted as Quraysh.

They said to one another, "This man has done what he has done, and you have seen it for yourselves. We cannot be sure that he will not fall upon us with his followers who are not of us; so come to a decision about him." When they began to deliberate, one of them said, "Keep him in fetters, lock him up, and wait for the same kind of death to overtake him which overtook other poets of his sort before him, Zuhayr, al-Nābighah[225] and others." The old man from Najd said, "No, by God, this is not judicious; if you were to imprison him as you say, news of what had happened to him would leak out to his companions from behind the door which you had shut upon him, and in no time at all they would fall upon you and snatch him away from your hands. Then their numbers would grow against you and they would seize power from you. This is not judicious, so consider something else."

They consulted again, and one of them said, "Let us expel him
from among us and banish him from our land; when he has left [1231]
us, by God, we will not care where he goes or where he settles. The harm which he has been doing will disappear, we shall be rid of him and we shall be able to put our affairs in order again and restore our social harmony to what it was before." The old man from Najd said, "By God, this is not judicious; do you not see the beauty of his discourse, the sweetness of his speech and how he dominates the hearts of men with the message which he brings? By God, if you expel him, I think it not unlikely that he will descend upon some tribe of the Arabs and win them over with this speech and discourse of his so that they follow him in his plans; then he will lead them against you, crush you with them, seize power from your hands and do with you what he wants. Come to some other decision about him."

225. Two of the most famous pre-Islamic poets. The circumstances of their deaths are obscure.

Abū Jahl b. Hishām said, "By God, I have an idea about him, which I do not think you have hit upon yet." "What is it, Abū al-Ḥakam?" they asked. He said, "I think that you should take one young, strong, well-born, noble young man from each clan; then we should give each young man a sharp sword; then they should make for him and strike him with their swords as one man and kill him. Thus we shall be relieved of him, and if they do this, the responsibility for shedding his blood will be divided up among all the clans, and the Banū ʿAbd Manaf[226] will not be able to wage war against the whole of their tribe, and will be content to take blood money from us, which we can pay them." The old man from Najd was saying, "What this man says is right. This is the correct decision; you have no other." Thereupon they dispersed, having agreed upon this.

The Messenger of God Escapes from the Attempt to Kill Him

Then Gabriel came to the Messenger of God and said, "Do not spend this night in the bed in which you usually sleep." When
[1232] the first third of the night had gone past, the young men gathered at his door and waited for him to go to sleep so that they could fall upon him. When the Messenger of God saw them there he said to ʿAlī b. Abī Ṭālib, "Sleep on my bed and wrap yourself up in my green Ḥaḍramī cloak; nothing unpleasant will befall you from them." The Messenger of God used to sleep in that cloak when he went to bed.

Abū Jaʿfar (al-Ṭabarī): At this point one authority adds the following words to this story: Muhammad said to ʿAlī, "If Ibn Abī Quḥāfah—that is, Abū Bakr—comes to you, tell him that I have gone to Thawr and ask him to join me; send me some food, hire a guide for me who can show me the road to al-Madīnah, and buy me a riding camel." Then the Messenger of God went off, and God blinded the sight of those who were lying in wait for him so that he departed without their seeing him.

Ibn Ḥumayd—Salamah—Muḥammad b. Isḥāq—Yazīd b. Ziyād—Muḥammad b. Kaʿb al-Quraẓī: They gathered against him,

226. This must mean only the subclans Hāshim and al-Muṭṭalib, since the other two subclans of ʿAbd Manāf were represented at the meeting.

and among them was Abū Jahl b. Hishām, who said, while they were waiting at his door, "Muḥammad claims that if you follow him in his religion, you shall be the kings of the Arabs and the non-Arabs, that after your death you shall be brought back to life and your lot shall then be gardens like the gardens of Jordan. He also claims that if you do not do this, you shall meet with slaughter from him, and that after your death you shall be brought back to life, and your lot shall then be a fire, in which you shall burn." Then the Messenger of God came out, took a handful of dust and said, "Yes, I do say that; and you are one of them." Then God took away their sight so that they could not see him, and Muḥammad
began to sprinkle the dust on their heads while reciting the fol- [1233]
lowing verses from Sūrat Yā' Sīn:

> Yā' Sīn. By the wise Qur'ān, you are one of those sent on a straight path ...

to the words:

> and we have set a barrier before them and a barrier behind them, and have covered them so that they do not see.[227]

By the time he had finished reciting these verses he had put dust on the heads of every one of them, after which he went to where he wished to go. Someone who had not been with them came to them and said, "What are you waiting here for?" They answered, "Muḥammad." He said, "God has frustrated you, for Muḥammad has gone out despite you; furthermore, he has put dust on the heads of every one of you, and has gone away about his business. Do you not see what has happened to you?"

Every man of them put his hand on his head and found dust on it; then they began to investigate, and saw 'Alī on the bed shrouded in the Messenger of God's cloak. They said, "By God, this is Muḥammad asleep in his cloak," and they continued in this fashion until morning came, when 'Alī rose up from the bed. Then they said, "By God, the person who spoke to us was telling the truth."

Among the passages of the Qur'ān revealed concerning that day and what they had agreed upon are the following:

---

227. 3:1-9.

> And when those who disbelieve plot against you to wound you fatally or to kill you or to drive you out; they plot, but God plots; and God is the best of plotters.

and:

> Or they say: he is a poet, one for whom we may await the accident of time. Say; await! I am with you among those who await.[228]

Some of them assert that Abū Bakr came to ʿAlī and asked him
[1234] about the Prophet of God. He told him that he had gone to the cave of Thawr and said, "If you have any business with him, join him there." Abū Bakr went out hastily and caught up with the Prophet of God on the road. The Messenger of God heard the sound of Abū Bakr coming in the darkness of the night and thought that he was one of the polytheists. He increased his pace and his sandal strap snapped, and he skinned his big toe on a stone. It bled profusely, and he walked even faster. Abū Bakr was afraid that he would cause the Messenger of God distress, and so he raised his voice and spoke to him. The Messenger of God recognized him, and stopped until Abū Bakr reached him. They then set off again, with the Messenger of God's foot pouring blood. The cave was reached at dawn and they went in together.

When morning came the group of people who were lying in wait for the Messenger of God went into his house. ʿAlī rose from his bed, and when they came close to him they recognized him and said, "Where is your companion?" He replied, "I do not know. Do you expect me to keep watch over him? You told him to leave, and he has left." They scolded him and beat him. Then they took him to the mosque and imprisoned him for a while, but after this they left him alone. Thus God delivered his Messenger from their plotting. About this event God revealed: "and when those who disbelieve plot against you to wound you fatally or to kill you or to drive you out; they plot, but God plots; and God is the best of plotters."[229]

---

228. 8:30; 52:30-31.
229. 8:30.

The Messenger of God Emigrates to al-Madīnah

Abū Ja'far (al-Ṭabarī): After this God gave his Messenger permission to emigrate.

'Alī b. Naṣr al-Jahḍamī—'Abd al-Ṣamad b. 'Abd al-Wārith; also 'Abd al-Wārith b. 'Abd al-Ṣamad b. 'Abd al-Wārith—his father ('Abd al-Ṣamad)—Abān al-'Aṭṭār—Hishām b. 'Urwah—'Urwah: When the Messenger of God's Companions had gone to al-Madīnah but before he himself left Mecca, and before the verse [1235]
was revealed in which they were commanded to fight,[230] Abū Bakr, who had not been commanded to go, asked Muḥammad's permission to leave with the rest of his companions. The Messenger of God kept him back, however, and said, "Give me a little time. I do not know. Perhaps I shall be given permission to depart." Abū Bakr had bought two riding camels and had prepared them for departure to al-Madīnah with the Messenger of God's Companions. When the Messenger of God asked him to wait and told him of the hope which he had that God would give him permission to leave, he kept the two camels in expectation of accompanying the Messenger of God, and fed them well and fattened them. When the Messenger of God's departure was delayed, Abū Bakr said to him, "Do you hope that permission will be given to you?" He replied, "Yes. Wait until it comes." He then waited patiently.

'Ā'ishah told me that on a certain day, while they were in their house at noon time, there being nobody with Abū Bakr except his daughters 'Ā'ishah and Asmā', the Messenger of God suddenly appeared while the noonday sun was at its height. It had been his habit to come to Abū Bakr's house every day without fail at the beginning of the day and at the end of it, and so when Abū Bakr saw the Prophet coming at noon he said to him, "O Prophet of God, only something special has brought you here." When he came in, the Prophet said to Abū Bakr, "Ask whoever is with you to leave." He answered, "There are no spies upon us here. These are only my two daughters." Then the Prophet said, "God has given me permission to depart for al-Madīnah." Abū Bakr said, "O Messenger of God, may I accompany you?" "Yes," he replied. Abū Bakr said, "Take one of the riding camels." These were the riding camels which he had been feeding in preparation for departure when per- [1236]

230. The verse was alleged to be 8:39; see above pp.1225, 1227, and n. 218.

mission was granted to the Messenger of God. He gave him one of them and said, "Take it, O Messenger of God, and ride it." The Prophet replied, "I accept it, for its price."

ʿĀmir b. Fuhayrah was a half-breed from the tribe of Azd belonging to al-Ṭufayl b. ʿAbdallāh b. Sakhbarah (who was Abū al-Ḥārith) b. al-Ṭufayl, who had the same mother as Abū Bakr's daughter ʿĀʾishah and his son ʿAbd al-Raḥmān. ʿĀmir b. Fuhayrah became a Muslim while he was their slave, and Abū Bakr bought him and set him free. He was a good Muslim. At the time when the Prophet and Abū Bakr set out, Abū Bakr had the rights to the milk of a flock of sheep which used to come to his family in the evening. Abū Bakr sent ʿĀmir with the sheep to Thawr, and he used to bring them in the evening to the Messenger of God in the cave there, which is the cave named by God in the Qurʾān.[231]

They sent ahead with their mounts a man from the Banū ʿAbd b. ʿAdī, a confederate of the family of al-ʿĀṣ b. Wāʾil of Banū Sahm of Quraysh. At that time, this man ʿAdī was a polytheist, but they hired him as a guide for the journey. During the nights which they spent in the cave ʿAbdallāh b. Abī Bakr used to come to them in the evening and bring them all the news of Mecca, and then return to Mecca by morning. ʿĀmir would bring the sheep every evening so that they could milk them, and would then drive them to pasture at daybreak, and spend the morning with other people's shepherds, so that nobody realized what he was doing. When the clamor about Muḥammad and Abū Bakr died down and news came to them that people were no longer talking about them, their guide brought them their camels and they set off, taking with them ʿĀmir b. Fuhayrah to serve them and assist them. Abū Bakr mounted him behind him and shared the saddle with him by
[1237] turns. There was nobody with them but ʿĀmir b. Fuhayrah and the brother of the Banū ʿAdī, who guided them along the road. He took them through the Meccan lowlands, then along a route parallel to the coast below ʿUsfān, then across country, rejoining the road after Qudayd, then along the al-Kharrār path, then across the pass of al-Marah, and then along a road called al-Mudlijah, between the ʿAmq road and the Rawḥāʾ road. He then met the ʿArj road, coming to a spring called al-Ghābir to the right of Rakūbah,

231. The verse is 9:40.

and then ascended the Baṭn Ri'm, finally arriving, one day at high noon, at the quarter of the Banū 'Amr b. 'Awf in (the south of) al-Madīnah. I have been told that the Messenger of God only stayed among them for two days, although the Banū 'Amr b. 'Awf assert that he stayed among them for longer than that. Then he led his camel, which followed him to the quarter of the Banū al-Najjār. There the Messenger of God showed them a drying floor in the midst of their dwellings.

Ibn Ḥumayd—Salamah—Muḥammad b. Isḥāq—Muḥammad b. 'Abd al-Raḥmān b. 'Abd Allāh b. al-Ḥuṣayn al-Tamīmī—'Urwah b. al-Zubayr—'Ā'ishah the wife of the Prophet:[232] The Messenger of God never failed to come to Abū Bakr's house at the two ends of the day, early morning and evening. When the day arrived upon which God gave his Messenger permission to emigrate and to go away from Mecca from among his tribe, the Messenger of God came to us in the heat of the day at a time at which it was not his custom to come. When Abū Bakr saw him he said, "The Messen- [1238]
ger of God can only have come at such an hour because of something special." When he came in, Abū Bakr rose from his bed, and the Messenger of God sat down. There was nobody with Abū Bakr except for myself and my sister Asmā', and when the Messenger of God said, "Send out those who are with you," he said, "O Prophet of God, these are my daughters; there is no need for that, may my father and mother be your ransom."

Then the Messenger of God said, "God has given me permission to leave Mecca and to emigrate." Abū Bakr said, "May I accompany you, O Messenger of God?" "You may accompany me." he replied. By God, I was never aware that anyone could weep for joy until that day when I saw Abū Bakr weeping for joy. Then he said, "O Prophet of God, these are my two riding camels which I have prepared for this." They hired as a guide for the road 'Abdallāh b. Arqad, a man from the Banū al-Dīl b. Bakr, whose mother was from (the Meccan clan of) the Banū Sahm b. 'Amr, a polytheist. They handed their two riding camels over to him and he kept them with him to pasture them until the appointed time.

According to what I (Ibn Isḥāq) have been told not a single person knew of the Messenger of God's departure when he went ex-

232. Ibn Hishām, *Sīrah,* 327–30.

cept for ʿAlī b. Abī Ṭālib and Abū Bakr al-Ṣiddīq and his family. As for ʿAlī b. Abī Ṭālib, the Messenger of God is said to have informed him that he was leaving and to have commanded him to stay behind in Mecca to hand back those things which people had entrusted to his custody. Everyone in Mecca who had any possession which he feared to lose would deposit it with the Messenger
[1239] of God because they knew of his honesty and reliability. When the Messenger of God decided upon departure, he went to Abū Bakr b. Abī Quḥāfah, and the two of them left by a window in the back of Abū Bakr's house and went to a cave in Thawr, a mountain below Mecca, and entered it. Abū Bakr told his son ʿAbdallāh to listen to what people were saying about them during the day and to bring them the day's news in the evening. He also told his *mawlā* ʿĀmir b. Fuhayrah to pasture his flocks during the day and to bring them to them in the cave in the evening. Abū Bakr's daughter Asmā' brought them enough food for their needs in the evening.

The Messenger of God and Abū Bakr spent three days in the cave. When Quraysh realized that he was missing, they offered a hundred she-camels for whoever would bring him back to them. ʿAbdallāh b. Abī Bakr spent his time among Quraysh listening to what they were plotting and to what they were saying about the Messenger of God and Abū Bakr. Then he would come to them in the evening and give them the news. ʿĀmir b. Fuhayrah, Abū Bakr's *mawlā,* pastured his flocks among the other Meccan shepherds, and brought Abū Bakr's sheep to the cave in the evening, when the two men would milk them and slaughter (one of) them. When ʿAbdallāh b. Abī Bakr left for Mecca the following morning, ʿĀmir b. Fuhayrah would follow after him with the sheep in order to erase his trail.

When the third day had gone past, and the people's interest in the two had died down, the man whom they had hired brought them their camels and Asmā' brought them their travelling provisions. She had forgotten to bring them a strap, and when they set off, she went to attach the travelling provisions and found that
[1240] there was no strap. She took off her girdle and used that as a strap to attach the provisions. Thereafter she was known as "She of the two girdles" on account of this incident.

When Abū Bakr brought the two riding camels to the Messenger of God, he gave him the better of the two and said, "Mount, may my father and mother be your ransom." The Messenger of God replied, "I will not ride a camel which does not belong to me." "It is yours, O Messenger of God whom I value more than my father and mother," he said. "No," said the Messenger of God. "What is the price which you paid for it?" He named the price, and the Messenger of God said, "I will take it for that price." Abū Bakr said, "It is yours, O Messenger of God." They mounted and set off, and Abū Bakr mounted behind himself his *mawlā* ʿĀmir b. Fuhayrah, who was to serve them during the journey.

Ibn Ḥumayd—Salamah—Muḥammad b. Isḥāq—Asmāʾ bt. Abī Bakr: When the Messenger of God and Abū Bakr left, a number of men of Quraysh, including Abū Jahl b. Hishām, came to us and stood at Abū Bakr's door. I went out to them and they said, "Where is your father, daughter of Abū Bakr?" I replied, "By God, I do not know where my father is." Abū Jahl raised his hand, for he was a loathsome and evil man, and gave me a blow on the cheek which knocked off my earring. Then they left, and for three days we did not know where the Messenger of God had gone. Then a man of the jinn came from the lower part of Mecca singing lines of verse in the manner of the Arabs, followed by people who were listening to his voice but could not see him, until at last he went out from the upper part of Mecca. He sang these lines:

May God the Lord of Men give his best recompense
    to two Companions who took their siesta, in the two
    tents of Umm Maʿbad.
They halted there bringing guidance and set off in the morning bearing it; [1241]
    may whoever becomes Muḥammad's Companion prosper!
May the Banū Kaʿb be given joy by the position of their
    young woman,
    and by her sitting as a lookout for the Believers.[233]

When we heard what he said we knew where the Messenger of God had gone, and that he was making for al-Madīnah. There were four of them, the Messenger of God, Abū Bakr, ʿĀmir b. Fuhayrah, and ʿAbdallāh b. Arqad, their guide.

Abū Jaʿfar (al-Ṭabarī)—Aḥmad b. al-Miqdām al-ʿIjlī—Hishām b.

233. Umm Maʿbad was a woman of the clan of Banū Kaʿb of the tribe of Khuzāʿah.

Muḥammad b. al-Sā'ib al-Kalbī—'Abd al-Ḥamīd b. Abī 'Abs b. Muḥammad b. Abī 'Abs b. Jabr—his father: In the night, Quraysh heard a voice on (the hill of) Abū Qubays saying;

If the two Sa'ds accept Islam, Muḥammad will no longer
fear the opposition of any opponent in Mecca.

[1242] The next morning Abū Sufyān said, "Who are the two Sa'ds? Sa'd Bakr? Sa'd Tamīm? Sa'd Hudhaym?" The following night they heard the voice saying:

Sa'd, Sa'd of the Aws, be a helper *(nāṣir)*
and Sa'd, Sa'd of the noble Khazraj,
Respond to him who calls you to right guidance,
and wish
through God for the object of desire in Paradise
of one who knows.
God's reward for the seeker after right guidance
is pavilioned gardens of Paradise.

In the morning, Abū Sufyān said, "By God it is Sa'd b. Mu'ādh and Sa'd b. 'Ubādah."[234]

The Messenger of God Arrives in al-Madīnah

Abū Ja'far (al-Ṭabarī): Their guide brought them to Qubā'[235] in the quarter of the Banū 'Amr b. 'Awf on Monday, the twelfth of Rabī' I (September 24, 622) when the heat of the forenoon had grown intense and the sun had almost reached its midpoint in the sky.

Ibn Ḥumayd—Salamah—Muḥammad b. Isḥāq—Muḥammad b. Ja'far b. al-Zubayr—'Urwah b. al-Zubayr—'Abd al-Raḥmān b. 'Uwaym b. Sā'idah—some men of his clan from the Companions of the Messenger of God:[236] When we heard that the Messenger of God had left Mecca and we were expecting his arrival, we used to go out after the morning prayer to the far side of our (lava-flow)

234. Sa'd b. Mu'ādh was the chief of the clan of 'Abd al-Ashhal of the tribe of the Aws, and was the leader of all the Muslims of al-Madīnah until he died of wounds received in the siege of al-Madīnah in A.D. 627. Sa'd b. 'Ubādah was chief of the clan of Sā'idah of the tribe of al-Khazraj; he was latterly the leading man of the Khazraj, and after A.D. 627 of the Muslims of al-Madīnah as a whole.

235. A district in the south of the oasis of al-Madīnah.

236. Ibn Hishām, *Sīrah,* 333-35.

ḥarrah to wait for him, and did not depart until the sun left us no shade to shelter in. When we could no longer find any shade we returned to our houses; this was during a hot period. When the day came on which the Messenger of God arrived, we sat as usual until there was no shade left and then went into our houses. The Messenger of God arrived after we had gone home, and the first person to see him was one of the Jews, who had observed what we were doing and knew that we were expecting the arrival of the Messenger of God. He shouted out at the top of his voice, "Banū Qaylah,[237] here is your good fortune who has come!" [1243]

We went out to where the Messenger of God was sitting in the shade of a palm tree with Abū Bakr, who was about the same age as he. Most of us had not seen the Messenger of God before then, and we crowded around without knowing him from Abū Bakr. Then the shade left the Messenger of God and Abū Bakr rose up and shaded him with his cloak, and we knew.

Some say that the Messenger of God lodged with Kulthūm b. Hidm the brother of the Banū ʿAmr b. ʿAwf, of (the subclan of) the Banū ʿUbayd, while others say that he lodged with Saʿd b. Khaythamah. Those who say that he lodged with Kulthūm b. Hidm say that when he came out of Kulthūm b. Hidm's house he sat to receive people in Saʿd b. Khaythamah's house. This was because Saʿd was a bachelor without any family, and those of the Messenger of God's Emigrant Companions who were unmarried were lodging with him. This is why it is said that Muḥammad lodged with Saʿd b. Khaythamah. The latter's house was called "the bachelors' house." God knows best which of these reports is correct; this is all that we have heard.

Abū Bakr b. Abī Quḥāfah lodged with Khubayb b. Isāf the brother of the Banū al-Ḥārith b. al-Khazraj at al-Sunḥ; but there are some who say that he lodged with Khārijah b. Zayd b. Abī Zuhayr the brother of the Banū al-Ḥārith b. al-Khazraj. [1244]

ʿAlī b. Abī Ṭālib remained in Mecca for three full days until he had returned to their owners on the Messenger of God's behalf the deposits which had been in his keeping. When ʿAlī had completed this task, he joined the Messenger of God and lodged with him with Kulthūm b. Hidm. ʿAlī used to say that he lodged at Qubāʾ

237. The tribes of the Aws and the Khazraj together.

for a night or two with a Muslim woman who had no husband. He used to tell the following story: "I was lodging at Qubā' with a Muslim woman who had no husband, and I noticed a person coming to her in the middle of the night and knocking on her door. She would open the door for him and he would give her something which he had with him. I had misgivings about this and said to her, 'Handmaid of God, who is this man who knocks on your door every night and who gives you something, I do not know what, and you a Muslim woman with no husband?' She answered, 'This is Sahl b. Ḥunayf b. Wāhib, who knows that I am a woman living on my own. In the evening he falls upon his people's idols, smashes them, and brings them to me, saying, "Use this as firewood."'" 'Alī used to tell this story about Sahl b. Ḥunayf after Sahl died while he was with 'Alī in Iraq.

Ibn Ḥumayd—Salamah—Muḥammad b. Isḥāq: This story was
[1245] related to me by 'Alī b. Hind b. Sa'd d. Sahl b. Ḥunayf— 'Alī b. Abī Ṭālib.

The Messenger of God remained at Qubā' among the Banū 'Amr b. 'Awf for Monday, Tuesday, Wednesday, and Thursday, and founded their mosque.[238] Then God caused him to leave them on Friday. The Banū 'Amr b. 'Awf assert that he remained among them longer than that, but God knows best. Some say that his stay at Qubā' lasted for ten days or so.

238. This presumably means that he discovered a suitable piece of ground and conducted prayers there, not that he started building anything. The Muslims of Qubā' may have continued to use the same ground for prayers.

The Beginning of the Prophetic Mission
(Continued)

Abū Jaʿfar (al-Ṭabarī): The early scholars differ as to the length of the Messenger of God's stay in Mecca after he became a prophet. Some say that the length of his stay there, until he emigrated to al-Madīnah, was ten years.

Those who say this:

Ibn al-Muthannā—Yaḥyā b. Muḥammad b. Qays al-Madanī, who is known as Abū Zukayr—Rabīʿah b. Abī ʿAbd al-Raḥmān—Anas b. Mālik: The Messenger of God received his mission at the age of forty and stayed in Mecca for ten years.

Al-Ḥusayn b. Naṣr al-Āmulī—ʿUbaydallāh b. Mūsā—Shaybān—Yaḥyā b. Abī Kathīr—Abū Salamah b. ʿAbd al-Raḥmān—ʿĀ'ishah and Ibn ʿAbbās: The Messenger of God remained in Mecca for ten years receiving revelation of the Qur'ān.

Ibn al-Muthannā—ʿAbd al-Wahhāb—Yaḥyā b. Saʿīd—Saʿīd b. al- [1246]
Musayyab: The Qur'ān was first revealed to the Messenger of God when he was aged forty-three, and he remained in Mecca for ten years.

Aḥmad b. Thābit al-Rāzī—Aḥmad—Yaḥyā b. Saʿīd—Hishām—ʿIkrimah—Ibn ʿAbbas: It was first revealed to the Prophet when he was aged forty-three, and he remained in Mecca for ten years.

Muḥammad b. Ismāʿīl—ʿAmr b. ʿUthmān al-Ḥimṣī—his father—Muḥammad b. Muslim al-Ṭā'ifī—ʿAmr b. Dīnār: The Messenger of God emigrated ten years after his emergence as a prophet.

Abū Jaʿfar (al-Ṭabarī): Others say that this is not so, and that he remained in Mecca for thirteen years after becoming a prophet.

Those who say this:

Ibn al-Muthannā—Ḥajjāj b. al-Minhāl—Ḥammād, that is, Ibn

Salamah—Abū Jamrah—Ibn ʿAbbās: The Messenger of God remained in Mecca for thirteen years receiving revelations.

Muḥammad b. Khalaf—Ādam—Ḥammād b. Salamah—Abū Jamrah al-Ḍubaʿī—Ibn ʿAbbās: The Messenger of God received his mission at the age of forty, and remained in Mecca for thirteen years.

Muḥammad b. Maʿmar—Rawḥ—Zakariyyā' b. Isḥāq—ʿAmr b. Dīnār—Ibn ʿAbbās: The Messenger of God remained in Mecca for thirteen years.

ʿUbayd b. Muḥammad al-Warrāq—Rawḥ—Hishām—ʿIkrimah—Ibn ʿAbbās: The Prophet received his mission at the age of forty and remained in Mecca for thirteen years receiving revelations; then he was commanded to emigrate.

Abū Jaʿfar (al-Ṭabarī): The account of those who say that the Messenger of God received his mission at the age of forty and remained in Mecca for thirteen years agrees with the account of Abū Qays Ṣirmah b. Abī Anas the brother of the Banū ʿAdī b. al-Najjār which is found in his *qaṣīdah* (poem) in which he says, describing how God ennobled them with Islam and how the Messenger of God came to stay with them:

He stayed among Quraysh for some ten years
    reminding people of Islam if he found a favorable friend,
Offering himself to the pilgrims,
    yet did not see anyone taking refuge in Islam or
    summoning others to it.
But when he came to us God gave victory to his religion,
    and he became joyful and satisfied at Ṭaybah.
He found a friend and his aim became secure
    and he had manifest support from God.
He related to us what Noah said to his people
    and what Moses saw when he answered the Caller.
He came to fear none of mankind,
[1248] whether near or far.
We expended the greater part of our wealth upon him
    and our own lives in the clamor of battle and at
    the time of consolation.
We know that there is nothing but God
    and we know that God is the best guide.

Abū Qays informs us in this poem that the length of the Messenger of God's stay among his people of Quraysh after he became a prophet and made public his revelations from God was some ten years.

Some of them say that he remained in Mecca for fifteen years.

Those who say this:

Al-Ḥārith–Ibn Sa'd—Muḥammad b. 'Umar–Ibrāhīm b. Ismā'īl—Dāwūd b. al-Ḥuṣayn—'Ikrimah—Ibn 'Abbās: He quoted the line by Abū Qays Ṣirmah b. Abī Anas except that he recited it as follows:

He stayed among Quraysh for fifteen years
reminding people of Islam if he found a favorable friend.

Abū Ja'far (al-Ṭabarī): It is related on the authority of al-Sha'bī that (the angel) Isrāfīl was associated with the Messenger of God [1249]
for three years before he received any revelation.

Al-Ḥārith—Ibn Sa'd—Muḥammad b. 'Umar al-Wāqidī—al-Thawrī—Ismā'īl b. Abī Khālid—al-Sha'bī: He (al-Wāqidi) also said that he had this from al-Manṣūr by dictation—al-Ash'ath—al-Sha'bī: Isrāfīl was associated with the Messenger of God's prophethood for three years. The Messenger of God was aware of him, but could not see his person. After that came Gabriel.

Al-Wāqidī: I mentioned that to Muḥammad b. Ṣāliḥ b. Dīnār, who said, "By God, nephew, I heard 'Abdallāh b. Abī Bakr b. Ḥazm and 'Āṣim b. 'Umar b. Qatādah conversing in the mosque. An Iraqi man was saying this to them and they both denied it, saying, 'We have neither heard nor learnt anything other than that it was Gabriel who was associated with him and used to bring him revelations from the day he became a prophet until he died.' "

Ibn al-Muthannā—Ibn Abī 'Adī—Dāwūd—'Āmir: Prophethood descended upon him when he was forty. Isrāfīl was associated with his prophethood for three years, and used to teach him the word and the deed,[239] but the Qur'ān was not revealed by his tongue. After three years had gone by Gabriel was associated with Muḥammad's prophethood and the Qur'ān was revealed by his

239. The Qur'ān presupposes that the religion of Islam had already been given certain forms, such as those of the *ṣalāt*, or worship; and this pre-Qur'ānic nonverbal revelation to Muḥammad would appear to be what is here ascribed to Isrāfīl.

tongue for ten years in Mecca and ten years in al-Madīnah.

Abū Ja'far (al-Ṭabarī): Perhaps those who say that the length of Muḥammad's stay in Mecca after the revelation was ten years count this period from the time that Gabriel brought him the revelation from God and he began to summon men to acknowledge that God is one, while those who say that the length of his stay
[1250] was thirteen years count from the beginning of the time that he became a prophet, when Isrāfīl was associated with him, this being the first three years in which he was not commanded to summon men to Islam.

A different account from the two which I have mentioned is related on the authority of Qatādah. This is as follows: Rawḥ b. 'Ubādah—Sa'īd—Qatādah: The Qur'ān was revealed to the Messenger of God for a period of eight years in Mecca and ten years in al-Madīnah) after the emigrated.

Al-Ḥasan used to say: Ten in Mecca and ten in al-Madīnah.

The Institution of the Islamic Calendar

The Date of the Institution of the Islamic Era

Abū Jaʿfar (al-Ṭabarī): It is said that when the Messenger of God came to al-Madīnah he ordered the establishing of a new era.[240]

Zakariyyā' b. Yaḥyā b. Abī Zā'idah—Abū ʿĀṣim—Ibn Jurayj—Abū Salamah—Ibn Shihāb: When the Prophet came to al-Madīnah, which was in Rabīʿ I (September 624), he ordered the establishing of a new era.

Abū Jaʿfar (al-Ṭabarī): It is said that they used to reckon the date by the number of months after Muḥammad's arrival (in al-Madīnah), until the (first) year was completed. It is also said that the first person to order the establishing of a chronology was ʿUmar b. al-Khaṭṭāb.

Reports on This Subject

Muḥammad b. Ismāʿīl—Abū Nuʿaym—Ḥibbān b. ʿAlī al-ʿAnazī—Mujālid al-Shaʿbī: Abū Mūsā al-Asharī wrote to ʿUmar saying, "Letters have come from you to us which do not have a date." ʿUmar assembled the people for consultation. Some said, "Date from the beginning of the Messenger of God's mission," while [1251]
others said, "From the Messenger of God's emigration, for that

240. It is very improbable that Muḥammad was concerned about this matter, and almost certainly true that the formal institution of the Islamic era was due to ʿUmar, the second Caliph. Doubtless, however, people spoke of events as so many months after Muḥammad's arrival in al-Madīnah, as Ṭabarī mentions below; and there are in fact several examples of such dating in his accounts of the earlier years at al-Madīnah.

distinguished between truth and falsehood."

Muḥammad b. Ismāʿīl—Qutaybah b. Saʿīd—Khālid b. Ḥayyān Abū Yazīd al-Kharrāz—Furāt b. Salmān—Maymūn b. Mihrān: A money order was brought before ʿUmar which fell due in (the month of) Shaʿbān. ʿUmar said, "Which Shaʿbān? The one which is coming or the one we are in now?" Then he said to the Messenger of God's Companions, "Contrive something for the people which they can recognize." Some said, "Write according to the chronology of the Greeks; it is said that they date their letters from the time of Alexander, but that was a long time ago." Others said, "Write according to the chronology of the Persians; it is said that whenever a king rises up amongst them he discards the era of his predecessors." In the end they agreed that they should see how long the Messenger of God had remained in al-Madīnah. They found this to be ten years, and the era was reckoned from the Messenger of God's emigration.

Umayyah b. Khālid and Abū Dāwūd al-Ṭayālisī—Qurrah b. Khālid al-Sadūsī—Muḥammad b. Sīrīn: A man rose up before ʿUmar b. al-Khaṭṭāb and said, "Institute a chronology." ʿUmar said, "What is that?" The man replied, "It is something which the non-Arabs do. They write, 'In such-and-such a month of such-and-such a year.'" ʿUmar b. al-Khaṭṭāb said, "This is good. Institute a chronology." They said, "Which year shall we begin from?" Some said, "From the beginning of Muḥammad's mission," and others said, "From his death." Finally they agreed upon his hijrah or emigration. Then they said, "From which month shall we begin?"
[1252] They said, "Ramaḍān," and then they said, "al-Muḥarram, for that is the month when people depart from their pilgrimage, and it is a sacred month." So they agreed upon al-Muḥarram.

Muḥammad b. Ismāʿīl—Saʿīd b. Abī Maryam; and ʿAbd al-Raḥmān b. ʿAbdallāh b. ʿAbd al-Ḥakam—his father; both from ʿAbd al-ʿAzīz b. Abī Ḥāzim—Abū Ḥāzim—Sahl b. Saʿd: Whenever people calculated the date, they did not reckon from the beginning of the Messenger of God's mission, nor from his death; they only reckoned from his arrival in al-Madīnah.

Muḥammad b. Ismāʿīl—Saʿīd b. Abī Maryam—Yaʿqūb b. Isḥāq—Muḥammad b. Muslim—ʿAmr b. Dīnār—ʿAbdallāh b. ʿAbbās: The era began in the year in which the Messenger of God came to al-Madīnah, which is the year in which ʿAbdallāh b. al-

Zubayr was born.

ʿAbd al-Raḥmān b. ʿAbdallāh b. ʿAbd al-Ḥakam—Yaʿqūb b. Isḥāq b. Abī ʿAbbād—Muḥammad b. Muslim al-Ṭā'ifī—ʿAmr b. Dīnār—Ibn ʿAbbās: The era began in the year in which the Messenger of God came ... (his comment is) followed by a report similar to the one above.

Muḥammad b. Ismāʿīl—Qutaybah b. Saʿīd—Nūḥ b. Qays al-Ṭāḥī—ʿUthmān b. Miḥsan: concerning the Qur'ānic verses "By the dawn, and ten nights,"[241] Ibn ʿAbbās used to say, "The dawn is al-Muḥarram, the dawn of the year."

Muḥammad b. Ismāʿīl—Abū Nuʿaym al-Faḍl b. Dukayn—Yūnus b. Abī Isḥāq—Abū Isḥāq—al-Aswad b. Yazīd—ʿUbayd b. ʿUmayr: Al-Muḥarram is God's month, and it is the beginning (that is the first month) of the year. In it, the Kaʿbah is clothed, [1253]
dating commences, and silver is struck. In it is a day upon which people repented, and God forgave them.

Aḥmad b. Thābit al-Rāzī—Aḥmad—Rawḥ b. ʿUbādah—Zakariyyā' b. Isḥāq—ʿAmr b. Dīnār: The first person to date letters was Yaʿlā b. Umayyah, when he was in the Yemen. The Prophet of God came to al-Madīnah in Rabīʿ I (September 624) and people began their chronology from the beginning of the year in which he came to al-Madīnah

ʿAli b. Mujāhid—Muḥammad b. Isḥaq—al-Zuhrī and Muḥammad b. Ṣāliḥ—al-Shaʿbī: The children of Ishmael dated from the fire of Abraham[242] until the building of the Kaʿbah, when Abraham and Ishmael built it. Then they dated from the building of the Kaʿbah until they dispersed, and every time a people departed from Tihāmah they dated from their departure. Those of the descendants of Ishmael who remained in Tihāmah dated from the departure from Tihāmah of Saʿd, Nahd, and Juhaynah, the sons of Zayd, until Kaʿb b. Lu'ayy died; then they dated from his death until the Year of the Elephant. After that they dated from the Elephant until ʿUmar b. al-Khaṭṭāb established the era of the hijrah. This was in the year 17 or 18 (A.D. 638 or 639).

ʿAbd al-Rahmān b. ʿAbdallāh b. ʿAbd al-Ḥakam—Nuʿaym b.

241. 89:1-2.

242. According to the Qur'ān (21:68–70, 29:24, 37:97), when Abraham attacked the idolatry of his people, they prepared a fire to burn him, but God saved him from them.

Ḥammād—al-Dārawardī—'Uthman b. 'Ubaydallāh b. Abī Rāfi'—Sa'īd b. al-Musayyab: 'Umar b. al-Khaṭṭāb assembled the people
[1254] and asked them, "From what day shall we begin our dating?" 'Alī said, "From the day on which the Messenger of God emigrated and abandoned the land of polytheism." 'Umar followed this advice.

Abū Ja'far (al-Ṭabarī): The acount given by 'Alī b. Mujāhid narrated from his authorities for the chronology of the descendants of Ishmael is not far from the truth, which is that it was not their custom to date from an established (and well-known) event which the majority of them could adopt, but that, when they dated an event, they did so from (a local happening, such as) a drought which took place in some part of their country, a barren year which befell them, the reign of a governor who ruled over them, or an event the news of which became widespread among them. This is shown by the way in which their poets differ in their dating; if they had had a dating from an established event and a generally adopted basis, this difference among them would not have arisen. An example of this can be seen in the lines of al-Rabī' b. Ḍabu' al-Fazārī:

Here I am, hoping for immortality, and yet
 my knowledge and my time of birth go back to Ḥujr,
The father of Imru' al-Qays – have you heard of him?
 How far from the mark! How long have I lived!

Here he dates his life by Ḥujr b. 'Amr, the father of Imru' al-Qays.[243]

Likewise Nābighah of the Banū Ja'dah says:

Whoever asks about my age, let him know
 that I was young at the time of the glanders.

Here he dates his life by an epidemic which afflicted them.

Another poet says:

I was still wearing boy's garments at the time
 when Ibn Hammām raided the encampment of Khath'am.

243. Imru' al-Qays is a well-known poet who is thought to have died about A.D. 550. See *EI* [2] s.v. Imru' al-Ḳays b. Ḥujr. He was the youngest son of Ḥujr, king of the tribe of Kindah. Al-Rabī' al-Fazārī and Nābighah al-Ja'dī are minor poets, of whom the latter (who is not to be confused with the famous Nābighah al-Dhubyānī) lived to become a Muslim.

All of these poets whose chronology I have quoted in these lines [1255] lived close in time to one another, and the events from which they dated were also close in time to one another, and yet they all chose different events. If they had had a recognized era, as the Muslims and other communities do today, they would not, God willing, have used other than that; but matters stood with them, I believe, as I have stated.

As for the Quraysh among the Arabs, the latest epoch which I have been able to establish as being used by them in computing dates before the emigration of the Prophet from Mecca to al-Madīnah is that of the Year of the Elephant, which is the year in which the Messenger of God was born. There were twenty years between the Year of the Elephant and the Sacrilegious War, fifteen years between the Sacrilegious War and the rebuilding of the Kaʿbah, and five years between the rebuilding of the Kaʿbah and the beginning of the Prophet's mission.

Summary of Meccan Chronology

Abū Ja'far (al-Ṭabarī): The Messenger of God received his call to prophethood at the age of forty. According to al-Sha'bī, Isrāfīl was associated with the Messenger of God's prophethood, for three years, this being before he was commanded to call people to Islam and to proclaim it openly. We have already quoted the narratives and stories to this effect. After three years, Gabriel was associated with his prophethood, and he commanded him to summon people openly to God. He did this for ten years while resident in Mecca, and then emigrated to al-Madīnah in Rabī' I fourteen years after becoming a prophet. He left Mecca for al-Madīnah on a Monday and arrived in al-Madīnah on Monday the twelfth of Rabī' I (September 24, 624).

Ibrāhīm b. Sa'īd al-Jawharī—Mūsā b. Dāwūd—Ibn Lahī'ah—Khālid b. Abī 'Imrān—Ḥanash al-Ṣan'ānī—Ibn 'Abbās: The Prophet was born on a Monday, became a prophet on a Monday, lifted the (Black) Stone on a Monday, left Mecca to emigrate to al-
[1256] Madīnah on a Monday, arrived in al-Madīnah on a Monday, and passed away on a Monday.

Ibn Ḥumayd—Salamah—Ibn Isḥāq—al-Zuhrī: The Messenger of God arrived in al-Madīnah on Monday, the twelfth of Rabī' I.

Abū Ja'far (al-Ṭabarī): If the matter of the Muslim chronology is as I have described it, then although it is based on the emigration it actually begins two months and twelve days before the Prophet's arrival in al-Madīnah. This is because the year begins in al-Muḥarram, and the Prophet arrived in al-Madīnah after this period of time had elapsed; the era did not begin with the time of his arrival but with the beginning of that year.

Abbreviations

EI[I] , *EI*[2] : *Encyclopaedia of Islam,* Ist ed., 2d ed., Leiden and London, 1913–42, 1960 – .
EI(S) : *The Shorter Encyclopedia of Islam,* Leiden 1953.
GAL : C. Brockelmann, *Geschichte der arabischen Literatur,* 2nd ed., vol. 1 Leiden 1943.
Guillaume : *The Life of Muhammad* (translation of Ibn Isḥaq), London 1955.
Lane : E.W. Lane, *An Arabic-English Lexicon,* London 1863 – 93.
Lisān : Ibn Manẓūr, *Lisān al-ʿArab.*
Watt, *Mecca:* W.M.Watt, *Muhammad at Mecca,* Oxford 1953.
Medina : *Muhammad at Medina,* Oxford 1956.

Bibliography of Cited Works

Goldziher, Ignaz, *Muslim Studies*, 2 vols., ed. S.M.Stern, London 1967, 1971.

Guillaume, A., *The Life of Muhammad: a Translation of (Ibn) Isḥaq's Sīrat Rasūl Allāh*, London 1955; puts Ibn Hishām's editorial notes into an appendix.

Ḥassān b. Thābit, *Dīwān*, ed. W.Arafat, 2 vols., London 1971.

Ibn Ḥabīb, *K. al-Munammaq*, Hyderabad 1964.

Ibn Ḥajar, *Tahdhīb al-Tahdhīb*, 12 vols., Hyderabad 1907 – 9.

Ibn Hishām, *Sīrat Rasūl Allāh*, ed. F.Wüstenfeld, Göttingen 1858, 1859; incorporates the *Sīrah* of Ibn Ishāq.

Ibn Manẓūr, *Lisān al-ʿArab*, various editions; a dictionary in twenty volumes.

Ibn Saʿd, *K. al-Ṭabaqat al-kabīr*, ed. E. Sachau et al., 9 vols., Leiden 1904 – 17; references are all vol I, part 1.

al-Masʿūdī, *Murūj al-dhahab*, ed. and trans. C.Barbier de Meynard and Pavet de Courteille, 9 vols., 1861 – 76.

Nöldeke, Th., *Geschichte des Qorāns* ², ed. F. Schwally, G.Bergstrasser, and O. Pretzl, 3 vols., Leipzig 1909 – 38.

Schacht, Joseph, *The Origins of Muhammadan Jurisprudence*, Oxford 1950.

Sezgin, Fuat, *Geschichte des arabischen Schrifttums*, vol. 1, Leiden 1967.

al-Wāqidī,*Kitāb al-Maghāzī*, ed. Marsden Jones, 3 vols., London 1966; *Muhammed in Medina*, abbreviated German translation by J. Wellhausen, Berlin 1882.

Watt, W.Montgomery, *Bell's Introduction to the Qur'ān*, Edinburgh 1970.

Muhammad at Mecca, Oxford 1953.

Muhammad at Medina, Oxford 1956.
Wellhausen, J., *Reste arabischen Heidentums*^{2}, Berlin 1897.

Index

The index contains all proper names of persons, places, tribal and other groups, and the like occuring in the foreword, the text, and the footnotes, except that some minor names from the early genealogies have been omitted. As far as the foreword and footnotes are concerned, however, only those names that belong to the medieval or earlier periods are listed.

The definite article al-, the abbreviations b. (ibn, son) and bt. (bint, daughter), and all parenthetical material ahve been disregarded in the alphabetical arrangement. Where a name occurs in both the text and the footnotes on the same page, only the page number is given.

Abbreviations: 'AA. = 'Abdallah; B. = Banu (sons of); M. = Muḥammad. An asterisk after a name indicates that it occurs only in the isnāds, the chains of transmitters. The letter "f." indicates one following page only.

Z